THE NEGRO CHURCH

The Negro Church

Report of a Social Study made under the direction of Atlanta University; together with the Proceedings of the Eighth Conference for the Study of the Negro Problems, held at Atlanta University, May 26th, 1903

EDITED BY

W. E. BURGHARDT Du BOIS

Corresponding Secretary of the Conference

A Reprint of the 1903 Edition with a
New Introduction by Alton B. Pollard III

CASCADE *Books* · Eugene, Oregon

THE NEGRO CHURCH
Report of a Social Study made under the direction of Atlanta University; together with the proceedings of the eighth Conference for the Study of the Negro Problems, held at Atlanta University, May 26th, 1903. With an Introduction by Alton B. Pollard III.

Cascade Books
A Division of Wipf and Stock Publishers
199 W. 8th Ave., Suite 3
Eugene, OR 97401
www.wipfandstock.com

ISBN 13: 978-1-60899-767-1

Cataloging-in-Publication data:

Du Bois, W. E. B. (1868–1963).

The Negro church : report of a social study made under the direction of Atlanta University; together with the proceedings of the eighth Conference for the Study of the Negro Problems, held at Atlanta University, May 26th, 1903 / W. E. B. Du Bois ; introduction by Alton B. Pollard III.

xxxviii + 296 p.; 25.4 cm.—Includes bibliographical references and index.

1. African American Churches. 2. African Americans—Religion. 3. Du Bois, W. E. B. (William Edward Burghardt), 1868–1963. 4. Conference for the Study of the Negro Problems (8th: 1903: Atlanta University). 5. Religion and sociology. I. Pollard, Alton B. (Alton Brooks), 1956–. II. Title.

BR563.N4 N43 2011

Manufactured in the U.S.A.

Cover image credit:
Untitled, Storefront Churches series 1957–61; photograph © Milton Rogovin 1952–2002; courtesy Center for Creative Photography, University of Arizona Foundation

For the Ancestors

The Negro Church is the only social institution of the Negroes which started in the African forest and survived slavery; under the leadership of priest or medicine man, afterward of the Christian pastor, the Church preserved in itself the remnants of African tribal life and became after emancipation the center of Negro social life. So that today the Negro population of the United States is virtually divided into church congregations which are the real units of race life.

—*Report of the Third Atlanta Conference, 1898*

Contents

Contents

The Negro Church: An Introduction

ALTON B. POLLARD III

Race, Religion, and the Politics of Knowledge

One of the principal means by which any discipline or profession seeks to introduce new or potential members to the guild is by way of narrative account, through the presentation of a distinguished history—complete with texts, theories, thinkers, and applications. Over the course of time and for strategic reasons, certain historical factors tend to be excluded and trivialized while others are emphasized and elevated to the official status of "canon." The production and dissemination of an authoritative history is basic to communicating to group members a collective sense of meaning, purpose, power, and identity. The history of an organization acts, as it were, as a kind of sacred script, ritual artifact, or fixed discourse on the way things naturally came to be. Simply stated, the past orders the present with a narrative truth beyond the power of mere mortals to change. For newcomers to the group, the metanarrative is transmitted with its special meaning both as a matter of course and as an important source of truth.

makes me think of this 'Classical Theories' course

Where the history of sociology in the United States is concerned, venerable canonical accounts have proven extraordinarily successful at concealing a long legacy of cultural and hierarchal power arrangements in the profession. For its part, the process of masking, silencing, and deception in the social study of religion has been equally opaque and problematic. Sociology's willful disregard of W. E. B. Du Bois as one of the founders of the discipline, including the study of religion, is recounted here as both rejoinder and primer in the politics of knowledge, in the politics of hierarchy (race, gender, sexuality, ability, and class, considered among others), and on which aspects of social and religious life deserve to be considered, researched, underscored, and known.[1] Despite encountering numerous "early restrictions" and

---

1. Segregated realities notwithstanding, the tradition of early African American social analysts was

adversities because of his race, Du Bois was a towering figure in the development of sociology in the United States from the very beginning, on his own terms, and in his own right.[2]

W. E. B. Du Bois was editor and principal investigator of *The Negro Church*, published in 1903. Issued as number eight in a series of social studies made by Du Bois at Atlanta University from 1896 to 1910, it is the series' longest work.[3] *The Negro Church* is a groundbreaking study in a number of respects. It is the first full-length treatment of the Black church in the United States. It is the first scholarly history of the Black religious experience in the United States. It is the first monograph on the sociology of religion in the United States. It is the first empirical study of religion to be done at a Black college or university and to be administered and led by Black scholars.

In short, *The Negro Church* is a landmark text conceived by one of the seminal minds of early social science in the United States. Yet and still, the work languishes in intellectual and historical obscurity. Despite its pioneering status, *The Negro Church* is scarcely referenced in the chronicles of sociology or religion in the United States or, for that matter, in more contemporary works on religion and society.[4] It can seldom be found on library shelves and is rarely considered in scholarly discourse. For that matter, few of Du Bois's writings on religion are referred to in the social-scientific literature.[5] These are but a few of the reasons why the appearance of this text for a new generation of students, scholars, researchers, and religious leaders is cause to celebrate. Recognition of *The Negro Church* is long overdue and justly deserved.

---

rich and considerable, including Anna Julia Cooper, Kelly Miller, Mary Church Terrell, and Ida B. Wells-Barnett, among others.

2. A header from one of the opening chapters of W. E. B. Du Bois, *The Negro Church: Report of a Social Study Made Under the Direction of Atlanta University; Together with the Proceedings of the Eighth Conference for the Study of the Negro Problems, Held at Atlanta University, May 26th, 1903* (Atlanta: Atlanta University Press, 1903), 10.

3. Publication of the series of Atlanta University Studies was completed in 1914.

4. Du Bois is not mentioned, for instance, in either Richard K. Fenn, ed., *The Blackwell Companion to Sociology of Religion*, Blackwell Companions to Religion 2 (Oxford: Blackwell, 2001); or William H. Swatos, Jr., *Faith of the Fathers: Science, Religion, and Reform in the Development of Early American Sociology* (Bristol, IN: Wyndham Hall, 1984). Du Bois receives four sentences and thus fares slightly better in the more recent compendium by William H. Swatos, Jr., ed., *Encyclopedia of Religion and Society* (Walnut Creek, CA: AltaMira, 1998), 144–45.

5. The most prominent exception is the Phil Zuckerman, Sandra L. Barnes, and Daniel Cady introduction to *The Negro Church* (Walnut Creek, CA: AltaMira, 2003). Arno Press also reissued the Atlanta University Publications in a single volume in 1968.

Scholarly Religion

Du Bois's most famous assessments of Black religion are found in *The Souls of Black Folk*, also published in 1903. There he wrote in culturally specific ways and in lyric social-scientific terms about the religious experience of people of African descent in the United States: "The Negro church of today is the social centre of Negro life in the United States, and the most characteristic expression of African character."[6] The basic anatomy of Black religion is described as being composed of three parts: "the Preacher, the Music, and the Frenzy," the latter a less than flattering designation for emotional religion.[7] Four of the book's chapters are unambiguously religious—"Of Our Spiritual Strivings," "Of the Faith of the Fathers" (previously published in 1900 as "The Religion of the American Negro"), "Of Alexander Crummell," and "Of the Passing of the First-Born"—while several other chapters resonate with deep religious sentiment and purpose. A leading historian and Du Bois scholar has even characterized the entire text as a sermon in prose.[8] Nineteen years earlier, in his very first published articles, Du Bois had chosen to emphasize aspects of Black religious life in his native town of Great Barrington, Massachusetts.[9] But it was not until the publication of *The Philadelphia Negro* in 1899 and the even more focused statistical studies of *The Negro Church* that Du Bois began in earnest to investigate the centrality of religion in African American life.

Du Bois's person and place in the world of science and letters was continuously made tentative by rampant and unrepentant racism in the American academy. Despite the marginalizing tendencies of his white contemporaries, in the end they were unable to diminish his accomplishments as one of the premier analysts of the United States context, inclusive of religion, at the dawn of the twentieth century. In point of fact, it was only a matter of time before Du Bois's own progressive social vision proved larger than the fledgling discipline of sociology he had helped to establish. During the early years of his career, however, he completely and uncritically embraced the norms of positivist science and confidently and enthusiastically immersed himself in the methods of empirical and statistical analysis, ethnography, and historiography—and more through his work on the Black church and other social dimensions of life in the Black community including the family, labor, and education among others.

6. Du Bois, *The Souls of Black Folk* (Greenwich, CT: Fawcett, [1903] 1963), 142.

7. Ibid., 141.

8. Herbert Aptheker, "W. E. B. Du Bois and Religion: A Brief Reassessment," *Journal of Religious Thought* 39 (Spring/Summer 1982) 8.

9. Essays found under the headings "Great Barrington News" and "From the Berkshire Hills" in the *New York Globe*, 29 September 1883 and 22 November 1884.

For the record it is here noted that Du Bois published his venerable work, *The Negro Church*, a decade or more earlier than such other renowned writings in the sociology of religion as Ernst Troeltsch's *The Social Teachings of the Christian Churches* (1912), Emile Durkheim's *The Elementary Forms of the Religious Life* (1915), and Max Weber's *The Protestant Ethic and the Spirit of Capitalism* (1920).[10] As brilliant and impressive as these works are, the fact still remains they are but theoretical formulations based on research conducted by someone else, that is, theories supported by secondary and often suspect source material.[11] Du Bois stands alone among his contemporaries in the employment of empirical methods and practices, which while no doubt rudimentary by today's standards, are nevertheless foundational to the early sociological study of religion.

Spiritual Strivings

Not surprisingly, efforts by contemporary scholars to understand Du Bois's religious views, personal and academic, are still quite piecemeal and incomplete.[12] Akin to the very religious expressions that Du Bois sought to study, his views on religion were critical, controversial, complementary, challenging, creative, and complex—reflecting an overt set of commitments and internal recognitions many researchers still find perplexing and contradictory—but which are in fact utterly and dialectically consistent. Over the course of his ninety-five years Du Bois defied easy either/or religious labels, all the while making his way from an early and staunch belief in the orthodox tenets of New England Puritanism to a fervent and unremitting faith in the "spiritual strivings" of Black folk the world over.

10. Ernst Troeltsch, *The Social Teaching of the Christian Churches*, 2 vols., Library of Theological Ethics (Louisville: Westminster John Knox, 1992); Emile Durkheim, *The Elementary Forms of the Religious Life*, trans. Joseph Ward Swain (New York: Free Press, 1965); Max Weber, *The Protestant Ethic and the Spirit of Capitalism*, trans. Talcott Parsons, Scribner Library (New York: Scribner, 1958).

11. For a more detailed account of many of these themes see my *Mysticism and Social Change: The Social Witness of Howard Thurman* (New York: Lang, 1992), 129–50.

12. Aptheker, "W. E. B. Du Bois and Religion"; Vincent Harding, "W. E. B. Du Bois and the Black Messianic Vision," in *Black Titan—W. E. B. Du Bois: An Anthology*, ed. John Henrik Clarke et al. (Boston: Beacon, 1970), 52–68; Manning Marable, "The Black Faith of W. E. B. Du Bois: Sociocultural and Political Dimensions of Black Religion," *The Southern Quarterly* 23 (Spring 1985) 15–33; Wilson Jeremiah Moses, *Afrotopia: The Roots of African American Popular History*, Cambridge Studies in American Literature and Culture 118 (Cambridge: Cambridge University Press, 1998); Barbara Dianne Savage, "W.E.B. Du Bois and 'The Negro Church,'" *Annals of the American Academy of Political and Social Science* 568 (2000) 235–49. See also the tribute by Martin Luther King Jr., "Honoring Dr. Du Bois," preface to *Dusk of Dawn* (New York: Schocken, [1940] 1968), vii–xvii. For general biographical information on Du Bois, see the definitive volumes by David Levering Lewis, *W. E. B. Du Bois—Biography of a Race, 1868–1919* (New York: Holt, 1993); and *W. E. B. Du Bois: The Fight for Equality and the American Century, 1919–1963* (New York: Holt, 2000).

From Du Bois's own recollections, we know that as a young man growing up in the town of Great Barrington, Massachusetts, during the 1870s he knew intimately the Protestant ethic of hard work, frugality, morality, and respectability. In the last of his autobiographies (he wrote three), he writes that he and his mother, Mary Silvina Burghardt Du Bois, a respected and devout Christian, worshipped on occasion at the new African Methodist Episcopal Zion (AMEZ) Church, which in his youthful inexperience seemed to him a curiously "segregated institution." However, due mainly to reasons of close proximity and white beneficence, they faithfully attended the First Congregational Church where they were "the only colored communicants."[13] Du Bois recognized early on that modest class distinctions existed between Great Barrington's local Protestant and Catholic churches, but given the town's small Black population, he had no real experience with the intrigues and trials of race until he went south at the age of seventeen to attend Fisk University in September 1885.

Du Bois's collegiate experience fundamentally shaped his life. All the teachers at Fisk were white—commonplace at the time for northern missionary-founded schools in the south—but many of his most transformative experiences came from the southern Black world around him. His strict moral and religious upbringing found reinforcement in the classroom context but was berated by some of his classmates, many of whom were older, more urbane, and certainly more experienced in the ways of the world. Like other Black collegians of the time, the small cadre of students at Fisk was typically confident and poised to assume their communal responsibility as the vanguard of scholars, activists, and propagandists for the race. Writes Du Bois: "At Fisk the problem of race was faced openly and essential racial equality asserted and natural inferiority strenuously denied."[14] All the social, intellectual, and religious dimensions of his southern experience began to congeal in the summers of 1886 and 1887. It was in the east Tennessee backcountry, where Du Bois was serving as an elementary schoolteacher, that he first experienced the radical contingency of the religion of the oppressed in the form of the Southern Negro revival:

> And so most striking to me, as I approached the village and the little plain church perched aloft, was the air of intense excitement that possessed that mass of Black folk. A sort of suppressed terror hung in the air and seemed to seize them—a pythian madness, a demoniac possession, that lent terrible reality to song and word. The Black and massive form of the preacher swayed and quivered as the words crowded to his lips and flew at us in singular eloquence. The people moaned and fluttered, and then the gaunt-cheeked brown woman beside me suddenly leaped straight into the air and

13. Du Bois, *The Autobiography of W. E. B. Du Bois* (New York: International, 1968), 88, 90.

14. Joe M. Richardson, *A History of Fisk University, 1865–1946* (University: University of Alabama Press, 1980), 48.

shrieked like a lost soul, while round about came wail and groan and out-
cry, and a scene of human passion such as I had never conceived before.[15]

What is this "essence?"

Here in the heart of Alexandria, Tennessee's Black community, Du Bois experienced something of the heart of the essence of Black religious life. In the simple
wood-framed tabernacles and unadorned houses of worship of rural southern Black
folk he encountered depths of spirituality unknown to him, a spirituality that he
found all the more powerful and unpretentious for being so unfamiliar. The nature
of his response was not confined merely to the rational or categorical, but clearly reflected the inherent paradox of the experience and also the stark contrast of his own
New England Puritan past. Still loyal to his Calvinistic upbringing, yet increasingly
alienated from the church of his youth, Du Bois was fiercely determined to make
sense of the religious datum that emanated from America's communities of African
descent and integrate it into his still embryonic worldview. The summer months of
1886 and 1887 provided him with an intimate introduction to his people as a race

"objective?"

and a dawning awareness that here also was an opportunity to engage in objective
social analysis that would culminate in his formal work as a sociologist from 1897
to 1906.

By Du Bois's senior year, Fisk University president Erastus Cravath was
enamored enough with the young man's talents to try and persuade him to accept
a scholarship to attend Hartford Seminary. As his autobiographical writings attest,
his social outlook had undergone dramatic transformation. In matters of personal
morality, however, he remained stoically and steadfastly Puritan:

> I believed too little in Christian dogma to become a minister. I was not
> without faith: I never stole material nor spiritual things; I not only never
> lied, but blurted out my conception of truth on the most untoward occa-
> sions; I drank no alcohol and knew nothing of women, physically or psy-
> chically, to the incredulous amusement of my more experienced fellows: I
> above all believed in work –systematic and tireless.[16]

Du Bois was a devout believer in the Protestant ethic and its implied power to
instill the cultural values needed for Black social and political progress. Upon joining the faculty of Wilberforce University in 1894, the flagship educational institution
of the African Methodist Episcopal (AME) Church, he had a chance encounter with
a group of students who were having informal worship. The acerbic young professor
soon found himself embroiled in a campus-wide controversy after he refused to lead
the students in prayer. After joining the Atlanta University faculty in 1897 he caused

15. Du Bois, *Autobiography*, 120; Du Bois, *Souls of Black Folk*, 140.
16. Du Bois, *Autobiography*, 124.

consternation once again by refusing to participate in religious services. Eventually, he agreed to read collects from the Episcopal *Book of Common Prayer* and finally began to write his own prayers.[17] His prayer glorifying the work ethic is illustrative:

> God teach us to work. Herein alone do we approach our Creator when we stretch our arms with toil, and strain with eye and ear and brain to catch the thought and do the deed and create the things that make life worth living. Let us learn quickly in our youth, O Father, that in the very doing, the honest humble determined striving, lies the realness of things, the great glory of life. Of all things there is fear and fading—beauty pales and hope disappoints; but blessed is the worker—his are the kingdoms of earth—Amen.[18]

[handwritten margin note: similarities to Marx here in some ways — the "species-being"]

[handwritten note: 'Doing' vs. 'Being' (where does contemplation come into play in this idea?)]

Without a doubt, the burgeoning worldview of Du Bois was also deeply transformed by the deteriorating state of race relations across the nation. The young scholar was coming to maturity during some of the longest and most bitter years of the Black American struggle for freedom. The fledgling hope to which late nineteenth-century Emancipation and Reconstruction had given rise shattered against the racism rife across the land. In the South and Border States anti-Negro hate groups maimed, murdered, raped, burned, and rioted in bigoted fury. Between 1885 and 1894 more than 1700 lynchings of Black men and women were recorded in the United States.[19] The Supreme Court handed down the *Plessy v. Ferguson* decision in 1896, making the ideology of "separate but equal" sacrosanct for the next sixty years. Social and political deconstruction, North and South, denied Black people the vote and offered them educational opportunities that were inferior at best; the courts dispensed their own brand of civil injustice, and discrimination barred Blacks from decent housing; those who could find jobs often had to withstand subhuman working conditions. White American society as a whole saw Black people—women, children and men—as lazy, insolent, libidinous, ignorant, irresponsible, uncultured, criminal, irredeemable, and in the final analysis, somewhat less than human. And, by and large, the scientific community concurred: Social Darwinists and other racialists proclaimed the culture of the Negro deficient and their inferiority natural and innate, that those who were of darker hue were unfit for full and equitable participation in the modern competitive world.

This was the social drama that powerfully fueled Du Bois's fierce loyalty and allegiance to the Black American estate. From the fall of 1887 to the spring of 1892 he

17. Ibid., 285. Most of Du Bois's extended family in New England was Episcopalian rather than Congregationalist. For a period of time, Du Bois also conducted evening devotions at Atlanta University.

18. W. E. B. Du Bois, *Prayers for Dark People*, ed. Herbert Aptheker (Amherst: University of Massachusetts Press, 1980), 62.

19. Du Bois, *Autobiography*, 124.

took up graduate residence at Harvard University (and postgraduate studies at the University of Berlin from 1892 to 1894) where he received the Bachelor and Master of Arts degrees and became the first African American to receive a doctorate from the famed institution. He quickly found acceptance in Boston's Black community, and especially among the Black Brahmins so-called—men and women of influence and status, relative terms in any case in a race- and gender-stratified and xenophobic United States. Du Bois also pursued his relationship with area Black churches, even agreeing to organize and participate in a play at the Charles Street AME Church.[20]

Du Bois was more than content to remain an outsider where certain aspects of the Black religious experience were concerned. His strict Puritan sensibilities were disturbed by the excessive emotionalism emblematic of Black worship and by the ineptitude and immorality of some of the clergy. At the same time, on spiritual and cultural as well as on intellectual grounds he understood his humanity and destiny to be altogether bound up with the Black masses. Du Bois was only just beginning to make a strong claim for a holistic definition of Black spirituality, one that embraced the transcendent worth, intrinsic value, and distinctive gifts of African-descended people. He demonstrated a near numinous faith in the values and virtues of his people, especially when rhapsodizing on the resilient Black rural southern (as opposed to the more prosaic Black urban northern) proletariat.

The faith of Du Bois in the wherewithal of the institutional Black church to champion Black American social progress was not nearly so transcendent or sublime however. In an 1891 paper delivered before the National Colored League of Boston he sternly admonished the church, stating, "a religion that won't stand the application of reason and common sense is not fit for an intelligent dog."[21] Much to the dismay of Du Bois and such other well-known Black public figures and intellectuals as Anna Julia Cooper, Reverend Francis J. Grimké, and Reverend Alexander Crummell, the Black church was overly steeped in emotionalism and excess while failing in its mission to translate sacred imperatives into social activism. This having been said, Du Bois's critique where the Black church is concerned was mild in comparison to his withering and incisive condemnation of the white church, a point that will be touched on later, and which has been well examined by others elsewhere.[22]

20. Du Bois, *Dusk of Dawn*, 36.
21. Cited in Marable, "The Black Faith of W. E. B. Du Bois," 21.
22. For an extensive treatment of Du Bois's views on the white church, see Moses, *Afrotopia*, 136–68.

The Negro Church

As a passionate observer of the national condition and a sensitive interpreter of Black life, Du Bois was keenly aware of the psychological subversions of late nineteenth- and early twentieth-century white racism and supremacy. In *The Souls of Black Folk*, he would write famously about this contingency and the critical hermeneutic adopted by Black America, artfully and exquisitely stated in a trio of metaphors: "twoness," "double consciousness" and, most often, "the Veil."

In *The Negro Church*, Du Bois expresses the same critical dialectic in different ways, primarily through scientific means. His intention was to do sociology from the standpoint of the oppressed, employing the tools of social analysis as a kind of double lens through which to effect societal change. Thus, even the subtitle of the book signals a dual heuristic project: "for the Study of the Negro Problems." On the one hand, Du Bois was committed in *The Negro Church* to probing, documenting and assessing the forms, functions, and potential of Black church life in America (read: "the *Negro* problems"). But the equally critical subtext for his work was to establish a peremptory challenge to white cultural hierarchy and racist conventions (read: "*the* Negro problems"). Again, it was the unspoken intent of Du Bois to establish prima facie evidence for social change through the methods, constructs, and vocabulary of the social sciences. Like the other Atlanta University reports, *The Negro Church* is a valuable historic example of the art of African American moral suasion through scholarship.

A thorough and meticulous scholar, Du Bois early on approached his work with the supreme confidence that empirical sociology would be a formidable ally in the Black struggle for equality and a counter to white supremacist pathologies. However, his hope in the redemptive power of an impartial scientific truth would soon be shattered upon the rocks of white racial supremacy, intransigence, and hostility. As he so famously penned years later in the autobiographical *Dusk of Dawn*, "Two considerations thereafter broke in upon my work and eventually disrupted it: first, one could not be a calm, cool, and detached scientist while Negroes were lynched, murdered, and starved; and secondly, there was no such definite demand for scientific work of the sort I was doing, as I had confidently assumed would be easily forthcoming."[23]

The Negro Church was Du Bois's most methodological and systemic presentation of Black religion. He emphasized the unparalleled role of the Black church in the social, organizational, moral, and spiritual life of Black people. Participant-observation

---

23. Du Bois, *Dusk of Dawn: An Essay toward an Autobiography of a Race Concept* (New York: Harcourt, Brace & World, 1940), 67–68.

studies were conducted by teams of researchers in six localities across the country: Richmond, Virginia; Chicago, Illinois; Thomas County, Georgia; Atlanta, Georgia; Greene County, Ohio; and Deland, Florida. The work also drew heavily on US government census data and the difficult-to-access records of Black denominational bodies. However, the book itself begins with a trans-Atlantic analysis of religion and culture in West African indigenous societies. While not extensively emphasizing the role of African retentions, early in his career, Du Bois was already committed to the notion that a vital understanding of African religious antecedents was imperative to making sense of Black religiosity in the Caribbean and the Americas. In the process, he became the first scholar to positively identify the African origins of the Black church throughout the African Diaspora, which church was never exclusively Christian in any case, calling it "the sole surviving social institution of the African fatherland."[24]

At the same time, some of Du Bois's cultural observations on African indigenous society in *The Negro Church* can only be described as pejorative, degrading, paternalistic and otherwise incongruous with his efforts to combat social Darwinism in the United States.[25] That much of his incipient Pan-Africanism is still indicative of the time and intellectually flawed is hardly surprising when one takes into account the fact that his doctrine of *Kulture* (culture) was formidably indebted to European theory. That he staked his entire discussion of the cultural significance of Africa for the African Diaspora on nonindigenous sources (principally the *Encyclopedia Britannica* and the work of German ethnographer Friedrich Ratzel) points to the real limitations of his knowledge about Africa circa 1903. Twenty-one years would pass before Du Bois experienced the African context firsthand, in 1924, when he traveled to Liberia at the age of fifty-six. In the interim, his knowledge about the culture and politics of Africa grew exponentially, and he would make amends through later writings and involvements for his early porous scholarship.

The Negro Church was the high point of Du Bois's progressive sociological search for truth about the significance of institutional Christianity for Black social and religious life. He characterized the "African church" as the "oldest Negro organization, dating in part from Africa itself, and here Negroes have had the most liberty and experience."[26] Due to the suppressive nature of white society in the United States, the

24. Du Bois, *The Negro Church* (New York: Arno, 1968), 5.

25. The following statement is a prime example: "But the central fact of African life, political, social and religious, is its failure to integrate—to unite and systematize itself in some conquering whole which should dominate the wayward parts" (ibid., 3). As many of my African and African Diasporan students have angrily and rightly noted, were it not for the historicity of the text and the later intellectual maturity of Du Bois, this sentence alone would literally negate the broader merits of the book.

26. Ibid., 154.

Black church was called upon to blend together family and ritual functions in an all-encompassing way. The functions of the church were far-reaching, so much so that it "became the center of amusements, of what little spontaneous economic activity remained, of education, and of all social intercourse."[27] As a result, the church was more often than not "a social institution first, and religious afterwards, but nevertheless, its religious activity is wide and sincere."[28] For Du Bois, the true strength and genius of the Black church was found in its dedication to preserving and upholding the humanity of Black folk and in its liberating vision of Christianity without caste distinctions. In *The Philadelphia Negro*, segments of which are revisited in *The Negro Church*, he early and positively concluded that because of their unique position in the Black community, "all movements for social betterment are apt to center in the churches" where the "race problem in all its phases is continually being discussed."[29]

Yet there was also never Du Bois without some trenchant form of critique. As a rule, his praise of the Black church was measured and reserved and, with rare exception, fleeting and faint. In *The Negro Church*, Du Bois is disarmingly cautious in his estimates of Black religious life. He is careful to differentiate between religion as moral precept and religion as emotive outlet. He indicates that the church as a social institution had yet to sufficiently concern itself with issues of social empowerment. Taking a cue from the remarkable legacies of Haitian revolutionary leader Toussaint L'Ouverture and radical antebellum preacher Nat Turner, whom Du Bois greatly admired and studied extensively while at Harvard, early twentieth-century Black America required an uncompromising political protest—an idea that was not readily or enthusiastically received by the largely conservative Black clergy of the time. Not only that, the leadership of the church had yet to advance the race in matters of personal and cultural formation: "In direct moral teaching and setting standards for the people . . . the church is timid, and naturally so, for its constitution is democracy tempered by custom."[30] He chided the churches further for what he saw as the distractions of extravagance, missed opportunity and internal dissension, which spoiled their greater purpose. Last but not least, the church suffered from a dearth of well-educated leadership. As a result, the well-being of local congregations and the broader community was destined to suffer as well.

For Du Bois, the moments of tension between his spiritual (African cultural) and puritanical (European cultural) values were constant and pedestrian, and sometimes episodic; so too were his efforts to reconcile sacred and social processes.

27. Ibid., 5.

28. Ibid., 110.

29. W. E. B. Du Bois, *The Philadelphia Negro* (Philadelphia: University of Pennsylvania Press, [1899] 1996), 205.

30. Du Bois, *The Negro Church*, 110.

Again, his achievement of a dialectical unity of opposites, his synthesis of African world and Hegelian ideals, the ability to consider the part and the whole, while alien to white cultured despisers was of one piece to him. As Manning Marable explains, "the central motif in his ideological biography" is "the ability to create sound political programs on the quicksand of racist violence and segregation."[31] So it was that Du Bois could well affirm the ideal of the church universal and strongly criticize Black churches for their naive acceptance and uncritical embrace of white Christian doctrine. However, if the Black church was criticized for its provincialism and lack of agency, the white church was more immoral and problematic still. Du Bois's criticism of white Christianity was tempered in *The Negro Church*, but not in general as evidenced by a torrid stream of articles and addresses over the years. Here however, he offers but modest words, along with principal co-analysts Mary Church Terrell and Kelly Miller, as a challenge to white America:

> Religious precepts would rob the white man of his prejudices and cause him to recognize the Fatherhood of God and the brotherhood of man. Christianity is contrary to the spirit of caste—spiritual kinship transcends all other relations. The race problem will be solved when Christianity gains control of the innate wickedness of the human heart, and men learn to apply in dealing with their fellows the simple principles of the Golden Rule and the Sermon on the Mount.[32]

Other more subtle and nuanced themes emerge in *The Negro Church*. Mary Church Terrell, one of the study's lead collaborators (along with Kelly Miller), is another pioneering scholar seldom referenced in social-science literature. Terrell was an author, educator, lecturer, and activist. A leading figure in the Black women's club movement, she was also cofounder of the National Association of Colored Women, and a charter member of the National Association for the Advancement of Colored People. Like her contemporaries Ida B. Wells, Fannie Williams, and Anna Julia Cooper, she undertook profound social analysis and advocacy from the standpoint of Black women. Like her male co-investigators Du Bois and Miller, Terrell was compelled by her social standing and moral standpoint to work to empower the Black dispossessed.[33]

---

31. Manning, "The Black Faith of W. E. B. Du Bois," 31.

32. Du Bois, *The Negro Church*, 208.

33. For further biographical information see Mary Church Terrell, *A Colored Woman in a White World* (New York: Hall, [1940] 1996). Hers is the first full-length published autobiography by an African American woman. Howard University sociologist Kelly Miller published such well-known works as *Radicals and Conservatives, and Other Essays on the Negro in America* (New York: Schocken [1908], 1968); and *Out of the House of Bondage* (New York: Schocken, [1914] 1971).

The Black elite of the time, women and men alike, recognized that class differences in the Black community were largely unperceived in a white world in which race was the first identifier imposed on them and gender the second. At the same time, the most silenced voices of the era belonged to Black women who were the bedrock of everyday congregational life and activity. Slavery had violated Black women, brutalized Black men, desecrated Black children, and virtually decimated every institution other than the Black church. At the beginning of the twentieth century, therefore, it was widely agreed in the Black community that a reverent and moral faith was needed to meet the severe challenges facing the race. Regrettably, little in the way of gendered and class analysis was given to this important subject in *The Negro Church*. Nevertheless, for Terrell, Miller, and Du Bois, what is abundantly clear is that Black women represented (and represent still) the best hope of Black people: "Upon the *women* of no race have the truths of the gospel taken a firmer and deeper hold than upon the colored women of the United States. For her protection and by her help a religious rebirth is needed."[34]

Some of the most poignant and informative sections of *The Negro Church* are the narrative statements and opinions of everyday people interspersed throughout. As social science, these vignettes have little direct value; as personal accounts, they offer us a more textured and intimate look at Black social and religious life at the turn of the last century. The explicit faith that Du Bois once held in the social sciences would never again be sustained after the Atlanta University Studies. For his part, he had well mastered the forms and modalities of empirical sociology, and they were found wanting. Scientific rigor had not resulted in religious or intellectual repentance or social reform on the part of whites in the United States as he had anticipated; seemingly unassailable, scientific racism, social Darwinism, and white supremacy still reigned. Nevertheless, what Arnold Rampersad had to say about Du Bois's sociological approach in the urban classic *The Philadelphia Negro*, published four years earlier, was no less true of his work in *The Negro Church*: "There is no special pleading, apart from the final appeal, no disposition of the evidence to create images that would have ideological consequences; there is, in other words, almost no hint of propaganda. His respect for truth was almost fundamentalist; his ideas on how best to move a nation were still politically and psychologically naïve."[35]

The Negro Church concludes with a set of resolutions signed by Terrell, Miller, and Du Bois. Their collective call is for a religious rebirth for Black people, one that

[handwritten marginal note: rather heartbreaking naïveté here]

34. Du Bois, *The Negro Church*, 207. The theme of women as the critical center of social uplift and moral awakening in Black communities is taken up further in the final Atlanta University study, *Morals and Manners among Negro Americans* (1914).

35. Arnold Rampersad, *The Art & Imagination of W. E. B. Du Bois* (New York: Schocken, 1990), 50.

would move the church away from mere "emotional fervor" and an inadequately prepared and easily corrupted leadership toward fulfilling its destiny as a "mighty social power" and the "most powerful agency in the moral development and social reform of 9,000,000 Americans of Negro blood."[36] As the principal investigator and author of *The Negro Church*, Du Bois had rigorously and methodically scrutinized the progress of the Black church. In the end, his was the difficult and necessitous task of reminding Black believers that people of African descent in the United States could afford nothing less than an uncompromising ethical, economic, and political leadership in the midst of a social order that maimed, raped, and lynched Black hopes, dreams, and aspirations.

The Negro Church thus marks both an end and a beginning in the religious scholarship of Du Bois. Despite his well-chronicled dislike for religious dogma, over the next six decades he continued to write frequently on religion, the Black church, and the social, moral, and political responsibility of religious institutions. Du Bois's editorials, poetry, and short stories are full of religious imagery, themes, and ideas. As a mature scholar and activist, Du Bois remained faithful to the God of Black resistance and liberation, even as his life's work assumed a myriad of political and ideological forms. Not only were God and Jesus Black, but Christ was extolled as "the greatest of religious rebels" and an emancipator of the world's colored and exploited masses.[37] For Du Bois, by far the greatest gift of Black faith was its radical reinterpretation of Christianity for an oppressive and prejudicial social order. Thus, to the white world, he expressed a seeming agnosticism; but his enduring and principled spiritual commitment was to the Black world. Du Bois held to a multifaceted faith in the religion of Black people, a faith that was commonly but not only Christian, and in the utter righteousness of their cause.[38] One of his final essays, published in 1962, was the introduction to Milton Rogovin's fine photographic study of storefront churches in inner-city Buffalo, New York.[39]

After the Atlanta University Studies, the sanctity of scientific investigation steadily gave way for Du Bois before the intransigent realities of white racial supremacy and indifference. He concluded that an immoral and unjust world required an analytical response of a different order and magnitude, one less "impartial" and "objective" and one considerably more active, engaged and transformative in the

36. Du Bois, *The Negro Church*, 208.

37. W. E. B. Du Bois, "Postscript," *Crisis* 35 (1928) 203–4; and "Shall We Fight for Freedom?" *Chicago Defender*, 13 April 1946.

38. Marable and Aptheker develop aspects of these contrasting themes in their respective works. See "The Black Faith of W. E. B. Du Bois" and "W. E. B. Du Bois and Religion."

39. W. E. B. Du Bois, Introduction to "Store Front Churches" by Milton Rogovin, *Aperture* 10:2 (1962) 64, 68, 77, 84.

end. As he now saw it, the compelling challenge was not how to do less but how to do more; how to find ever more probing, progressive, and preemptive ways to mobilize his people, Black people, in the process transforming the dominant social order. Already, in 1903, Du Bois's tone was starting to change as his intellectual, moral, and aesthetic selves met in a pragmatic and prophetic dance. At the dawn of the twentieth century, he had authored two volumes of immense importance to the study of African American religion and culture that were published in the same year: *The Negro Church* and *The Souls of Black Folk*. The former was a natural and necessary precursor to the latter. Du Bois's sociological self was beginning to give way to even greater expressions of the soul.

The Black Church in the United States since Du Bois

In the years since Du Bois published *The Negro Church*, the African American community has undergone momentous and labyrinthine change. By the middle of the twentieth century, the largely Southern agrarian population had become predominately urban (and later suburban) as Blacks "voted with their feet" against Jim Crow segregation and the heinousness of white brutality for the "promised land" of the urban and mostly Northern industrial cities. The religious ramifications were considerable. The period between the First and Second World Wars witnessed what Gayraud Wilmore has called the "deradicalization of the Black church" as even the most modest forms of social critique gave way to a near exclusive emphasis on individual care and transformation in the midst of the white American maelstrom.[40] Much of the more radical hope of Black religion thus had to operate outside the traditional churches, as African Americans raised troubling new questions about the spiritual malaise of the Black church and its seeming preoccupation with white Christian values.

Out of the ensuing ecclesial schizophrenia emerged important new religious formations: the Holiness, Pentecostal, and Apostolic churches; the African Orthodox Church of Marcus Garvey; and such preachers of note as Rosa A. Horn, Ida B. Robinson, Father Divine, and Daddy Grace. Out of Newark, New Jersey, came Master Wali Fard and the Moorish Science Temple, with a message that was pro-Black, and perhaps even more important, non-Christian. In Detroit, Michigan, a small group of believers called the Temple People came under the influential leadership of Elijah Muhammad to become the Nation of Islam and a powerful voice of judgment on racist white America. These and other new religious movements rep-

40. See especially the introduction to the second edition of Gayraud Wilmore's *Black Religion and Black Radicalism: An Interpretation of the Religious History of Afro-American People* (Maryknoll, NY: Orbis, 1983), vii–x.

resented some of the most subversive expressions and transcendent hopes of Black people as they sought to create agency, dignity, and integrity in their lives.

In 1948, Du Bois, who had long since distanced himself from the contagion of the institutional Black church, still saw its prophetic possibilities and continued to express his support in the most public and provocative of ways. Speaking before an audience at Wilberforce University he offered these prescient words: "Our religion, with all its dogma, demagoguery, and showmanship, can be a center to teach character, right conduct and sacrifice. There lies here a career for a Negro Gandhi and a host of earnest followers."[41] Du Bois was right of course. Just over the horizon loomed the profoundly sacramental and Black-led struggle for the transformation of the nation—in civil rights, Black consciousness, and womanist activity—and enabling new paradigms for the witness of the church.

The Black-led freedom movement of the 1950s and beyond was an intense evocation of powerful and prolonged experiences that for the better part of three hundred years had sought to dismantle the institutional apparatus of racism. The scope and magnitude of these militant new protests were of a scale previously unknown and firmly identified with local church leadership—the Reverend Dr. Martin Luther King Jr., the Southern Christian Leadership Conference, and the Student Nonviolent Coordinating Committee among others. C. Eric Lincoln indicates that these were the watershed years when the "Negro Church" died and was reborn in the form of the "Black Church."[42] In the half century since, Black sociopolitical objectives and spiritual imperatives have been joined in intermittent fashion, at times spectacularly so but more often not, as Black religious communions still struggle to embrace the call to resistance, liberation, and social change as part of their divine mandate.

One cannot know for certain what Du Bois would have to say about the impact of Black congregational life in the United States more than one hundred years later (in my mind's eye he would not be surprised by contemporary Black church developments but deeply disappointed and chagrined), but some contemporary sociological observations are in order nonetheless. In a study of Black faith-based institutions that I conducted several years ago in Atlanta, Georgia, my findings were that a significant number of churches and mosques uncritically equated their social service provisions, while widespread and certainly important, with social justice advocacy and involvement, a less frequent and even more visionary undertaking.[43]

41. Cited in Aptheker, "W. E. B. Du Bois and Religion," 11.

42. See C. Eric Lincoln, *The Black Church since Frazier*, in *The Negro Church in America*, by E. Franklin Frazier; *The Church since Frazier* (New York: Schocken, 1974).

43. Alton B. Pollard III, "Black Churches, Black Empowerment, and Atlanta's Civil Rights Legacy," in *Black Churches and Local Politics*, ed. R. Drew Smith and Frederick C. Harris (Lanham, MD: Rowman & Littlefield, 2005), 3–22.

Take as an example the historic churches along Atlanta's spiritual main street Auburn Avenue: Ebenezer Baptist, Wheat Street Baptist, and Big Bethel African Methodist Episcopal—churches that are being challenged by an arresting array of residential problems ranging from job losses to gentrification. As a result, these well known congregations are strategically dedicating more of their material and spiritual resources to issues of neighborhood revitalization, community development and social justice. Roughly analogous to Sweet Auburn, located on the other side of downtown is the historic Vine City Community. On the corner of Northside Drive and Martin Luther King Jr. Drive, sits a cluster of attractive and affordable pastel-colored townhomes, the result of the work of a consortium of eleven congregations called the Vine City Housing Ministry. In Southeast Atlanta, the Atlanta Masjid of Al-Islam has made a strong educational investment in the East Lake community with the establishment of a community center, elementary school, and high school. All these congregations have become vital resources for their immediate neighborhoods, yet they are virtually nonfactors in Atlanta city or Fulton County public policy formulation. My investigations had only just begun to consider the impact of Atlanta's mostly suburban Black megachurches. However, data from recent studies of the megachurch phenomenon nationwide suggests such congregations have yet to establish a liberative ethos or presence in the wider community, their unique positioning and significant institutional capacity notwithstanding.[44]

Atlanta is popularly described as a modern-day Mecca for African Americans, and not without good reason. As of this writing, African Americans lead city government including the mayor, the president of the city council, the chiefs of the police and fire departments, and the superintendent of schools. The city is an urban enclave of unparalleled political power, civic involvement, economic prosperity, and social and cultural opportunity for some of America's citizens of African descent. At the same time, large numbers of Blacks remain trapped behind high poverty lev-

---

44. R. Drew Smith and Tamelyn Tucker-Worgs define the minimum threshold for megachurches as two thousand persons in weekly attendance. In Atlanta, as in many communities, it has become commonplace for congregations to hold two or more worship services. See Smith and Tucker-Worgs, "Megachurches: African American Churches in Social and Political Context," in *The State of Black America 2000* (New York: National Urban League, 2000), 171–97. Other important studies of the burgeoning Black megachurch phenomenon include Ronald Waters and Tamelyn Tucker-Worgs, "Black Churches and Electoral Engagement in the Nation's Capital," in *Black Churches and Local Politics*, eds. R. Drew Smith and Frederick C. Harris (Lanham, MD: Rowman & Littlefield, 2005), 99–116; Milmon F. Harrison, *Righteous Riches: The Word of Faith Movement in Contemporary African American Religion* (Oxford: Oxford University Press, 2005); Shayne Lee, *T. D. Jakes: America's New Preacher* (New York: New York University Press, 2005); Stephanie Y. Mitchem, *Name It and Claim It? Prosperity Preaching in the Black Church* (Cleveland: Pilgrim, 2007); and Jonathan L. Walton, *Watch This! The Ethics and Aesthetics of Black Televangelism* (New York: New York University Press, 2009).

els and low expectations with respect to quality of life and substantive economic change. That there are serious and long-standing problems in this post-civil rights city owes to a litany of factors—the white elite's concentrated monopolization of capital, a corresponding shift in race relations from white electoral dominance to containment management strategies (less overt, similar results) including but not limited to long-inadequate public schools, lack of job training and education, manufacturing jobs lost to the suburbs and exurbs, suburban government's curtailment of public transportation, past and present discrimination in housing and employment, the shortcomings of public agencies, and the migration of the Black middle class to adjoining counties.

As a result, economic empowerment has emerged in the Black faith-based community as one of the chief strategies required to respond to the current social crisis.[45] Some congregations have decided, largely independent of one another, that intermediate entrepreneurial solutions to achieving economic capacity—ranging from job-training programs, small business incubators, investment projects, and public-private collaborations to credit unions—are the best means to effect change and intervention in an uncertain economic and political environment. A few examples will suffice. Wheat Street Baptist Church sponsors a federal credit union (the first Black church to sponsor a credit union in the country) that has provided more than $10 million in loans to thousands of applicants over the last forty years. Antioch Baptist Church North has launched a landmark joint-venture partnership with the city of Atlanta and the business community to develop a ninety-acre, $86 million mixed use development that is anticipated to provide more than a thousand jobs and seventy new residential units to the area, which includes the impoverished Herndon Homes housing development and the Vine City neighborhood. In Atlanta's West End, the Shrine of the Black Madonna #9 has long operated a very popular and profitable Cultural Center and Bookstore and extensive economic self-help ventures, including three apartment complexes totaling 125 units.[46] Big Bethel AME, the city's oldest African American congregation, has purchased thirteen neighborhood properties for about $1 million, with the prophetic and pragmatic intent to restore the people and proud heritage of Auburn Avenue.

Similar indicators of Black-church economic activity are evidenced across the country. In Oakland, California, the Allen Temple Baptist Church sponsors a 125-unit housing development for the elderly, a credit union with $1 million in assets,

45. Smith and Tucker-Worgs, "Megachurches: African American Churches in Social and Political Context," 104. While only partially applicable in the theological sense, my use of the phrase "Black churches" is sociological shorthand for all Black faith-based institutions.

46. According to member reports, the Shrine is at present considering selling its apartment holdings.

a blood bank, and other community-service projects. In North Philadelphia, the Deliverance Evangelistic Church owns and operates the Hope Plaza Shopping Center, anchored by a leading supermarket chain, a McDonald's restaurant, and other merchants. Allen AME Church in Jamaica, New York, with a senior center, accredited school, oil consortium, and hundreds of housing units, has become one of the leading nonprofit corporations in the country and the second-largest African American employer in the city of New York. Churches such as Trinity United Church of Christ in Chicago, Union Baptist Church in Baltimore, The Sanctuary at Kingdom Square in Capital Heights, Maryland, First AME in Los Angeles, Olivet Institutional Baptist Church in Cleveland, Hartford Memorial Baptist Church in Detroit, and Concord Baptist Church in Brooklyn, among others, have established landmark ministries of social outreach and community development.[47]

In Kansas City, Missouri, small and median-sized churches have astutely leveraged their resources in the interest of a more comprehensive service than any one church could achieve alone with the establishment of the Community Development Corporation of Kansas City (CDC-KC). The Linwood Shopping Center was constructed in 1986 through this umbrella effort that represents dozens of churches in the Kansas City area. Seven years later a second shopping center, Linwood Square, was opened as an incubus for aspiring entrepreneurs. In 2001, the CDC-KC announced an even more ambitious project, a mixed-use development including retail stores, a one-hundred-room hotel, four hundred units of housing, and restaurants. A decade later, at a projected cost of $90 million and after a series of political delays, completion of Citadel Plaza is still fully anticipated.[48]

It is helpful to compare for a moment what these and other local congregations have done to extend empowerment into the surrounding community with some of the more popular television ministries and predominantly Black megachurches of today. Often, one of the most popular teachings of these ministries is the prosperity gospel, whose insular message and promise is "health and wealth" in this life. — *Yikes* In Atlanta, as elsewhere, "name-it-and-claim-it" and "highly-favored" teachings on prosperity abound and are frequently proclaimed as one of the general perks of church membership, yet there is little to indicate that this highly individualistic message possesses any broad restorative potential for the larger Black community. The long-term civic impact of such ministries, however, is a story that is only begin-

47. Some of these churches are highlighted in the foreword by C. Eric Lincoln to Gregory J. Reed's *Economic Empowerment through the Church: A Blueprint for Progressive Community Development* (Grand Rapids: Zondervan, 1994), 11–17.

48. Further information on the Community Development Corporation of Kansas City is found at the following website: http://www.lisc.org/kansascity/CDCKC.htm/.

ning to unfold. What the above churches of even the most modest means have done megachurch ministries can undoubtedly do and more. The Christian New Testament reminds us "to whom much has been given, much will be required" (Luke 12:48).

The more constructive efforts of Atlanta's Black churches to promote economic and social equality are themselves often confounded by problems of religious isolation and division. Although individual churches are making important, and even significant, contributions to the broader community, they rarely try to establish alliances with other churches or leading neighborhood development and nonprofit agencies. A noteworthy exception is the Concerned Black Clergy of Metropolitan Atlanta, Inc. (CBC), a critical mass of clergy and laity (with an active membership of 125 churches), who come together weekly to address critical community issues. On Atlanta's Southside the CBC is partnering with banking concerns and the county housing authority to work on affordable housing and other investment projects. Even the leadership of an organization like the CBC, as important as it is, does not disprove the general rule however. By and large, progressive Black communions everywhere have yet to seriously consider that tackling the root problems of the Black community will require a far more organized and intentional structural witness than is currently in place.

African American congregations must take the courageous next step and direct their still formidable resources to public policy advocacy and education, engaging the complex underlying structural and systemic forces that work against community building. For example, the negative distribution of goods and services in Black communities everywhere is but one major social policy trend that awaits a concerted response from Black churches. The wholesale shift of economic activity away from the urban center, with tragic consequences for the poor, is yet another compelling concern. Finally, it is important to ascertain and to respond to what causes so many Black religious bodies—whether small, marginalized, mainstream, multicultural, or megachurch—to focus with such passion on their own entrepreneurial interests to the economic neglect of the surrounding community. The endemic problems facing Atlanta's Black churches, communities, and people serve as a sobering reminder that Du Bois's call one hundred years ago for a prophetic moral agency is still as urgent as ever.

In the end, the work of personal transformation and community empowerment requires far more than what the institutional forms of Black religion alone can hope to accomplish. For all his harsh criticism of Black churches, the incredible breadth of Du Bois's Atlanta University studies illustrates how well he understood this truth, perhaps more so than most of us do today. We now have a broad array of organizations and enterprises in the Black community that have to be called upon to be accountable to the whole.

"the Black churched"

Still this does not in the least relieve the Black churched of their social no less religious responsibility. Tragically, for too many churches the recognition that there was a shift in the political terrain after the 1950s and 1960s, that the struggle for freedom moved from the steps of the courthouse and city hall and into the hallowed chambers of legislative assemblies, corporate boardrooms, and executive suites, appears never to have really occurred.[49] Now as never before a learned, strong and resourceful ministry and laity must be joined with the best that the Black religious scholarly tradition has to offer.[50] As we move well into the twenty-first century, as the racial lessons of the recent past continue to fade ipso facto from the collective memory—a reflection of the powerful and prolonged processes that now and again stall the African American freedom movement—pressing questions remain: How (and how well) will the Black faith community respond? What spiritual sensibilities will be involved in the affairs of everyday life? What theological and ethical resources will be brought to bear in light of current social struggles? What public policy and civic commitments will be made? These issues and more are at the center of the contemporary study of Black religion.

The Social Study of Black Religion

From the pioneering work of Du Bois in *The Negro Church* and *The Souls of Black Folk* to the present time, the role of the African American religious researcher has remained essentially unchanged. By 1960, only a handful of new studies on Black religion in the United States had been produced: Carter G. Woodson's *The History of the Negro Church* (1921); Benjamin E. Mays and Joseph Nicholson's *The Negro's Church* (1933); Benjamin Mays's *The Negro's God as Reflected in His Literature* (1938); a col-

---

49. Compelling analysis of the sociopolitical and economic difficulties confronting contemporary Black churches is presented in recent studies—Frederick C. Harris, *Something Within: Religion in African American Political Activism* (Oxford: Oxford University Press, 1999); Omar M. McRoberts, *Streets of Glory: Church and Community in a Black Urban Neighborhood* (Chicago: University of Chicago Press, 2003); R. Drew Smith, ed., *New Day Begun: African American Churches and Civic Culture in Post–Civil Rights America* (Durham: Duke University Press, 2003); and Smith, ed., *Long March Ahead: African American Churches and Public Policy in Post-Civil Rights America* (Durham: Duke University Press, 2005); Michael Leo Owens, *God and Government in the Ghetto: The Politics of Church-State Collaboration in Black America* (Chicago: University of Chicago Press, 2007); and Barbara Dianne Savage, *Your Spirits Walk Beside Us: The Politics of Black Religion* (Cambridge: Harvard University Press, 2008), among others.

50. The case for a better-educated and more resourceful Black clergy is made convincingly by C. Eric Lincoln and Lawrence H. Mamiya in *The Black Church in the African American Experience* (Durham: Duke University Press, 1990), 399–400.

lection of essays by Zora Neale Hurston, which were later published as *The Sanctified Church* (circa 1930s); Arthur Huff Fauset's *Black Gods of the Metropolis* (1944); and the posthumous work by E. Franklin Frazier, *The Negro Church in America* (1964).[51] The response of the white academic community to these researchers and their publications did not substantively deviate from that of their predecessors to Du Bois. Most white scholars remained oblivious to the idea that there was anything of merit to study in the Black religious tradition or for that matter that anyone else would want to do so.

Social studies of the Black church and Black religion have grown appreciably over the last half century. Leading the way in terms of contemporary social analysis was C. Eric Lincoln's celebrated study of the Nation of Islam, *The Black Muslims in America*, published in 1961 and followed by such writings as *The Black Experience in Religion* (1973), an excursus into the diversity of Black religious experiencing—African American churches, Black sectarian groups, and Caribbean and African religions—and his *Black Church Since Frazier* (1974). In 1965 ethicist George Kelsey wrote *Racism and the Christian Understanding of Man*, a powerful critique of racism as idolatry. In 1969 James Cone produced the watershed work, *Black Theology and Black Power*, followed by *A Black Theology of Liberation* (1970), and *The Spirituals and the Blues* (1972). Historical tours de force included Gayraud Wilmore's *Black Religion and Black Radicalism* (1972), Albert Raboteau's *Slave Religion* (1977), and Vincent Harding's *There Is a River* (1981). A seminal text from the history of religions was Charles H. Long's *Significations* (1985), whose essays on the religion of Blackness and the religions of the oppressed remain unsurpassed. Other influential researchers and texts of this generation merit discussion: Joseph R. Washington's *Black Religion* (1964), Albert Cleage's *The Black Messiah* (1968), Henry Mitchell's *Black Preaching* (1970), J. Deotis Roberts's *Liberation and Reconciliation* (1971), William R. Jones's *Is God a White Racist?* (1973), C. Eric Lincoln and Lawrence Mamiya's *Black Religion and the African American Experience* (1990), and James Cone's *Martin & Malcolm & America* (1991) come immediately and appreciatively to mind; even though they receive but brief mention here. The late 1970s and early 1980s saw the emergence of the next generation of Black religious intellectuals, most notably the pioneering womanist and feminist scholars Jacquelyn Grant, Katie Cannon, Delores Williams, Cheryl Townsend Gilkes, and Evelyn Higginbotham; and also Peter Paris, James Washington, Cornel West, and Cain Hope Felder, among others.

51. Other scholars who gave notable attention to African American religion during this period are St. Clair Drake, George Edmund Haynes, Melville Herskovits, Charles S. Johnson, Kelly Miller, and Howard Thurman.

Today another generation of Black religious scholars has emerged to explore the vast datum of Black religious life. Much like their predecessors, the current generation of researchers reflects the Du Boisian qualities of progressive intellectual vision and growth. Characteristically interdisciplinary or multidisciplinary in perspective and preparation, they are theologian, historian, ethicist, phenomenologist, biblical interpreter, Africanist, anthropologist, womanist, psychologist, political scientist, queer theorist, economist, sociologist, aesthete, and preacher—depending on what is called for by the context. Most by definition are researchers whose approach to African American religion and life is multiple, comparative, and more theoretically innovative than in the past. With varying degrees of investment in more nuanced approaches to identity and formation, their writings reflect the continuing struggle to restructure understandings of Black oppression, survival, resistance, and liberation by refracting race through the multiple lenses of religion, region, gender, class, sexuality, ecology and other categories of analysis. For Black religious scholars, religion never has been and is not now an uninteresting or insular phenomenon but an ever-potential source for social change. Akin to Du Bois, they promote religiously grounded social change through incisive and prophetic scholarship. Less clear, however, is to what degree the academy and the churches of today are better prepared than in the time of Du Bois to embrace new empirical and interpretive perspectives for change.

The questions and concerns that persons of African descent in this country struggle with on a daily basis, the vast schedule of needs that give shape to much of Black social and religious life, are vaster still. None may be more controversial or important than those relating to issues of intraracial and interracial identity, that is, establishing what constitutes inclusive and exclusive prerogatives and recognitions.[52] At present, the set of criteria commonly used to determine racial legitimacy is sufficiently confused and complicated to produce a broad array of responses and sometimes contradictory results: educational attainment, material accumulation, social class ascension, skin tone, color consciousness, gendered patterns, sexual relationships, generational perspectives, dual heritages, and endogenous relations with immigrants from Africa, the Caribbean, South America, and elsewhere in the Diaspora over the last third of a century: these and more figure prominently in the equation. On the other hand, there is a clear consensus among America's communities of African descent on the matter of state indifference and the inequitable delivery of health care, housing, education, employment, and other social services. Even in the present presidential age, the state of affairs of the nation's Black estate has far

---

52. While there is a general consensus that race is not a biological classification, its philosophical and social manifestations remain fully hegemonic.

from appreciably changed. Finally, there is a growing awareness of the interlocking and coalescent nature of degradations based on race, gender, sexuality, ecology, and ethnicity. In multitudinous ways, these issues and more are influenced by and in turn influence the Black religious landscape.

Akin to Du Bois, and seemingly anomalous to social science, for most contemporary Black scholars the collection and analysis of social data has no enduring value apart from its social manifestations and ethical implications. Today researchers who study the forms, expressions, and meanings of Black religion usually have a keen and common awareness of the promise and peril resident in Black life in general. The Black scholar-activist does not take less seriously than other researchers the criteria of sound scientific method and data collection and interpretation but refuses to make the knowledge an end in itself. Instead, Black scholars reflexively and with integrity consider another view, one which holds in critical and creative tension the idea that the religious motivations and beliefs of the community are worthy of recognition and may even represent more than the sum of their parts.[53] Such an understanding rests on and abides in a Du Boisian ethic of painstaking and prophetic scholarship for the empowerment of Black people. Du Bois's sense of moral purpose—his way of approaching social justice and the common good—is wise ancestral counsel as we continue to search for answers to the numerous personal, social, and sacred questions that abound. In the spirit of Du Bois, Terrell, and Miller, and that radiantly dark "cloud of witnesses" (Hebrews 11), Black scholars of religion, joined by others of like conviction, are now more prepared than ever to embrace new empirical and interpretive perspectives, for the advancement of knowledge and in the name of justice.[54]

53. For some representative works, see the following: Marla F. Frederick, *Between Sundays: Black Women and Everyday Struggles of Faith* (Berkeley: University of California Press, 2003); Teresa Fry Brown, *Weary Throats and New Songs: Black Women Proclaiming God's Word* (Nashville: Abingdon, 2003); Cheryl Townsend Gilkes, *"If it Wasn't for the Women . . .": Black Women's Experience and Womanist Culture in Church and Community* (Maryknoll, NY: Orbis, 2001); Dwight N. Hopkins, *Heart and Head: Black Theology—Past, Present, and Future* (New York: Palgrave, 2002); Charles H. Long, *Significations: Signs, Symbols, and Images in the Interpretation of Religion* (Philadelphia: Fortress, 1986); Jacob K. Olupona, ed., *African Spirituality: Forms, Meanings, and Expressions* (New York: Crossroad, 2000); R. Drew Smith, ed., *New Day Begun: African American Churches and Civic Culture in Post-Civil Rights America* (Durham: Duke University Press, 2003); and Vincent L. Wimbush, ed., *African Americans and the Bible: Sacred Texts and Social Textures* (New York: Continuum, 2000).

54. For a fuller treatment of contemporary themes in Black religion, see Alton B. Pollard III and Love Henry Whelchel, eds., *How Long this Road: Race, Religion and the Legacy of C. Eric Lincoln* (New York: Palgrave Macmillan, 2003).

Preface

A study of human life today involves a consideration of conditions of physical life, a study of various social organizations, beginning with the home, and investigations into occupations, education, religion and morality, crime and political activity. The Atlanta Cycle of studies into the Negro problem aims at exhaustive and periodic studies of all these subjects so far as they relate to the American Negro. Thus far, in the first eight years of the ten-year cycle, we have studied physical conditions of life (Reports No. 1 and No. 2), social organization (Reports No. 2 and No. 3), and economic activity (Reports No. 4 and No. 7), and Education (Reports No. 5 and No. 6). This year we take up the important subject of the NEGRO CHURCH, studying the religion of Negroes and its influence on their moral habits.

materialism

Such a study could not be made exhaustive for lack of funds and organization. On the other hand, the United States government and the churches themselves have published a great deal of material and it is possible from this and limited investigations in various typical localities to make a study of some value.

So, not necessarily claiming an exhaustive study

This investigation bases its results on the following data:

United States Census of 1800.
Minutes of Conferences.
Reports of Conventions, Societies, etc.
Catalogues of Theological Schools.
Two hundred and fifty special reports from pastors and officials.
One hundred and seventy-five special reports from colored laymen.
One hundred and seventeen special reports from heads of schools and prominent men, white and colored.
Fifty-four special reports from Southern white persons. *] interesting*
Thirteen special reports from Colored Theological Schools.
One hundred and nine special reports from Northern Theological Schools.
Answers from 1,300 school children.

Local studies in —

Richmond, Virginia.	Atlanta, Georgia.
Chicago, Illinois.	Greene County, Ohio.
Thomas County, Georgia.	Deland, Florida.

General and periodical literature.

In the preparation of this report the editor begs to acknowledge his indebtedness to the several hundred persons who have so kindly answered his inquiries; to students in Atlanta University and Virginia Union University, who have made special investigations; and particularly to Professor B. F. Williams, Mr. M. N. Work, Mr. R. R. Wright, Jr., and F. J. Grimke has kindly allowed the use of his unpublished report, made to the Hampton Conference in 1901; Mr. J. W. Cromwell has loaned us the results of his historical researches, and Dr. A. M. MacLean has given us the results of a valuable local study. The proof-reading was largely done by Mr. A. G. Dill.

Atlanta University has been conducting studies similar to this for the past seven years. The results, distributed at a nominal sum, have been widely used.

Notwithstanding this success the further prosecution of these important studies is greatly hampered by the lack of funds. With meager appropriations for expenses, lack of clerical help and necessary apparatus, the Conference cannot cope properly with the vast field of work before it.

We appeal therefore to those who think it worth while to study this, the greatest group of social problems that has ever faced the Nation, for substantial aid and encouragement in the further prosecution of the work of the Atlanta Conference.

Select Bibliography of Negro Churches

A brief statement of the rise and progress of the testimony of the religious society of Friends against slavery and the slave-trade. Philadelphia: Joseph and William Kite. 1843.

Ernest H. Abbott. Religious life in America. A record of personal observation. New York: The Outlook, 1902. XII, 730 pp. 80.

Nehemiah Adams. A South side view of slavery. 80. Boston, 1854.

Richard Allen, first bishop of the A. M. E. Church. The life, experience and gospel labors of the Rt. Rev. Richard Allen. Written by himself. Philadelphia, 1833.

Richard Allen and Jacob Tapisco. The doctrine and discipline of the A. M. E. Church. Philadelphia, 1819.

Matthew Anderson. Presbyterianism and its relation to the Negro. Philadelphia, 1897.

A statistical inquiry into the condition of the people of color of the city and districts of Philadelphia. Philadelphia, 1849, 1856 and 1859.

Samuel J. Baird. A collection of the acts, deliverances and testimonies of the Supreme Judiciary of the Presbyterian Church, from its origin in America to the present time, with notes and documents explanatory and historical, constituting a complete illustration of her polity, faith and history. Philadelphia: Presbyterian Board of Publications.

J. C. Ballagh. A history of slavery in Virginia. Johns Hopkins University Studies. Extra vol., No. 24. Baltimore, 1902.

Albert Barnes. Inquiry into the scriptural views of slavery. Philadelphia, 1857.

John S. Bassett. History of slavery in North Carolina. Johns Hopkins University studies. Baltimore, 1899.

———. Slavery and servitude in the colony of North Carolina. Baltimore: The Johns Hopkins Press, April and May, 1896.

David Benedict. A general history of the Baptist denomination in America and other parts of the world. Boston, 1813.

Edward W. Blyden. Christianity, Islam and the Negro race. With an introduction by the Hon. Samuel Lewis. 2d edition. London: W. B. Whittingham & Co. 432 pp. 80.

George Bourne. Man-stealing and Slavery denounced by the Presbyterian and Methodist Churches. Boston: Garrison and Knapp.

Jeffrey R. Brackett. Notes on the progress of the colored people of Maryland since the war. A supplement to the Negro in Maryland, a study of the institution of slavery. Baltimore: J. Hopkins Univ., 1890. 96 pp. 80.

———. The Negro in Maryland. A study of the institution of slavery. Baltimore: N. Murray (6) 268 pp. 80. (Johns Hopkins University studies in historical and political science.) Extra vol. 6.

William Burling. An address to the elders of the church upon the occasion of some Friends compelling certain persons and their posterity to serve them continually and arbitrarily, without regard to equity or right, not heeding whether they give them anything near so much as their labor deserveth. 1718. In Lay, All Slave Keeper Apostates. pp. 6-10.

Rev. Dr. R. F. Campbell. The race problem in the South. Pamphlet, 1899.

W. E. Burghardt Dubois. 1900. The religion of the American Negro. New World, vol. 9 (Dec. 1900) 614-625.

———. The Philadelphia Negro. A Social Study. Philadelphia, 1899: Ginn & Co.

———. The Negroes of Farmville, Va. 38 pp. Bulletin U.S. Department of Labor, Jan. 1898.

———. Some efforts of American Negroes for their own social betterment. Report of an investigation under the direction of Atlanta University, together with the proceedings of the third Conference for the study of the Negro problems, held at Atlanta University, May 25-26. 1898. Atlanta, Ga. (Atlanta University, 1898. 66 pp.)

———. The Souls of Black Folk. Chicago, 1903.

William Douglass. Sermons preached in the African Protestant Episcopal Church of St. Thomas. Philadelphia, 1854.

Annals of St. Thomas's Church. Philadelphia, 1862.

Bryan Edwards. History, civil and commercial, of the British Colonies in the West Indies. London, 1807.

Friends. A brief testimony of the progress of the Friends against slavery and the slave-trade. 1671-1787. Philadelphia, 1843.

William Goodell. The American slave code in theory and practice. Judiciary decisions and illustrative facts. New York, 1853.

H. Gregoire. Enquiry concerning the intellectual and moral faculties, etc., of Negroes. Brooklyn, 1810.

L. M. Hagood. The Colored Man in the Methodist Episcopal Church. Cincinnati.

Bishop J. W. Hood. One Hundred Years of the A. M. E. Zion Church.

Edward Ingle. The Negro in the District of Columbia. Johns Hopkins University studies. Vol. XI. Baltimore, 1893.

Samuel M. Janney. History of the religious Society of Friends. Philadelphia, 1859–1867.

Chas. C. Jones. The religious instruction of the Negroes in the United States. Savannah, 1842.

Absalom Jones. A Thanksgiving sermon on account of the abolition of the African slave-trade. Philadelphia, 1808.

Robert Jones. Fifty years in the Lombard Street Central Presbyterian Church. Philadelphia, 1894. 170 pp.

Fanny Kemble. A journal of a residence on a Georgia plantation. New York, 1863.

Walter Laidlow, editor. The Federation of Churches and Christian Workers in New York City. New York, 1896-1897.

Lucius C. Matlack. The history of American slavery and Methodism from 1780–1849. New York, 1849.

Holland McTyeire. A history of Methodism, comprising a view of the rise of this revival of spiritual religion in the first half of the eighteenth century. Nashville, Tenn.: Southern Methodist Publishing House, 1887.

Minutes, Annual Conferences, A. M. E. Church.

Minutes, Annual Conferences, C. M. E. Church.

Minutes, Annual Conferences, M. E. Church.

Minutes, Annual Conferences, A. M. E. Z. Church.

Minutes, General Conferences, A. M. E. Church.

Minutes, General Conferences, C. M. E. Church.

Minutes, General Conferences, M. E. Church.

Minutes, General Conferences, A. M. E. Z. Church.

Minutes, National Baptist Convention.

Edward Needles. Ten years' progress or a comparison of the state and condition of the colored people in the city and county of Philadelphia from 1837–1847. Philadelphia, 1849.

Daniel A. Payne. History of the A. M. E. Church. Nashville, 1891.

L. Garland Penn and J. W. E. Bowen. The United Negro: his problems and his progress. Containing the addresses and proceeding of the Negro Young People's

Christian and Educational Congress, held August 6–11, 1902. Atlanta, Ga.: D. E. Luther Publishing Co., 1902, XXX, 600 pp. Plates, portraits. 120.

Reports, Freedmen's Aid Society, Presbyterian Church.

Robert R. Semple. History of the rise and progress of Baptists in Virginia. Richmond, 1810.

William J. Simmons. Men of Mark, Eminent, Progressive and Rising. Cleveland, Ohio.

Slavery as it is: The testimony of a thousand witnesses. Publication of Anti-Slavery Society. New York, 1839.

George Smith. History of Wesleyan Methodism. London, 1862.

David Spencer. Early Baptists of Philadelphia. Philadelphia, 1877.

William B. Sprague. Annals of the American Pulpit. New York, 1858.

Benjamin T. Tanner. An outline of history and government for A. M. E. Churchman. Philadelphia, 1884.

———. An apology for African Methodism. Baltimore, 1867.

H. M. Turner. Methodist Polity. Philadelphia.

United States Census, 1890. Churches.

A. W. Wayman. My Recollections of A. M. E. Ministers. Philadelphia, 1883.

S. D. Weld. American Slavery as it is: testimony of thousands of witnesses. New York, 1839.

Stephen B. Weeks. Anti-slavery sentiment in the South. Washington, D.C., 1898.

———. Southern Quakers and Slavery. Baltimore, 1896.

George W. Williams. History of the Negro race in America. New York, 1883.

White. The African Preacher.

1

Primitive Negro Religion

The prominent characteristic of primitive Negro religion is Nature worship with the accompanying strong belief in sorcery. There is a theistic tendency: "Almost all tribes believe in some supreme god without always worshiping him, generally a heaven and rain god; sometimes, as among the Cameroons and in Dahomey, a sun-god. But the most widely-spread worship among Negroes and Negroids, from west to northeast and south to Loango, is that of the moon, combined with a great veneration of the cow."[*] The slave trade so mingled and demoralized the west coast of Africa for four hundred years that it is difficult today to find there definite remains of any great religious system. Ellis tells us of the spirit belief of the Ewne people; they believe that men and all Nature have the indwelling "Kra," which is immortal. That the man himself after death may exist as a ghost, which is often conceived of as departed from the "Kra," a shadowy continuing of the man. So Bryce, speaking of the Kaffirs of South Africa, a branch of the great Bantu tribe, says:

> To the Kaffirs, as to the most savage races, the world was full of spirits— spirits of the rivers, the mountains, and the woods. Most important were the ghosts of the dead, who had power to injure or help the living, and who were, therefore, propitiated by offerings at stated periods, as well as on occasions when their aid was especially desired. This kind of worship, the worship once most generally diffused throughout the world, and which held its ground among the Greeks and Italians in the most flourishing period of ancient civilization, as it does in China and Japan today, was, and is, virtually the religion of the Kaffirs.

[*] Professor C. P. Thiele, in Encyclopedia Britannica, 9th ed., XX, p. 362.

The supreme being of the Bantus is the dimly conceived Molimo, the Unseen, who typifies vaguely the unknown powers of nature or of the sky. Among some tribes the worship of such higher spirits has banished fetishism and belief in witchcraft, but among most of the African tribes the sudden and violent changes in government and social organization have tended to overthrow the larger religious conceptions and leave fetishism and witchcraft supreme. This is particularly true on the west coast among the spawn of the slave traders.

There can be no reasonable doubt, however, but that the scattered remains of religious systems in Africa today among the Negro tribes are survivals of the religious ideas upon which the Egyptian religion was based, and that the basis of the religion of Egypt was "of a purely Negritian character."[†]

The early Christian church had an Exarchate of fifty-two dioceses in Northern Africa, but it probably seldom came in contact with purely Negro tribes on account of the Sahara. The hundred dioceses of the patriarchate of Alexandria, on the other hand, embraced Libya, Pentapolis, Egypt, and Abyssinia, and had a large number of Negroid members. In Western Africa, after the voyage of Da Gama, there were several kingdoms of Negroes nominally Catholic, and the church claimed several hundred thousand communicants. These were on the slave coast and on the eastern coast.

Mohammedanism entered Africa in the seventh and eighth centuries and has since that time conquered nearly all Northern Africa, the Soudan, and made inroads into the populations of the west coast. "The introduction of Islam into Central and West Africa has been the most important if not the sole preservation against the desolations of the slave-trade,"[†] and especially is it preserving the natives against the desolations of Christian rum.

[†] Encyclopedia Britannica, 9th ed., XX, p. 362.
[†] Blyden, *Meth. Quar. Review*, Jan. 1871. See also his Christianity, Islam and the Negro Race.

2

Effect of Transplanting

It ought not to be forgotten that each Negro slave brought to America during the four centuries of the African slave trade was taken from definite and long-formed habits of social, political, and religious life. These ideas were not the highest, measured by modern standards, but they were far from the lowest, measured by the standards of primitive man. The unit of African tribal organization was the clan or family of families ruled by the patriarch or his strongest successor; these clans were united into tribes ruled by hereditary or elected chiefs, and some tribes were more or less loosely federated into kingdoms. The families were polygamous, communistic groups, with one father and as many mothers as his wealth and station permitted; the family lived together in a cluster of homes, or sometimes a whole clan or village in a long, low apartment house. In such clans the idea of private property was but imperfectly developed, and never included land. The main mass of visible wealth belonged to the family and clan rather than to the individual; only in the matter of weapons and ornaments was exclusive private ownership generally recognized.

The government, vested in fathers and chiefs, varied in different tribes from absolute despotisms to limited monarchies, almost republican. Viewing the Basuto National Assembly in South Africa, Mr. Bryce recently wrote:

> "The resemblance to the primary assembles of the early peoples of Europe is close enough to add another to the arguments which discredit the theory that there is any such thing as an 'Aryan Type' of institutions."*

In administering justice and protecting women these governments were as effective as most primitive organizations.

The power of religion was represented by the priest or medicine man. Aided by an unfaltering faith, natural sharpness and some rude knowledge of medicine, and

* Impressions of S. Africa, 3rd ed., p. 352.

3

supported by the vague sanctions of a half-seen world peopled by spirits, good and evil, the African priest wielded a power second only to that of the chief, and often superior to it. In some tribes the African priesthood was organized and something like systematic religious institutions emerged. But the central fact of African life, political, social and religious, is its failure to integrate—to unite and systematize itself in some conquering whole which should dominate the wayward parts. This is the central problem of civilization and while there have arisen from time to time in Africa conquering kingdoms, and some consolidation of power in religion, it has been continually overthrown before it was strong enough to maintain itself independently. What have been the causes of this? They have been threefold: the physical peculiarities of Africa, the character of external conquest, and the slave-trade—the "heart disease of Africa." The physical peculiarities of the land shut out largely the influence of foreign civilization and religion and made human organization a difficult fight for survival against heat and disease; foreign conquest took the form of sudden incursions, causing vast migrations and uprooting of institutions and beliefs, or of colonizations of strong, hostile and alien races, and finally for four centuries the slave-trade fed on Africa, and peaceful evolution in political organization or religious belief was impossible.

Especially did the slave-trade ruin religious evolution on the west coast; the ancient kingdoms were overthrown and changed, tribes and nations mixed and demoralized, and a perfect chaos of ideas left. Here it was that animal worship, fetishism and belief in sorcery and witchcraft strengthened their sway and gained wider currency than ever.

The first social innovation that followed the transplanting of the Negro was the substitution of the West Indian plantation for the tribal and clan life of Africa. The real significance of this change will not appear at first glance. The despotic political power of the chief was now vested in the white master; the clan had lost its ties of blood relationship and became simply the aggregation of individuals on a plot of ground, with common rules and customs, common dwellings, and a certain communism in property. The two greatest changes, however, were, first, the enforcement of severe and unremitted toil, and, second, the establishment of a new polygamy—a new family life. These social innovations were introduced with much difficulty and met determined resistance on the part of the slaves, especially when there was community of blood and language. Gradually, however, superior force and organized methods prevailed, and the plantation became the unit of a new development. The enforcement of continual toil was not the most revolutionary change which the plantation introduced. Where this enforced labor did not descend to barbarism and slow murder, it was not bad discipline; the African had the natural indolence of a tropical nature which had never felt the necessity of work; his first great awakening came with hard labor, and a pity it was, not that he worked, but that voluntary labor on his part was not from the first encouraged and rewarded. The vast and overshadowing change that the plantation system introduced was the change in the status of women—the new polygamy. This new polygamy had all the evils and not one of the safeguards of the African prototype. The African system was a complete protection for girls, and a strong protection for wives against everything but the tyranny of the husband; the plantation polygamy left the chastity of Negro women absolutely unprotected in law, and practically little guarded in custom. The number of wives of a native African was limited and limited very effectually by the number of cattle he could command or his prowess in war. The number of wives of a West India slave was limited chiefly by his lust and cunning. The black females, were they wives or growing girls, were the legitimate prey of the men, and on this system there was one, and only one, safeguard, the character of the master of the plantation. Where the master was himself lewd and avaricious the degradation of the women was complete. Where, on the other hand, the plantation system reached its best development, as in Virginia, there was a fair approximation of a monogamic marriage system among the slaves; and yet even here, on the best conducted plantations, the protection of Negro women was but imperfect; the seduction of girls was frequent, and seldom did an illegitimate child bring shame, or an adulterous wife punishment to the Negro quarters.

And this was inevitable, because on the plantation the private home, as a self-protective, independent unit, did not exist. That powerful institution, the polygamous African home, was almost completely destroyed and in its place in America arose sexual promiscuity, a weak community life, with common dwelling, meals and child-nurseries. The internal slave trade tended to further weaken natural ties. A small number of favored house servants and artisans were raised above this—had their private homes, came in contact with the culture of the master class, and assimilated much of American civilization. Nevertheless, broadly speaking, the greatest social effect of American slavery was to substitute for the polygamous Negro home a new polygamy less guarded, less effective, and less civilized.

At first sight it would seem that slavery completely destroyed every vestige of spontaneous social movement among the Negroes; the home had deteriorated; political authority and economic initiative was in the hands of the masters, property, as a social institution, did not exist on the plantation, and, indeed, it is usually assumed by historians and sociologists that every vestige of internal development disappeared, leaving the slaves no means of expression for their common life, thought, and striving. This is not strictly true; the vast power of the priest in the African state has already been noted; his realm alone—the province of religion and medicine—remained largely unaffected by the plantation system in many important particulars. The Negro priest, therefore, early became an important figure on the plantation and found his function as the interpreter of the supernatural, the comforter of the sorrowing, and as the one who expressed, rudely, but picturesquely, the longing and disappointment and resentment of a stolen people. From such beginnings arose and spread with marvellous rapidity the Negro Church, the first distinctively Negro American social institution. It was not at first by any means a Christian Church, but a mere adaptation of those heathen rites which we roughly designate by the term Obe Worship, or "Voodoism." Association and missionary effort soon gave these rites a veneer of Christianity, and gradually, after two centuries, the Church became Christian, with a simple Calvinistic creed, but with many of the old customs still clinging to the services. It is this historic fact that the Negro Church of today bases itself upon the sole surviving social institution of the African fatherland that accounts for its extraordinary growth and vitality. We easily forget that in the United States today there is a Church organization for every sixty Negro families. This institution, therefore, naturally assumed many functions which the other harshly suppressed social organs had to surrender; the Church became the center of amusements, of what little spontaneous economic activity remained, of education, and of all social intercourse.

3

The Obeah Sorcery

Let us now trace this development historically. The slaves arrived with a strong tendency to Nature worship and a belief in witchcraft common to all. Beside this some had more or less vague ideas of a supreme being and higher religious ideas, while a few were Mohammedans, and fewer Christians. Some actual priests were transported and others assumed the functions of priests, and soon a degraded form of African religion and witchcraft appeared in the West Indies, which was known as Obi,* or sorcery. The French Creoles called it "Waldensian" (Vaudois), because of the witchcraft charged against the wretched followers of Peter Waldo, whence comes the dialect name of Voodoo or Hoodoo, used in the United States. Edwards gives as sensible an account of this often exaggerated form of witchcraft and medicine as one can get:

> As far as we are able to decide from our own experience and informa-
> tion when we lived in the island, and from the current testimony of all
> the Negroes we have ever conversed with on the subject, the professors
> of Obi are, and always were, natives of Africa, and none other; and they
> have brought the science with them from thence to Jamaica, where it is so
> universally practiced, that we believe there are few of the large estates pos-
> sessing native Africans, which have not one or more of them. The oldest
> and most crafty are those who usually attract the greatest devotion and
> confidence; those whose hoary heads, and a somewhat peculiarly harsh
> and forbidding aspect, together with some skill in plants of the medical
> and poisonous species, have qualified them for successful imposition

---

* Obi (Obeah, Obiah or Obia), is the adjective: Obe or Obi, the noun. It is of African origin, probably connected with Egyptian Ob, Aub, or Obron, meaning serpent. Moses forbids Israelites ever to consult the demon Ob, i.e., "Charmer, Wizard." The Witch of Endor is called Oub or Ob. Oubaous is the name of the Baselisk or Royal Serpent, emblem of the Sun, and, according to Horus Appollo, " ancient oracular Deity of Africa." —Edwards, West Indies, II, pp. 106–119.

upon the weak and credulous. The Negroes in general, whether Africans or Creoles, revere, consult, and fear them. To these oracles they resort, and with the most implicit faith, upon all occasions, whether for the cure of disorders, the obtaining revenge for injuries or insults, the conciliating of favor, the discovery and punishment of the thief or adulterer, and the prediction of future events. The trade which these imposters carry on is extremely lucrative; they manufacture and sell their Obeis adapted to the different cases and at different prices. A veil of mystery is studiously thrown over their incantations, to which the midnight hours are allotted, and every precaution is taken to conceal them from the knowledge and discovery of the White people.[†]

At first the system was undoubtedly African and part of some more or less general religious system. It finally degenerated into mere imposture. There would seem to have been some traces of blood sacrifice and worship of the Moon, but unfortunately those who have written on the subject have not been serious students of a curious human phenomenon, but rather persons apparently unable to understand why a transplanted slave should cling to heathen rites.

[†] Edwards: West Indies, II, 108–109.

4

Slavery and Christianity

The most obvious reason for the spread of witchcraft and persistence of heathen rites among Negro slaves was the fact that at first no effort was made by masters to offer them anything better. The reason for this was the widespread idea that it was contrary to law to hold Christians as slaves. One can realize the weight of this if we remember that the Diet of Worms and Sir John Hawkins' voyages were but a generation apart. From the time of the Crusades to the Lutheran revolt the feeling of Christian brotherhood had been growing, and it was pretty well established by the end of the sixteenth century that it was illegal and irreligious for Christians to hold each other as slaves for life. This did not mean any widespread abhorrence of forced labor from serfs or apprentices and it was particularly linked with the idea that the enslavement of the heathen was meritorious, since it punished their blasphemy on the one hand and gave them a change for conversion on the other.

When, therefore, the slave-trade from Africa began it met only feeble opposition here and there. That opposition was in nearly all cases stilled when it was continually stated that the slave-trade was simply a method of converting the heathen to Christianity. The corollary that the conscience of Europe immediately drew was that after conversion the Negro slave was to become in all essential respects like other servants and laborers, that is bound to toil, perhaps, under general regulations, but personally free with recognized rights and duties.

Most colonists believed that this was not only actually right, but according to English law. And while they early began to combat the idea they continually doubted the legality of their action in English courts. In 1635 we find the authorities of Providence islands condemning Mr. Reshworth's behavior concerning the Negroes who ran away, as indiscreet, "arising, as it seems, from a groundless opinion that

Christians may not lawfully keep such persons in a state of servitude during their strangeness from Christianity," and injurious to themselves. *

The colonies early began cautiously to declare that certain distinctions lay between "Christian" inhabitants and slaves, whether they were Christians or not. Maryland, for instance, proposed a law, in 1638, which failed of passage. It was:

> "For the liberties of the people" and declared "all Christian inhabitants (slaves only excepted) to have and enjoy all such rights, liberties, immunities, privileges and free customs, within this province, as any natural born subject of England hath or ought to have or enjoy in the realm of England, saving in such cases as the same are or may be altered or changed by the laws and ordinances of this province." †

The question arose in different form in Massachusetts when it was enacted that only church members could vote. If Negroes joined the church, would they become free voters of the commonwealth? It seemed hardly possible. ‡ Nevertheless, up to 1660 or thereabouts it seemed accepted in most colonies and in the English West Indies that baptism into a Christian church would free a Negro slave. Massachusetts first apparently attacked this idea by enacting in 1641 that slavery should be confined to captives in just wars "and such strangers as willingly sell themselves or are sold to us," meaning by "strangers" apparently heathen, but saying nothing as to the effect of conversion. Connecticut adopted similar legislation in 1650 and Virginia declared in 1661 that Negroes "are incapable of making satisfaction" for time lost in running away by lengthening their time of service, thus implying that they were slaves for life, and Maryland declared flatly in 1663 that Negro slaves should serve "*durante cita.*" In Barbadoes the Council presented, in 1663, an act to the Assembly recommending the christening of Negro children and the instruction of all adult Negroes to the several ministers of the place.

At the same time in the ready-made Duke of York's laws sent over to the new colony of New York in 1664 the old idea seems to prevail:

> "No Christian shall be kept in bondslavery, villenage, or captivity, except such who shall be judged thereunto by authority, or such as willingly have sold or shall sell themselves, in which case a record of such servitude shall be entered in the Court of Sessions held for that jurisdiction where such masters shall inhabit, provided that nothing in the law contained shall be to the prejudice of master or dame who have or shall by any indenture or

---

* Sainsbury: Calendar of State Papers, 1574–1660, ¶ 262.
† Williams' History of the Negro Race, I, 239.
‡ *Ibid.* I, 190.

covenant take apprentices for term of years, or other servants for term of years or life." *

It was not until 1667 that Virginia finally plucked up courage to attack the issue squarely and declared by law:

> "Baptisme doth not alter the condition of the person as to his bondage or freedom, in order that diverse masters freed from this doubt may more carefully endeavor the propagation of Christianity." *

Following this Virginia took three further decisive steps in 1670, 1682, and 1705. First she declared that only slaves imported from Christian lands should be free. Next she excepted Negroes and mulattoes from even this restriction unless they were born of Christians and were Christians when taken in slavery. Finally only personal Christianity in Africa or actual freedom in a Christian country excepted a Virginia Negro slave from life-long slavery. †

This changing attitude of Christians toward Negroes was reflected in Locke's Fundamental Constitutions for Carolina in 1670, one article of which said:

> "Since charity obliges us to wish well to the souls of all men, and religion ought to alter nothing in any man's civil estate or right, it shall be lawful for slaves as well as others to enter themselves and to be of what church or profession any of them shall think best, and thereof be as fully members as any freeman. But yet no slave shall hereby be exempted from that civil dominion his master hath over him, but be in all things in the same state and condition he was in before." ‡

So much did this please the Carolinians that it was one of the few articles re-enacted in the Constitution of 1698. In 1671 Maryland was moved to pass "An Act for the Encouraging of the Importation of Negroes and Slaves." This law declared that conversion or the holy sacrament of baptism should not be taken to give manu-mission in any way to slaves or their issue who had become Christians or had been or should be baptized either before or after their importation to Maryland, "any opinion to the contrary notwithstanding."

It was explained that this law was passed because "several of the good people of this province have been discouraged from importing or purchasing therein any Negroes or other slaves; and such as have imported or purchased any there have neglected—to the great displeasure of Almighty God and the prejudice of the souls

---

* Williams I, 139.

† Ballagh, pp. 47–52.

‡ Bassett: Slavery in Colony of N. C., p. 41.

of those poor people—to instruct them in the Christian faith, and to permit them to receive the holy sacrament of baptism for the remission of their sin, under the mistaken and ungrounded apprehension that their slaves by becoming Christians would thereby be freed." * This law was re-enacted in 1692 and 1715.

It is clear from these citations that in the seventeenth century not only was there little missionary effort to convert Negro slaves, but that there was on the contrary positive refusal to let slaves be converted, and that this refusal was one incentive to explicit statements of the doctrine of perpetual slavery for Negroes. The French Code Noir of 1685 made baptism and religious instruction of Negroes obligatory. We find no such legislation in English colonies. On the contrary, the principal Secretary of State is informed in 1670 that in Jamaica the number of tippling houses has greatly increased, and many planters are ruined by drink. "So interests decrease, Negroes and slaves increase. There is much cruelty, oppression, rape, whoredoms, and adulteries." †

In Massachusetts John Eliot and Cotton Mather both are much concerned that "so little care was taken of their (the Negroes') precious and immortal souls," which were left to "a destroying ignorance merely for fear of thereby losing the benefit of their vassalage."

So throughout the colonies it is reported in 1678 that masters, "out of covetousness," are refusing to allow their slaves to be baptized; and in 1700 there is an earnest plea in Massachusetts for religious instruction of Negroes since it is "notorious" that masters discourage the "poor creatures" from baptism. In 1709 a Carolina clergyman writes to the secretary of the Society for the Propagation of the Gospel in England that only a few of 200 or more Negroes in his community were taught Christianity, but were not allowed to be baptized. Another minister writes, a little later, that he prevailed upon a master after much importuning to allow three Negroes to be baptized. In North Carolina in 1709 a clergyman of the Established Church complains that masters will not allow their slaves to be baptized for fear that a Christian slave is by law free. A few were instructed in religion, but not baptized. The Society for the Propagation of the Gospel combated this notion vigorously. Later, in 1732, Bishop Berkeley reports that few Negroes have been received into the church. ‡

This state of affairs led to further laws, and the instructions to some of the royal Governors contain a clause ordering them to "find out the best means to facilitate and encourage the conversion of Negroes and Indians to the Christian religion." §

* Brackett, p. 29.

† Sainsbury's Calendars, 1669–74, ¶ 138.

‡ Brackett, p. 31. Bassett: Slavery in Colony of N. C., p. 46.

§ Instructions of Lord Cornbury of Va., 702. Williams I, 140.

New York hastened to join the States which sought to reassure masters, declaring in 1706:

> "Whereas, Divers of her Majesty's good subjects, inhabitants of this colony, now are, and have been willing that such Negroes, Indian and Mulatto slaves, who belong to them, and desire the same, should be baptized, but are deterred and hindered therefrom by reason of a groundless opinion that hath spread itself in this colony, that by the baptizing of such Negro, Indian or Mulatto slaves, they would become free, and ought to be set at liberty. In order, therefore, to put an end to all such doubts and scruples as have, or hereafter any time may arise about the same:
>
> "Be it enacted, etc., That the baptizing of a Negro, Indian, or Mulatto slave shall not be any cause or reason for the setting them, or any of them, at liberty.
>
> "And be it, etc., That all and every Negro, Indian, Mulatto and Mestee bastard child and children, who is, are, and shall be born of any Negro, Indian, or Mestee, shall follow the state and condition of the mother and be esteemed, reputed, taken and adjudged a slave and slaves to all intents and purposes whatsoever." [†]

In 1729 an appeal from several colonies was made to England on the subject in order to increase the conversion of blacks. The Crown Attorney and Solicitor General replied that baptism in no way changed the slave's status. [§]

[†] Williams I, p. 141.
[§] Brackett, p. 30.

5

Early Restrictions

"In the year 1624, a few years after the arrival of the first slave ship at Jamestown, Va., a Negro child was baptized and called William, and from that time on in almost all, if not all, the oldest churches in the South, the names of Negroes baptized into the church of God can be found upon the registers." ‖

It was easy to make such cases an argument for more slaves. James Habersham, the Georgia companion of the Methodist Whitefield, said about 1730:

> "I once thought it was unlawful to keep Negro slaves, but I am now induced to think God may have a higher end in permitting them to be brought to this Christian country, than merely to support their masters. Many of the poor slaves in America have already been made freemen of the heavenly Jerusalem and possibly a time may come when many thousands may embrace the gospel, and thereby be brought into the glorious liberty of the children of God. These, and other considerations, appear to plead strongly for a limited use of Negroes; for, while we can buy provisions in Carolina cheaper than we can here, no one will be induced to plant much."

In other cases there were curious attempts to blend religion and expediency, as for instance, in 1710, when a Massachusetts clergyman evolved a marriage ceremony for Negroes in which the bride solemnly promised to cleave to her husband "so long as God in his Providence" and the slave-trade let them live together!

The gradual increase of these Negro Christians, however, brought peculiar problems. Clergymen, despite the law, were reproached for taking Negroes into the church and still allowing them to be held as slaves. On the other hand it was not easy to know how to deal with the black church member after he was admitted. He must either be made a subordinate member of a white church or a member of a Negro

‖ Archdeaeon J. H. M. Pollard.

church under the general supervision of whites. As the efforts of missionaries, like Dr. Bray, slowly increased the number of converts, both these systems were adopted. But the black congregations here and there soon aroused the suspicion and fear of the masters, and as early as 1715 North Carolina passed an act which declared:

> That if any master or owner of Negroes or slaves, or any other person or persons whatsoever in the government, shall permit or suffer any Negro or Negroes to build on their, or either of their, lands, or any part thereof, any house under pretense of a meeting-house upon account of worship, or upon any pretense whatsoever, and shall not suppress and hinder them, he, she, or they so offending, shall, for every default, forfeit and pay fifty pounds, one-half toward defraying the contingent charges of the government, the other to him or them that shall sue for the same."[*]

This made Negro members of white churches a necessity in this colony, and there was the same tendency in other colonies. "Maryland passed a law in 1723 to suppress tumultuous meetings of slaves on Sabbath and other holy days," a measure primarily for good order, but also tending to curb independent religious meetings among Negroes. In 1800 complaints of Negro meetings were heard. Georgia in 1770 forbade slaves "to assemble on pretense of feasting," etc., and "any constable," on direction of a justice, is commanded to disperse any assembly or meeting of slaves "which may disturb the peace or endanger the safety of his Majesty's subjects; and every slave which may be found at such meetings, as aforesaid, shall and may, by order of such justice, immediately be corrected, without trial, by receiving on the bare back twenty-five stripes, with a whip, switch, or cowskin," etc.[†] In 1792 in a Georgia act "to protect religious societies in the exercise of their religious duties," punishment was provided for persons disturbing white congregations, but "no congregation or company of Negroes shall upon pretense of divine worship assemble themselves" contrary to the act of 1770. Whether or not such acts tended to curb the really religious meetings of the slaves or not it is not easy to know. Probably they did, although at the same time there was probably much disorder and turmoil among slaves, which sought to cloak itself under the name of the church. This was natural, for such assemblies were the only surviving African organizations, and they epitomized all there was in slave life outside of forced toil.

It gradually became true, as Brackett says, that "any privileges of church-going which slaves might enjoy depended much, as with children, on the disposition of the masters."[‡] In some colonies, like North Carolina, masters continued indifferent

[*] Lapsed in 1741. See Laws of 1715, Ch. 46, Sec. 18; Bassett: Colony, p. 50.

[†] Prince's Digest, 447.

[‡] Brackett, pp. 108–110.

throughout the larger part of the eighteenth century. In New Hanover county of that state out of a thousand whites and two thousand slaves, 307 masters were baptized in 1742, but only nine slaves. The English are told of continued indifference in Massachusetts, the Connecticut General Assembly is asked in 1738 if masters ought not to promise to train slaves as Christians, and instructions are repeatedly given to Governors on the matter, with but small results.[§]

[§] Bassett: Colony, p. 49; Williams I, p. 188.

6

The Society for the Propagation of the Gospel[φ]

"The Society for the Propagation of the Gospel in Foreign Parts" was incorporated under William III, on the 16th day of June, 1701, and the first meeting of the society under its charter was the 27th of June of the same year. Thomas Laud, Bishop of Canterbury, Primate and Metropolitan of all England, was appointed by his majesty the first president.

This society was formed with the view, primarily, of supplying the destitution of religious institutions and privileges among the inhabitants of the North American colonies, members of the established church of England; and, secondarily, of extending the gospel to the Indians and Negroes. The society entered upon its duties with zeal, being patronized by the king and all the dignitaries of the Church of England.

They instituted inquiries into the religious condition of all the colonies, responded to "by the governors and persons of the best note," (with special reference to Episcopacy), and they perceived that their work "consisted of three great branches: the care and instruction of our people settled in the colonies; the conversion of the Indian savages, and the conversion of the Negroes." Before appointing missionaries they sent out a traveling preacher, the Rev. George Keith (an itinerant missionary), who associated with himself the Rev. John Talbot. Mr. Keith preached between North Carolina and Piscataqua river in New England, a tract above eight hundred miles in length, and completed his mission in two years, and returned and reported his labors to the society.

The annual meetings of this society were regularly held from 1702 to 1819 and 118 sermons preached before it by bishops of the Church of England, a large number of them distinguished for piety, learning, and zeal.

[φ] This section is taken largely from Charles Colcock Jones' "The religious Instruction of the Negroes," Savannah, 1842.

In June, 1702, the Rev. Samuel Thomas, the first missionary, was sent to the colony of South Carolina. The society designed he should attempt the conversion of the Yammosee Indians; but the governor, Sir Nathaniel Johnson, appointed him to the care of the people settled on the three branches of Cooper river, making Goose creek his residence. He reported his labors to the society and said "that he had taken much pains also in instructing the Negroes, and learned twenty of them to read." He died in October, 1706. He was succeeded by a number of missionaries.

"In 1709 Mr. Huddlestone was appointed school-master in New York city. He taught forty poor children out of the society funds, and publicly catechized in the steeple of Trinity Church every Sunday in the afternoon, 'not only his own scholars, but also the children, servants and slaves of the inhabitants, and above one hundred usually attended him.'

"The society established also a catechizing school in New York city in 1704, in which there were computed to be about 1,500 Negro and Indian slaves. The society hoped their example would be generally followed in the colonies. Mr. Elias Neau, a French Protestant, was appointed catechist, who was very zealous in his duty, and many Negroes were instructed and baptized.

"In 1712 the Negroes in New York conspired to destroy all the English, which greatly discouraged the work of their instruction. The conspiracy was defeated, and many Negroes taken and executed. Mr. Neau's school was blamed as the main occasion of the barbarous plot; two of Mr. Neau's students were charged with the plot; one was cleared and the other was proved to have been in the conspiracy, but guiltless of his master's murder. 'Upon full trial the guilty Negroes were found to be such as never came to Mr. Neau's school; and, what is very observable, the persons whose Negroes were found most guilty were such as were the declared opposers of making them Christians.' In a short time the cry against the instruction of the Negroes subsided: the governor visited and recommended the school. Mr. Neau died in 1722, much regretted by all who knew his labors." He was succeeded by Rev. Mr. Wetmore, who afterwards was appointed missionary to Rye in New York. After his removal "the rector, church wardens, and vestry of Trinity Church in New York city" requested another catechist, "there being about 1,400 Negro and Indian slaves, a considerable number of whom had been instructed in the principles of Christianity by the late Mr. Neau, and had received baptism and were communicants in their church. The society complied with this request and sent over Rev. Mr. Colgan in 1726, who conducted the school with success."*

* Cf. Atlanta University Publications, No. 6.

The society looked upon the instruction and conversion of the Negroes as a principal branch of its care, esteeming it a great reproach to the Christian name that so many thousands of persons should continue in the same state of pagan darkness under a Christian government and living in Christian families as they lay under formerly in their own heathen countries. The society immediately from its first institution strove to promote their conversion, and inasmuch as its income would not enable it to send numbers of catechists sufficient to instruct the Negroes, yet it resolved to do its utmost and at least to give this work the mark of its highest approbation. Its officers wrote, therefore, to all their missionaries that they should use their best endeavors at proper times to instruct the Negroes, and should especially take occasion to recommend zealously to the masters to order their slaves, at convenient times, to come to them that they might be instructed.

The history of the society goes on to say: "It is a matter of commendation to the clergy that they have done thus much in so great and difficult a work. But, alas! what is the instruction of a few hundreds in several years with respect to the many thousands uninstructed, in several years with respect to the may thousands uninstructed, unconverted, living, dying, utter pagans. It must be confessed what hath been done is as nothing with regard to what a true Christian would hope to see effected." After stating several difficulties in respect to the religious instruction of the Negroes, it is said: "But the greatest obstruction is the masters themselves do not consider enough the obligation which lies upon them to have their slaves instructed." And in another place, "the society have always been sensible the most effectual way to convert the Negroes was by engaging their masters to countenance and promote their conversion." The bishop of St. Asaph, Dr. Fleetwood, preached a sermon before the society in the year 1711, setting forth the duty of instructing the Negroes in the Christian religion. The society thought this so useful a discourse that they printed and dispersed abroad in the plantations great numbers of that sermon in the same year; and in the year 1725 reprinted the same and dispersed again great numbers. The bishop of London, Dr. Gibson, (to whom the care of plantations abroad, as to religious affairs, was committed,) became a second advocate for the conversion of Negroes, and wrote two letters on the subject. The first in 1727, "addressed to masters and mistresses of families in the English plantations abroad, exhorting them to encourage and promote the instruction of their Negroes in the Christian faith. The second in the same year, addressed to the missionaries there, directing them to distribute the said letter, and exhorting them to give their assistance towards the instruction of the Negroes within their several parishes."

The society were persuaded this was the true method to remove the great obstruction to their conversion, and hoping so particular an application to the masters and mistresses from the See of London would have the strongest influence, they printed ten thousand copies of the letter to the masters and mistresses, which were sent to all the colonies on the continent and to all the British islands in the West Indies, to be distributed among the masters of families, and all other inhabitants. The society received accounts that these letters influenced many masters of families to have their servants instructed. The bishop of London soon after wrote "an address to serious Christians among ourselves, to assist the Society for Propagating the Gospel in carrying on this work."

In the year 1783, and the following, soon after the separation of our colonies from the mother country, the society's operations ceased, leaving in all the colonies forty-three missionaries, two of whom were in the Southern States—one in North and one in South Carolina. The affectionate valediction of the society to them was issued in 1785. "Thus terminated the connection of this noble society with our country, which, from the foregoing notices of its effort, must have accomplished a great deal for the religious instruction of the Negro population."

7

The Moravians, Methodists, Baptists, and Presbyterians*

The Moravians or United Brethren were the first who formally attempted the establishment of missions exclusively to the Negroes.

A succinct account of their several efforts, down to the year 1790, is given in the report of the Society for the Propagation of the Gospel among the Heathen, at Salem, N.C., October 5th, 1837, by Rev. J. Renatus Schmidt, and is as follows:

> "A hundred years have now elapsed since the Renewed Church of the Brethren first attempted to communicate the gospel to the many thousand Negroes of our land. In 1737 Count Zinzendorf paid a visit to London and formed an acquaintance with General Oglethorpe and the trustees of Georgia, with whom he conferred on the subject of the mission to the Indians, which the brethren had already established in that colony (in 1735). Some of these gentlemen were associates under the will of Dr. Bray, who had left funds to be devoted to the conversion of the Negro slaves in South Carolina; and they solicited the Count to procure them some missionaries for this purpose. On his objecting that the Church of England might hesitate to recognize the ordination of the Brethren's missionaries, they referred the question to the Archbishop of Canterbury, Dr. Potter, who gave it as his opinion 'that the Brethren being members of an Episcopal Church, whose doctrines contained nothing repugnant to the Thirty-nine Articles, ought not to be denied free access to the heathen.' This declaration not only removed all hesitation from the minds of the trustees as to the present application, but opened the way for the labors of the Brethren amongst the slave population of the West Indies, a great and blessed work, which has, by the gracious help of God, gone on increasing even to the present day.

---

* This section is largely based on Jones. See §6.

"Various proprietors, however, avowing their determination not to suffer strangers to instruct their Negroes, as they had their own ministers, whom they paid for that purpose, our brethren ceased from their efforts. It appears from the letters of Brother Spangenburg, who spent the greater part of the year 1749 at Philadelphia and preached the gospel to the Negroes in that city, that the labors of the Brethren amongst them were not entirely fruitless. Thus he writes in 1751: 'On my arrival in Philadelphia, I saw numbers of Negroes still buried in all their native ignorance and darkness, and my soul was grieved for them. Soon after some of them came to me, requesting instruction, at the same time acknowledging their ignorance in the most affecting manner. They begged that a weekly sermon might be delivered expressly for their benefit. I complied with their request and confined myself to the most essential truths of scripture. Upwards of seventy Negroes attended on these occasions, several of whom were powerfully awakened, applied for further instruction, and expressed a desire to be united to Christ and his church by the sacrament of baptism, which was accordingly administered to them.'"

At the request of Mr. Knox, the English Secretary of State, an attempt was made to evangelize the Negroes of Georgia. "In 1774 the Brethren, Lewis Muller, of the Academy at Niesky, and George Wagner, were called to North America and in the year following, having been joined by Brother Andrew Broesing, of North Carolina, they took up their abode at Knoxborough, a plantation so called from its proprietor, the gentleman above mentioned. They were, however, almost constant sufferers from the fevers which prevailed in those parts, and Muller finished his course in October of the same year. He had preached the gospel with acceptance to both whites and blacks, yet without any abiding results. The two remaining Brethren being called upon to bear arms on the breaking out of the war of independence, Broesing repaired to Wachovia, in North Carolina, and Wagner set out in 1779 for England."

In the great Northampton revival, under the preaching of Dr. Edwards in 1735-6, when for the space of five or six weeks together the conversions averaged at least "four a day," Dr. Edwards remarks: "There are several Negroes who, from what was seen in them then and what is discernible in them since, appear to have been truly born again in the late remarkable season."

Direct efforts for the religious instruction of Negroes, continued through a series of years, were made by Presbyterians in Virginia. They commenced with the Rev. Samuel Davies, afterwards president of Nassau Hall, and the Rev. John Todd, of Hanover Presbytery.

In a letter addressed to a friend and member of the "Society in London for promoting Christian knowledge among the poor" in the year 1755, he thus expresses himself: "The poor neglected Negroes, who are so far from having money to purchase books, that they themselves are the property of others, who were originally African savages, and never heard of the name of Jesus or his gospel until they arrived at the land of their slavery in America, whom their masters generally neglect, and whose souls none care for, as though immortality were not a privilege common to them, as with their masters; these poor, unhappy Africans are objects of my compassion, and I think the most proper objects of the society's charity. The inhabitants of Virginia are computed to be about 300,000 men, the one-half of which number are supposed to be Negroes. The number of those who attend my ministry at particular times is uncertain, but generally about 300, who give a stated attendance; and never have I been so struck with the appearance of an assembly as when I have glanced my eye to that part of the meeting-house where they usually sit, adorned (for so it has appeared to me) with so many black countenances, eagerly attentive to every word they hear and frequently bathed in tears. A considerable number of them (about a hundred) have been baptized, after a proper time for instruction, having given credible evidence, not only of their acquaintance with the important doctrines of the Christian religion, but also a deep sense of them in their minds, attested by a life of strict piety and holiness. As they are not sufficiently polished to dissemble with a good grace, they express the sentiments of their souls so much in the language of simple nature and with such genuine indications of sincerity, that it is impossible to suspect their professions, especially when attended with a truly Christian life and exemplary conduct. There are multitudes of them in different places, who are willingly and eagerly desirous to be instructed and embrace every opportunity of acquainting themselves with the doctrines of the gospel; and though they have generally very little help to learn to read, yet to my agreeable surprise, many of them by dint of application in their leisure hours, have made such progress that they can intelligibly read a plain author, and especially their Bibles; and pity it is that any of them should be without them.

"The Negroes, above all the human species that I ever knew, have an ear for music and a kind of ecstatic delight in psalmody, and there are no books they learn so soon or take so much pleasure in as those used in that heavenly part of divine worship."

The year 1747 was marked, in the colony of Georgia, by the authorized introduction of slaves. Twenty-three representatives from the different districts met in Savannah, and after appointing Major Horton president, they entered into sundry resolutions, the substance of which was, "that the owners of slaves should educate the young and use every possible means of making religious impressions upon the minds of the aged, and that all acts of inhumanity should be punished by the civil authority."

Methodism was introduced in New York in 1766, and the first missionaries were sent out by Mr. Wesley from New York in 1769. One of these says: "The number of blacks that attend the preaching affects me much." The first regular conference was held in Philadelphia, 1773. From this year to 1776 there was a great revival of religion in Virginia under the preaching of the Methodists in connection with Rev. Mr. Jarrett of the Episcopal Church, which spread through fourteen counties in Virginia and two in North Carolina. One letter states "the chapel was full of white and black;" another, "hundreds of Negroes were among them, with tears streaming down their faces." At Roanoke another remarks: "In general the white people were within the chapel and the black people without."

At the eighth conference in Baltimore in 1780 the following question appeared in the minutes: "Question 25. Ought not the assistant to meet the colored people himself and appoint helpers in his absence, proper white persons, and not suffer them to stay late and meet by themselves? Answer. Yes." Under the preaching of Mr. Garretson in Maryland "hundreds, both white and black, expressed their love for Jesus."

The first return of colored members distinct from white occurs in the minutes of 1786: White 18,791, colored 1,890. "It will be perceived from the above," says Dr. Bangs in his history of the Methodist Episcopal Church, "that a considerable number of colored persons had been received into the church, and were so returned in the minutes of the conference. Hence it appears that at an early period of the Methodist ministry in this country it had turned its attention to this part of the population."

In 1790 it was again asked: "What can be done to instruct poor children, white and black, to read? Answer. Let us labor as the heart and soul of one man to establish Sunday-schools in or near the place of public worship. Let persons be appointed by the bishops, elders, deacons, or preachers, to teach gratis all that will attend and have a capacity to learn, from 6 o'clock in the morning till 10 and from 2 p.m. till 6, where it does not interfere with public worship. The council shall compile a proper school-book to teach them learning and piety." The experiment was made, but it proved unsuccessful and was discontinued. The number of colored members this year was 11,682.

The first Baptist church in this country was founded in Providence, R.I., by Roger Williams in 1639. Nearly one hundred years after the settlement of America "only seventeen Baptist churches had arisen in it." The Baptist church in Charleston, S.C., was founded in 1690. The denomination advanced slowly through the middle and Southern States, and in 1790 it had churches in them all. Revivals of religion were enjoyed, particularly one in Virginia, which commenced in 1785 and continued until 1791 or 1792. "Thousands were converted and baptized, besides many who joined the Methodists and Presbyterians. A large number of Negroes were admitted to the Baptist Churches during the seasons of revival, as well as on ordinary occasions. They were, however, not gathered into churches distinct from the whites south of Pennsylvania except in Georgia."

"In general the Negroes were followers of the Baptists in Virginia, and after a while, as they permitted many colored men to preach, the great majority of them went to hear preachers of their own color, which was attended with many evils."

"Towards the close of 1792 the first colored Baptist Church in the city of Savannah began to build a place of worship. The corporation of the city gave them a lot for the purpose. The origin of this church—the parent of several others—is briefly as follows:

George Leile or Lisle, sometimes called George Sharp, was born in Virginia about 1750. His master sometime before the American war removed and settled in Burke county, Georgia. Mr. Sharp was a Baptist and a deacon in a Baptist church, of which Rev. Matthew Moore was pastor. George was converted and baptized under Mr. Moore's ministry. The church gave him liberty to preach."*

About nine months after George Leile left Georgia, Andrew, surnamed Bryan, a man of good sense, great zeal, and some natural elocution, began to exhort his black brethren and friends. He and his followers were reprimanded and forbidden to engage further in religious exercises. He would, however, pray, sing, and encourage his fellow-worshippers to seek the Lord. Their persecution was carried to an inhuman extent. Their evening assemblies were broken up and those found present were punished with stripes! Andrew Bryan and Sampson, his brother, converted about a year after him, were twice imprisoned, and they with about fifty others were whipped. When publicly whipped, and bleeding under his wounds, Andrew declared that he rejoiced not only to be whipped, but would freely suffer death for the cause of Jesus Christ,

and that while he had life and opportunity he would continue to preach Christ. He was faithful to his vow and, by patient continuance in well-doing, he put to silence and shamed his adversaries, and influential advocates and patrons were raised up for him. Liberty was given Andrew by the civil authority to continue his religious meet-

---

* See *infra*.

ings under certain regulations. His master gave him the use of his barn at Brampton, three miles from Savannah, where he preached for two years with little interruption.

The African church in Augusta, Ga., was gathered by the labors of Jesse Peter, and was constituted in 1793 by Rev. Abraham Marshall and David Tinsley. Jesse Peter was also called Jesse Golfin on account of his master's name—living twelve miles below Augusta.

The number of Baptists in the United States this year was 73,471, allowing one-fourth to be Negroes the denomination would embrace between 18,000 and 19,000.

The returns of colored members in the Methodist denomination from 1791 to 1795, inclusive, were 12,884, 13,871, 16,227, 13,814, 12,179.

The Methodists reported in 1796, 11,280 colored members. The recapitulation of the numbers for 1797 is given by states:

Massachusetts	8	Maryland	5,106
Rhode Island	2	Virginia	2,190
Connecticut	15	North Carolina	2,071
New York	238	South Carolina	890
New Jersey	127	Georgia	148
Pennsylvania	198	Tennessee	42
Delaware	823	Kentucky	57

Making a total of 12,215 Negroes; nearly one-fourth of the whole number of members were colored. There were three only in Canada.

The year 1799 is memorable for the commencement of that extraordinary awakening which, taking its rise in Kentucky and spreading in various directions and with different degrees of intensity, was denominated "the great Kentucky revival." It continued for about four years, and its influence was felt over a large portion of the Southern States. Presbyterians, Methodists, and Baptists participated in this work. In this revival originated camp-meetings, which gave a new impulse to Methodism. From the best estimates the number of Negroes received into the different communions during this season must have been between four and five thousand.

In 1800 there were in connection with the Methodists 13,452 Negroes. The bishops of the Methodist Episcopal Church were authorized to ordain African preachers in places where there were houses of worship for their use, who might be chosen by a majority of the male members of the society to which they belonged and could procure a recommendation from the preacher in charge and his colleagues on the circuit to the office of local deacons. Richard Allen, of Philadelphia, was the first colored man who received orders under this rule.

"The fact, however, is worthy of remembrance that, while the Indians—some of whom received us as guests and sold us their land at almost no compensation at all, and others were driven back to make us room, and with whom we had frequent and bloody wars, and we became, from time to time, mutual scourges—received some eminent missionaries from the colonists, and had no inconsiderable interest awakened for their conversion; the Africans who were brought over and bought by us for servants, and who wore out their lives as such, enriching thousand from Massachusetts to Georgia, and were members of our households, never received from the colonists themselves a solitary missionary exclusively devoted to their good, nor was there ever a single society established within the colonies, that we know of, with the express design of promoting their religious instruction!"

8

The Sects and Slavery

The approach of the Revolution brought heart-searching on many subjects, and not the least on slavery. The agitation was noticeable in the legislation of the time, putting an end to slavery in the North and to the slave-trade in all states. Religious bodies particularly were moved. In 1657 George Fox, founder of the Quakers, had impressed upon his followers in America the duty of converting the slaves, and he himself preached to them in the West Indies. The Mennonite Quakers protested against slavery in 1688, and from that time until the Revolution the body slowly but steadily advanced, step-by-step, to higher ground until they refused all fellowship to slaveholders. Radical Quakers, like Hepburn and Lay, attacked religious sects and Lay called preachers "a sort of devils that preach more to hell than they do to heaven, and so they will do forever as long as they are suffered to reign in the worst and mother of all sins, slave-keeping."

In Virginia and North Carolina this caused much difficulty owing to laws against manumission early in the nineteenth century, and the result was wholesale migration of the Quakers.[*]

Judge Sewall, among the Massachusetts Congregationalists, had declared, in 1700, that slavery and the slave-trade were wrong, but his protest was unheeded. Later, in 1770 and after, strong Congregational clergymen, like Samuel Hopkins and Ezra Stiles, attacked slavery, but so democratic a church could take no united action. Although Whitefield came to defend the institution, John Wesley, founder of the Methodists, called the slave-trade the "sum of all villanies," and the General Conference in America, 1780, declared slavery "contrary to the laws of God, man, and nature and hurtful to society." From this high stand, however, the church quickly and rather ignominiously retreated. By 1780 it only sought the destruction of slavery

---

[*] Cf. Week's Southern Quakers and Slavery; Thomas: Attitude, etc.

"by all wise and prudent means," while preachers were allowed to hold their slaves in slave states. In 1787 the General Conference urged preachers to labor among slaves and receive worthy ones into full membership and "to exercise the whole Methodist discipline among them." Work was begun early among the slaves and they had so many members that their churches in the south were often called Negro churches. The church yielded further ground to the pro-slavery sentiment in 1816, but in 1844 the censure of a bishop who married a slaveholder rent the church in twain on the question.

The Baptists had Negro preachers for Negro members as early as 1773. They were under the supervision of whites and had no voice in general church affairs. The early Baptists held few slaves, and they were regarded as hostile to slavery in Georgia. The Philadelphia Association approved of abolition as early as 1789, and a Virginia Association urged emancipation in the legislature about the same time. In Kentucky and Ohio the Baptist Associations split on the question. The Baptists early interested themselves in the matter of slave marriages and family worship, and especially took spiritual care of the slaves of their own members. They took a stand against the slave-trade in 1818 and 1835. After the division on the subject of missions the Missionary Baptist began active proselyting among the slaves.

The Presbyterian Synod of 1787 recommended efforts looking toward gradual emancipation, and in 1795 the question of excluding slave-holders was discussed, but it ended in an injunction of "brotherly love" for them. In 1815, 1818, and 1835 the question was dismissed and postponed, and finally in 1845 the question was dropped on the ground that Christ and the Apostles did not condemn slavery. At the time of the war the church finally divided.

9

Toussaint L'Ouverture and Nat Turner

"The role which the great Negro Toussaint, called L'Ouverture, played in the history of the United States has seldom been fully appreciated. Representing the age of revolution in America, he rose to leadership through a bloody terror, which contrived a Negro "problem" for the Western hemisphere, intensified and defined the anti-slavery movement, became one of the causes, and probably the prime one, which led Napoleon to sell Louisiana for a song; and, finally, through the interworking of all these effects, rendered more certain the final prohibition of the slave-trade by the United States in 1807."[*]

The effect of the revolution on the religious life of the Negro was quickly felt. In 1800, South Carolina declared:

"It shall not be lawful for any number of slaves, free Negroes, mulattoes, or mestizoes, even in company with white persons, to meet together and assemble for the purpose of mental instruction or religious worship, either before the rising of the sun or after the going down of the same. And all magistrates, sheriffs, militia officers, etc., etc., are hereby vested with power, etc., for dispersing such assemblies."[†]

On petition of the white churches the rigor of this law was slightly abated in 1803 by a modification which forbade any person, before 9 o'clock in the evening, "to break into a place of meeting wherein shall be assembled the members of any religious society in this State, provided a majority of them shall be white persons, or otherwise to disturb their devotions unless such persons, etc., so entering said place [of worship] shall first have obtained from some magistrate, etc., a warrant, etc., in case a magistrate shall be then actually with a distance of three miles from

[*] DuBois' Suppression of the Slave-Trade, p. 70.
[†] Goodell, 329.

such place of meeting; otherwise the provisions, etc., [of the Act of 1800] to remain in full force."‡

So, too, in Virginia the Haytian revolt and the attempted insurrection under Gabriel in 1800 led to the Act of 1804, which forbade all evening meetings of slaves. This was modified in 1805 so as to allow a slave, in company with a white person, to listen to a white minister in the evening. A master was "allowed" to employ a religious teacher for his slaves.§ Mississippi passed similar restrictions.

By 1822 the rigor of the South Carolina laws in regard to Negro meetings had abated, especially in a city like Charleston, and one of the results was the Vesey plot.

"The sundry religious classes or congregations, with Negro leaders or local preachers, into which were formed the Negro members of the various churches of Charleston, furnished Vesey with the first rudiments of an organization, and at the same time with a singularly safe medium for conducting his underground agitation. It was customary, at that time, for these Negro congregations to meet for purposes of worship entirely free from the presence of whites. Such meetings were afterwards forbidden to be held except in the presence of at least one representative of the dominant race. But during the three or four years prior to the year 1822 they certainly offered Denmark Vesey regular, easy and safe opportunities for preaching his gospel of liberty and hate. And we are left in no doubt whatever in regard to the uses to which he put those gatherings of blacks.

"Like many of his race, he possessed the gift of gab, as the silver in the tongue and the gold in the full or thick-lipped mouth are oftentimes contemptuously characterized. And, like many of his race, he was a devoted student of the Bible, to whose interpretation he brought like many other Bible students not confined to the Negro race, a good deal of imagination and not a little of superstition, which, with some natures, is perhaps but another name for the desires of the heart. Thus equipped, it is no wonder that Vesey, as he poured over the Old Testament scriptures, found many points of similitude in the history of the Jews and that of the slaves in the United States. They were both peculiar peoples. They were both Jehovah's peculiar peoples, one in the past, the other in the present. And it seemed to him that as Jehovah bent his ear, and bared his arm once in behalf of the one, so would he do the same for the other. It was all vividly real to his thought, I believe, for to his mind thus had said the Lord.

"He ransacked the Bible for apposite and terrible texts whose commands in the olden times, to the olden people, were no less imperative upon the new times and the new people. This new people was also commanded to arise and destroy their enemies and the city in which they

‡ Stroud, 93–4; Goodell, 329.

§ Stroud, 94; Ballagh, 95.

dwelt, 'both man and woman, young and old, with the edge of the sword.' Believing superstitiously as he did in the stern and Nemesis-like God of the Old Testament he looked confidently for a day of vengeance and retribution for the blacks. He felt, I doubt not, something peculiarly applicable to his enterprise and intensely personal to himself in the stern and exultant prophecy of Zachariah, fierce and sanguinary words, which were constantly in his mouth: 'Then shall the Lord go forth and fight against those nations as when he fought in the day of battle.' According to Vesey's lurid exegesis 'those nations' in the text meant beyond peradventure the cruel masters and Jehovah was to go forth to fight against them for the poor slaves and on whichever side fought that day the Almighty God on that side would assuredly rest victory and deliverance.

"It will not be denied that Vesey's plan contemplated the total annihilation of the white population of Charleston. Nursing for many dark years the bitter wrongs of himself and race had filled him without doubt with a mad spirit of revenge and had given to him a decided predilection for shedding the blood of his oppressors. But if he intended to kill them to satisfy a desire for vengeance he intended to do so also on broader ground. The conspirators, he argued, had no choice in the matter, but were compelled to adopt a policy of extermination by the necessity of their position. The liberty of the blacks was in the balance of fate against the lives of the whites. He could strike that balance in favor of the blacks only by the total destruction of the whites. Therefore the whites, men, women, and children, were doomed to death." *

The plot was well-laid, but the conspirators were betrayed. Less than ten years after this plot was discovered and Vesey and his associates hanged, there broke out the Nat Turner insurrection in Virginia. Turner was himself a preacher.

"He was a Christian and a man. He was conscious that he was a Man and not a 'thing;' therefore, driven by religious fanaticism, he undertook a difficult and bloody task. Nathaniel Turner was born in Southampton county, Virginia, October 2, 1800. His master was one Benjamin Turner, a very wealthy and aristocratic man. He owned many slaves, and was a cruel and exacting master. Young 'Nat' was born of slave parents, and carried to his grave many of the superstitions and traits of his father and mother. The former was a preacher, the latter a 'mother in Israel.' Both were unlettered but, nevertheless, very pious people. The mother began when Nat was quite young to teach him that he was born, like Moses, to be the deliverer of his race. She would sing to him snatches of wild, rapturous songs and repeat portions of prophecy she had learned from the preachers of those times. Nat listened with reverence and awe, and believed everything

* Grimke: Right on the Scaffold (Pub. American Negro Academy), pp. 11–12.

his mother said. He imbibed the deep religious character of his parents, and soon manifested a desire to preach. He was solemnly set apart to 'the gospel ministry' by his father, the church, and visiting preachers. He was quite low in stature, dark, and had the genuine African features. His eyes were small, but sharp, and gleamed like fire when he was talking about his 'mission' or preaching from some prophetic passage of scripture. It is said that he never laughed. He was a dreamy sort of a man, and avoided the crowd. Like Moses he lived in the solitudes of the mountains and brooded over the condition of his people. There was something grand to him in the rugged scenery that nature had surrounded him with. He believed that he was a prophet, a leader raised up by God to burst the bolts of the prison-house and set the oppressed free. The thunder, the hail, the storm-cloud, the air, the earth, the stars, at which he would sit and gaze half the night all spake the language of the God of the oppressed. He was seldom seen in a large company, and never drank a drop of ardent spirits. Like John the Baptist, when he had delivered his message, he would retire to the fastness of the mountain or seek the desert, where he could meditate upon his great work." *

[handwritten marginal note: a very romantic portrait]

In the impression of the Richmond *Enquirer* of the 30th of August, 1831, the first editorial or leader is under the caption of "The Banditte." The editor says:

"They remind one of a parcel of blood-thirsty wolves rushing down from the Alps; or, rather like a former incursion of the Indians upon the white settlements. Nothing is spared; neither age nor sex respected—the helplessness of women and children pleads in vain for mercy. . . . The case of Nat Turner warns us. No black man ought to be permitted to turn preacher through the country. The law must be enforced—or the tragedy of Southampton appeals to us in vain." †

Mr. Gray, the man to whom Turner made his confession before dying, said:

"It has been said that he was ignorant and cowardly and that his object was to murder and rob for the purpose of obtaining money to make his escape. It is notorious that he was never known to have had a dollar in his life, to swear an oath or drink a drop of spirits. As to his ignorance, he certainly never had the advantages of education, but he can read and write, and for natural intelligence and quickness of apprehension is surpassed by few men I have ever seen. As to his being a coward, his reason as given for not resisting Mr. Phipps, shows the decision of his character. When he saw Mr. Phipps present his gun, he said he knew it was impossible for him to escape as the woods were full of men. He, therefore, thought it was better for him to surrender and trust to fortune for his escape.

* Williams II, pp. 85–86.

† Quoted in *Ibid*, p. 90.

"He is a complete fanatic or plays his part most admirably. On other subjects he possesses an uncommon share of intelligence, with a mind capable of attaining anything, but warped and perverted by the influence of early impressions. He is below the ordinary stature, though strong and active, having the true Negro face, every feature of which is strongly marked. I shall not attempt to describe the effect of his narrative, as told and commented on by himself, in the condemned hole of the prison; the calm, deliberate composure with which he spoke of his late deeds and intentions; the expression of his fiend-like face when excited by enthusiasm, still bearing the stains of the blood of the helpless innocence about him, clothed with rags and covered with chains, yet daring to raise his manacled hand to heaven, with a spirit soaring above the attributes of man. I looked on him and the blood curdled in my veins." *

The Turner insurrection is so connected with the economic revolution which enthroned cotton that it marks an epoch in the history of the slave. A wave of legislation passed over the South prohibiting the slave from learning to read and write, forbidding Negroes to preach, and interfering with Negro religious meetings. Virginia declared, in 1831, that neither slaves or free Negroes might preach, nor could they attend religious service at night without permission. In North Carolina slaves and free Negroes were forbidden to preach, exhort to teach "in any prayer-meeting or other association for worship where slaves of different families are collected together" on penalty of not more than thirty-nine lashes. Maryland and Georgia had similar laws. The Mississippi law of 1831 said: It is "unlawful for any slave, free Negro, or mulatto to preach the gospel" upon pain of receiving thirty-nine lashes upon the naked back of the presumptuous preacher. If a Negro received written permission from his master he might preach to the Negroes in his immediate neighborhood, providing six respectable white men, owners of slaves, were present. † In Alabama the law of 1832 prohibited the assembling of more than five male slaves at any place off the plantation to which they belonged, but nothing in the act was to be considered as forbidding attendance at places of public worship held by white persons. No slave or free person of color was permitted to "preach, exhort, or harangue any slave or slaves, or free persons of color, except in the presence of five respectable slaveholders or unless the person preaching was licensed by some regular body of professing Christians in the neighborhood, to whose society or church the Negroes addressed properly belonged."

In the District of Columbia the free Negroes began to leave white churches in 1831 and to assemble in their own.

* Williams II, pp. 91–92.
† Williams II, 163.

10

Third Period of Missionary Enterprise

The efforts to convert Negroes in America fall in three main periods. The first period was early in the eighteenth century after it was decided that baptism did not free slaves. Results at this time were meager, and the effort spasmodic. A second period came about the time of the Revolution, and had larger results. C. C. Jones says of the conditions, 1790–1820, that:

> It is not too much to say that the religious and physical condition of the Negroes were both improved during this period. Their increase was natural and regular, ranging every ten years, between 34 and 36 percent. As the old stock from Africa died out of the country the grosser customs, ignorance and paganism of Africa, died with them. Their descendants, the country-born, were better looking, more intelligent, more civilized, more susceptible of religious impressions.
>
> "On the whole, however, but a minority of the Negroes and that a small one, attended regularly the house of God, and taking them as a class, their religious instruction was extensively and most seriously neglected.

The third period followed after the depression of the thirties. This depression was severe, and lasted nearly twenty-years. (1830s)

The Presbyterian Synod of South Carolina and Georgia, in 1833, published a statement in which they said of the slaves:

> There are over two millions of human beings in the condition of heathen and some of them in a worse condition. They may justly be considered the heathen of this country, and will bear a comparison with heathen in any country in the world. The Negroes are destitute of the gospel, and ever will be under the present state of things. In the vast field extending from an entire state beyond the Potomac, [i.e., Maryland], to the Sabine river [at the time our southwestern boundary,] and from the Atlantic to the Ohio,

there are, to the best of our knowledge, not twelve men exclusively devoted to the religious instruction of the Negroes. In the present state of feeling in the South, a ministry of their own color could neither be obtained nor tolerated. But do not the Negroes have access to the gospel through the stated ministry of the whites? We answer, no. The Negroes have no regular and efficient ministry: as a matter of course, no churches; neither is there sufficient room in the white churches for their accommodation. We know of but five churches in the slaveholding states built expressly for their use. These are all in the state of Georgia. We may now inquire whether they enjoy the privileges of gospel in their own houses, and on our plantations? Again we return a negative answer. They have no Bibles to read by their own firesides. They have no family altars; and when in affliction, sickness or death, they have no minister to address to them the consolations of the gospel, nor to bury them with appropriate services. *

The Presbyterian Synod of Kentucky, in 1834, said:

Slavery deprives its subjects, in a great measure, of the privileges of the gospel. The law, as it is here, does not prevent free access to the scriptures; but ignorance, the natural result of their condition, does. The Bible is before them. But it is to them a sealed book. Very few of them enjoy the advantages of a regular gospel ministry. †

The Synod of South Carolina and Georgia returned to the subject, in 1834, and declared:

The gospel, as things now are, can never be preached to the two classes (whites and blacks) successfully in conjunction. The galleries or back seats on the lower floor of white churches are generally appropriated to the Negroes, when it can be done without inconvenience to the whites. When it cannot be done conveniently, the Negroes must catch the gospel as it escapes through the doors and windows. If the master is pious, the house servants alone attend family worship, and frequently few or none of them, while the field hands have no attention at all. So as far as masters are engaged in the work [of religious instruction of slaves], an almost unbroken silence reigns on this vast field.*

To this the Rev. C. C. Jones, of Georgia, adds:

We cannot cry out against the Papists for withholding the scriptures from the common people, and the keeping them in ignorance of the way of life, for we withhold the Bible from our servants, and keep them in ignorance of it while we will not use the means to have it read and explained to them. *

* Goodell, pp. 333–35.
† Jones, 167–68; Goodell, p. 335–36.

In 1838 the Methodist Conference of South Carolina appointed a missionary to labor among the colored people, but the enterprise was soon suppressed by the principal citizens. The Greenville (S.C.) *Mountaineer* of November 2, 1838, contained the particulars: A committee was appointed, who addressed a note to the missionary requesting him to desist. This was backed up by James S. Pope and 352 others. The document argues at length the incompatibility of slavery with the "mental improvement and religious instruction" of slaves. "Verbal instruction," say they, "will increase the desire of the black population to learn. We know of upwards of a dozen Negroes in the neighborhood of Cambridge who can now read, some of whom are members of your societies at Mount Lebanon and New Salem. Of course, when they see themselves encouraged, they will supply themselves with Bibles, hymn books, and catechisms! Open the missionary sluice, and the current will swell in its gradual onward advance. We thus expect that a progressive system of improvement will be introduced, or will follow, from the nature and force of circumstances, and, if not checked (though they may be shrouded in sophistry and disguise), will ultimately revolutionize our civil institutions. We consider the common adage that 'knowledge is power,' and as the colored man is enlightened, his condition will be rendered more unhappy and intolerable. Intelligence and slavery have no affinity with each other." The document refers to the laws of the state, and hopes that "South Carolina is yet true to her vital interests," etc., etc. [*]

Bishop Capers testifies about this time that there was the most urgent need for preaching among Negroes. Of the Negroes around Wilmington, N.C., he says: "A numerous population of this class in that town and vicinity were as destitute of any public instruction (or, probably, instruction of any kind as to spiritual things) as if they had not been believed to be men at all, and their morals were as depraved as, with such a destitution of the gospel among them, might have been expected." To this state of things the masters were indifferent; for, adds the bishop, "it seems not to have been considered that such a state of things might furnish motives sufficient to induce pure-minded men to engage, at great inconvenience or even personal hazard, in the work of improving them." Such work, on the other hand, seems to have been regarded as unnecessary, if not unreasonable. Conscience was not believed to be concerned.

As the result of such appeals a reaction set in about 1835, and the Methodists and Baptists especially were active among the slaves. A minister in Mississippi testified that he had charge of the Negroes of five plantations and three hundred slaves; another in Georgia visited eighteen plantations every two weeks. "The own-

[*] Goodell, p. 336–7

ers have built three good churches at their own expense, all framed; 290 members have been added, and about 400 children are instructed." Another traveling minister declared, in 1841, that in many places, like Baltimore, Alexandria, and Charleston, the Negroes had large, spacious churches, and he thinks there were 500,000 Negro church members at the time, which is probably an exaggeration.

Charles C. Jones writes, in 1842, that:

"The Negro race has existed in our country for two hundred and twenty-two years, in which time the gospel has been brought within the reach of, and been communicated to, multitudes.

"While there have been but few societies, and they limited in extent and influence, formed for the special object of promoting the moral and religious instruction of the Negroes, and while there have been comparatively but few missionaries exclusively devoted to them, yet they have not been altogether overlooked by their owners, nor neglected by the regular ministers of the various leading denominations of Christians, as the facts adduced in this sketch testify.

"Yet it is a remarkable fact in the history of the Negroes in our country that their regular, systematic religious instructions has never received in the churches at any time that general attention and effort which it demanded, and the people have consequently been left, both in the free and in the slave states, in great numbers, in moral darkness, and destitution of the means of grace."

"In 1848 an enterprise was begun for the more thorough-going evangelization of the colored people in Charleston, S.C., under the auspices of the Rev. Dr. J. B. Adger and the session of the Second Presbyterian church. In 1859 a church building costing $25,000, contributed by the citizens of Charleston, was dedicated. From the first the great building was filled, the blacks occupying the main floor, and the whites the galleries, which seated two hundred and fifty persons. The Rev. J. L. Girardeau, one of the greatest preachers in the South, was for years the pastor of this church. The close of the war found it with exactly five hundred colored members, and nearly one hundred white." *

There were thirteen colored churches in Baltimore in 1847, supported largely, but not altogether, by free Negroes. In 1854 one-fourth of the slaves of South Carolina were said to be Methodists; one-third of the Presbyterians of that state were black, and one-half of the Baptists of Virginia. In 1859 there were 468,000 Negro church members reported in the South, of whom 215,000 were Methodists and 175,000 Baptists. †

* Campbell: Some Aspects, etc.; and Jones.
† Cf. Ingle Side Lights, pp. 273–74

Even at this time many restrictions on Negro religion remained. In Maryland camp-meetings were forbidden, and all meetings save at regular churches and with the consent of white preachers. There were also many local laws restricting worship. In other states the laws of the thirties remained in force or were strengthened. Moreover, even the church organizations working among Negroes were careful in their methods. The North Carolina Baptist Convention adopted a report concerning the religious instruction of the colored people, with a series of resolutions, concluding as follows:

"*Resolved*, That by religious instructions be understood verbal communications on religious subjects?" [*]

Moreover, the masters clung to the idea that the chief use of religion among slaves was to make them "obey their masters." When it was charged that slaves were not allowed to read the Bible, one naïve answer was that it was read to them, especially "those very passages which inculcate the relative duties of masters and servants."

An intelligent Negro, Lundsford Lane, thus describes the religious instruction of slaves:

> I was permitted to attend church, and this I esteem a great blessing. It was there I received much instruction, which I trust was a great benefit to me. I trusted, too, that I had experienced the renewing influences of divine grace. I looked upon myself as a great sinner before God, and upon the doctrine of the great atonement, through the suffering and death of the Savior, as a source of continual joy to my heart. After obtaining from my mistress a written permit, a thing always required in such cases, I had been baptized and received into fellowship with the Baptist denomination. Thus in religious matters I had been indulged in the exercise of my own conscience; this was a favor not always granted to slaves. There was one hard doctrine to which we as slaves were compelled to listen, which I found difficult to receive. We were often told by the ministers how much we owed to God for bringing us over from the benighted shores of Africa and permitting us to listen to the sound of the gospel. In ignorance of any special revelation that God had made to master, or to his ancestors, that my ancestors should be stolen and enslaved on the soil of America to accomplish their salvation, I was slow to believe all my teachers enjoined on this subject. How surprising, then, this high moral end being accomplished, that no proclamation of emancipation had before this been made! Many of us were as highly civilized as some of our masters, and as to piety in many instances their superiors. I was rather disposed to believe that God had originally granted me temporal freedom, which wicked men had

[*] Goodell, p. 336.

taken from me—which now I had been compelled to purchase at great cost. There was one kind-hearted clergyman whom I used often to hear; he was very popular among the colored people. But after he had preached a sermon to us in which he urged from the Bible that it was the will of heaven from all eternity that we should be slaves, and our masters be our owners, many of us left him, considering, like the doubting disciple of old, "This is a hard saying; who can hear it?" [†]

So, too, Dr. Caruthers says although many of the slaves were pious they owed for this "no thanks to slavery or the slave laws." Even after the war the reconstruction legislation of states like Mississippi sought especially to restrain Negro preachers and imposed, in 1865, upon Negroes exercising the functions of a minister without a license from a regularly organized church a fine of $10–$100, and liability to imprisonment not more than thirty days. [‡]

[†] Bassett: State, pp. 51–52.

[‡] Garner: Reconstruction, p. 115.

11

The Earlier Churches and Preachers

(BY MR. JOHN W. CROMWELL)

The original colored churches in different sections of the country came about in one of the following ways:

1. They were in some cases the result of special missionary effort on the part of the whites.

2. They were brought about by direct discrimination against the blacks made by the whites during divine worship.

3. They were the natural sequence, when, on account of increase in members, it became necessary for congregations to divide, whereupon the blacks were evolved as distinct churches, but still under the oversight, if not the exclusive control, of the whites.

4. They were, in not a few cases, the preference of colored communicants themselves, in order to get as much as possible the equal privileges and advantages of government denied them under the existing system.

The establishment of these churches took place about the same time in sections more distant from each other then than now, for it was before the time of the railroad, the use of the steamboat or the telegraph; so that their coming into existence at the same time must be attributed to a correspondence of general causes.

The first regular church organization of which I know was a Baptist Church at Williamsburg, Va., in the year 1776. Following it were three Baptist Churches in the year 1778, one in Augusta and two in Savannah, Ga.; the Episcopal Church, St. Thomas, in Philadelphia, in 1791; Bethel Church, Philadelphia, in 1794; Zion

Methodist Church, New York city, in 1796; Joy Street Baptist Church, Boston, in 1807; Abyssinian Baptist Church, New York, in 1808; First Baptist, St. Louis, 1830.

So far as the establishment is concerned of those colored Methodist Churches which evolved the A.M.E. and the A.M.E. Zion denominations, persecution by the whites was the moving cause. They were compelled to protect themselves against the yoke sought to be imposed on them, by worshipping among themselves. The one movement in Philadelphia, the other in New York, moved in parallel, often in rival lines. New York and Philadelphia were soon in free states and their methods were those of free men, in name at least, while the establishment of colored Methodist Churches in the South, as in Maryland, under the direction of the whites, illustrated one of the instances of special missionary effort.

The colored Baptist Church in the South came mostly into existence mainly through the third inciting cause mentioned.

The Presbyterian Church, as found among the colored people, came about through the operation of two causes: the desire of the colored people to be by themselves and that of the whites to strengthen their denomination among this class.

The first colored Episcopal Churches, both in New York and Philadelphia, resulted directly from causes similar to those which gave rise to the Methodist Churches in the same localities.

Of the men mainly instrumental by reason of their position as pioneers in organizing these first churches in the different colored denominations a word is needed.

First in order came Richard Allen. He was one of the leaders in the free African Society. From the members of this body came the leaders, almost the organization itself, both of the Bethel Methodist and the St. Thomas Episcopal Churches in the city of Philadelphia.

Richard Allen was born February 12, 1760, old style, a slave in Philadelphia. At an early age he gave evidence of a high order of talent for leadership. He was converted while quite a lad and licensed to preach in 1782. In 1797 he was ordained a deacon by Bishop Francis Asbury, who had been entrusted by John Wesley with the superintendence of the work in America. April 11, 1816, at the general conference of the African Methodist Churches, held in the city of Philadelphia, he was elected their first bishop. Under his administration the work was vigorously prosecuted in all directions. He died in 1831, universally lamented.

He possessed talents as an organizer to the highest order. He was a born leader and an almost infallible judge of human nature. He was actively identified with every forward movement among the colored people, irrespective of denomination, and died, leaving a greater influence upon the colored people of the North than any other man of his times. He was one of the promoters, as well as one of the chief actors, in the first national convention of colored men in the United States ever held, which was in Philadelphia in the year 1830.

Absalom Jones, who certainly comes next in point of time, was born a slave in Sussex, Del., November 6, 1746. At the age of sixteen he was taken to Philadelphia. He was married in 1770, purchased his wife, and afterward succeeded in obtaining his own liberty. Like his co-laborer, Richard Allen, with whom he was associated in the African Society, he was quite thrifty and became the owner of several pieces of real estate. His education was quite limited, so much so that a dispensation was necessary to admit of his ordination, to which a condition was annexed that this church (St. Thomas) should not have the power of sharing in the government of the Episcopal Church in the diocese of Pennsylvania. Rev. Wm. Douglass, subsequently a rector of this church, in his "Annals of St. Thomas Episcopal Church," says of Absalom Jones, that he was impressive in his style of preaching, though his forte was not in the pulpit. It was his mild and easy manners, his habits as a pastor, his public spirit, that strengthened him in public estimation. He says that "he was of medium height, dark complexion, with stout frame, bland and open countenance, yet indicative of firmness. Whenever he appeared in public he donned the costume of the profession, black dress coat, breeches and vest of the same color, with top-boots or shoes with buckles and black stockings." After a ministry of twenty-two years, he died February 13, 1818, aged 71 years.

Rev. John Gloucester, the first colored minister to act as pastor of the first colored Presbyterian Church, was a man thoroughly consecrated to his cause. He possessed a fair English education, which he received from private sources. He was a pioneer of Presbyterian ministers; four of his own sons, Jeremiah, John, Stephen, and James became Presbyterian ministers, and from the Sunday-school of his church three other well known ministers went forth—Rev. Amos to Africa, Rev. H. M. Wilson to New York, and Rev. Jonathan C. Gibbs, who died in Florida after having been Secretary of State and State Superintendent of Schools.

Mr. Gloucester, like Allen and Jones, was born a slave, in Kentucky, about the year 1776. Such was his intelligence that he was purchased by Rev. Gideon Blackburn, one of the leaders of the Presbyterian denomination in Kentucky. The records show that when Rev. Gloucester was ordained, Dr. Blackburn was the moderator of the presbytery. On the appointment of Rev. Gloucester to the first African Presbyterian church his master liberated him. One of the attractions of Rev. Gloucester was his rich musical voice that was pronounced as something phenomenal. In prayer his power was manifest.

His character was so simple and Christian that he won many friends of both races. He was not only preacher, but pastor and adviser of his people in their temporal matters. He traveled extensively North and South in nearly every city, raising the money with which he liberated his wife and children. He even crossed the ocean, where he met with great success.

After fifteen years of service in the church, during which time it rapidly increased in members, from 22 to 300, he died May 2, 1822, a victim of consumption, in the forty-sixth year of his age.

Now it is not to be inferred that these were the only men deserving of special notice as pioneers. By no means. We allude to them because of their relation to the historical churches. There were Harry Hosier, who traveled with Bishop Asbury, and who often filled appointments for him; Rev. Daniel Coker of Baltimore, and Rev. Peter Spencer of Delaware, who organized the Protestant branch of colored Methodism.

Circumstances were somewhat similar in other parts of the country. With the increase of the colored population and its distribution to other centers, other religious societies sprang up, so that wherever you find any number of these people in the earlier decades of the republic you find a church, often churches, out of all proportion to the population.

In the West, it may be stated, that colored churches were not the result of secessions or irregular wholesale withdrawals from the white churches as in the East. They sprang up directly in the path of the westward migration of colored people from the South and the East.

In the South the whites were in complete and absolute control, in church as in state. Colored people attended and held membership in the same church as the whites, though they did not possess the same rights or privileges. They either had special services at stated times or they sat in the galleries. There may have been deep protests against such un-Christian treatment, but we may rest assured that these were by no means loud, however deep. It was when this membership increased to very large numbers that separate churches for colored people, rather than of the colored people, were established. In the South, as in the North, this membership was principally in the Baptist and Methodist churches, and to these denominations did these separate colored churches belong, with exceptions so rare that they may be named as to cities or districts where it was otherwise.

Outside of the few ministers of the A.M.E. and the A.M.E. Zion churches in the border states, it is doubtful if there were a score of colored pastors in full control of colored churches in the South before the war. Nevertheless, there were a few colored ministers so very conspicuous by their work as pioneers as to deserve special notice here. It is possible to refer briefly only to a few.

Taking them in the order of time there was the Rev. George Lisle, a native of Virginia, the slave or body servant of a British officer. Throughout that struggle he preached in different parts of the country. As one of the results of his labors we find one of the very first colored churches of any denomination in the country organized, especially that in 1788 at Savannah, Ga., by Rev. Andrew Bryan, whom Lisle had baptized. Compelled to leave the United States at the close of the war, Lisle went to Jamaica, where he organized a church with four members in 1783. By 1790 he had baptized more than 400 persons on that island. In 1793 he built there the very first non-Episcopal religious chapel, to which there were belonging, in 1841, 3,700 members. That white Baptist missionaries subsequently went to the West Indies is to be attributed to Rev. Lisle's work, for they were brought there as a direct result of his correspondence with ecclesiastical authorities in Great Britain.

Next we have Lott Carey, also a native of Virginia, born a slave in Charles City county, about 1780. His father was a Baptist. In 1804 Lott removed to Richmond, where he worked in a tobacco factory and from all accounts was very profligate and wicked. In 1807, being converted, he joined the First Baptist Church, learned to read, made rapid advancement as a scholar, and was shortly afterwards licensed to preach.

After purchasing his family, in 1813, he organized, in 1815, the African Missionary Society, the first missionary society in the country, and within five years raised $700 for African missions.

trend – purchasing own family

That Lott Carey was evidently a man of superior intellect and force of character is to be evidenced from the fact that his reading took a wide range—from political economy, in Adam Smith's Wealth of Nations, to the voyage of Captain Cook. That he was a worker as well as a preacher is true, for when he decided to go to Africa his employers offered to raise his salary from $800 to $1000 a year. Remember, that this was over eighty years ago. Carey was not seduced by such a flattering offer, for he was determined. His last sermon in the old First Church in Richmond must have been exceedingly powerful, for it was compared by an eye-witness, a resident of another state, to the burning, eloquent appeals of George Whitefield. Fancy him as he stands there in that historic building ringing the changes on the word "freely," depicting the willingness with which he was ready to give up his life for service in Africa.

He, as you may already know, was the leader of the pioneer colony to Liberia, where he arrived even before the agent of the Colonization Society. In his new home his abilities were recognized, for he was made vice governor and became governor, in fact, while Governor Ashmun was absent from the colony in this country. Carey did not allow his position to betray the cause of his people, for he did not hesitate to expose the duplicity of the Colonization Society and even to defy their authority, it would seem, in the interests of the people.

While casting cartridges to defend the colonists against the natives in 1828, the accidental upsetting of a candle caused an explosion that resulted in his death.

Carey is described as a typical Negro, six feet in height, of massive and erect frame, with the sinews of a Titan. He had a square face, keen eyes, and a grave countenance. His movements were measured; in short, he had all the bearings and dignity of a prince of the blood.

12

Some Other Ante-Bellum Preachers

Six noted Negro preachers have been mentioned: Nat Turner, the revolutionist; Richard Allen, the founder of the African Methodist; Absalom Jones, the first Negro Episcopal rector; Harry Hosier, the companion of Bishop Asbury; George Lisle, the West Indian missionary, and Lott Carey, the African missionary. To these may be added the names of Lemuel Haynes, John Chavis, Henry Evans, James Varick, Jack of Virginia, Ralph Freeman, and Lunsford Lane, forming thirteen remarkable characters. "Lemuel Haynes was born in Hartford, Conn., July 18, 1753. His father was an African, his mother a white woman. He received the honorary degree of A.M. from Middlebury College in 1804. After completing a theological course he preached in various places and settled in West Rutland, Vt., in 1788, where he remained for thirty years, and became one of the most popular preachers in the state. He was characterized by subtle intellect, keen wit, and eager thirst for knowledge. His noted sermon from Genesis 3:4 was published and passed through nine or ten editions. His controversy with Hosea Ballou became of world-wide interest. The life of Lemuel Haynes was written by James E. Cooley, New York, 1848." [*] John Chavis was a full-blooded Negro, born in Granville County, N.C., near Oxford, in 1763. He was born free and was sent to Princeton, and studied privately under Dr. Witherspoon, where he did well. He went to Virginia to preach to Negroes. In 1802, in the county court, his freedom and character were certified to and it was declared that he had passed "through a regular course of academic studies" at what is now Washington and Lee University. In 1805 he returned to North Carolina, where he in 1809 was made a licentate in the Presbyterian Church and preached. His English was remarkably pure, his manner impressive, his explanations clear and concise. For a long time he taught school and had the best whites as pupils—a United States

[*] Report U.S. Bureau of Education, 1900–1, p. 857.

senator, the sons of a chief justice of North Carolina, a governor of the state and many others. Some of his pupils boarded in his family, and his school was regarded as the best in the State. "All accounts agree that John Chavis was a gentleman," and he was received socially among the best whites and asked to table. In 1830 he was stopped from preaching by the law. Afterward he taught a school for free Negroes in Raleigh. [†]

Henry Evans was a full-blooded Virginia free Negro and was the pioneer of Methodism in Fayetteville, N.C. He found the Negroes there, about 1800, without religious instruction. He began preaching and the town council ordered him away; he continued and whites came to hear him. Finally the white auditors outnumbered the black, and sheds were erected for Negroes at the side of the church. The gathering became a regular Methodist Church, with a white and Negro membership, but Evans continued to preach. He exhibited "rare self-control before the most wretched of castes! Henry Evans did much good, but he would have done more good had his spirit been untrammeled by this sense of inferiority." [‡]

His dying words uttered as he stood, aged and bent beside his pulpit, are of singular pathos:

> "I have come to say my last word to you. It is this: None but Christ. Three times I have had my life in jeopardy for preaching the gospel to you. Three times I have broken ice on the edge of the water and swam across the Cape Fear to preach the gospel to you; and, if in my last hour I could trust to that, or anything but Christ crucified, for my salvation, all should be lost and my soul perish forever." [*]

Early in the nineteenth century Ralph Freeman was a slave in Anson county, N.C. He was a full-blooded Negro, and was ordained and became an able Baptist preacher. He baptized and administered communion, and was greatly respected. When the Baptists split on the question of missions he sided with the anti-mission side. Finally the law forbade him to preach.[†]

Lunsford Lane was a Negro who bought his freedom in Raleigh, N.C., by the manufacture of smoking tobacco. He later became a minister and was intelligent, and had the confidence of many of the best people. [‡]

James Varick was a free Negro of New York, and is memorable as the first bishop of the Zion Methodists.

[†] Bassett, State, North Carolina, pp. 73–76. Cf. also Ballagh: Slavery in Virginia.

[‡] Bassett, State, North Carolina, pp. 58–59.

[*] *Ibid., loc .cit.*

[†] Ibid., p. 64.

[‡] *Ibid.*, p. 50. Cf. p. 29.

The story of Jack of Virginia is best told in the words of a Southern writer:

"Probably the most interesting case in the whole South is that of an African preacher of Nottoway county, popularly known as 'Uncle Jack,' whose services to white and black were so valuable that a distinguished minister of the Southern Presbyterian Church felt called upon to memorialize his work in a biography.

"Kidnapped from his idolatrous parents in Africa, he was brought over in one of the last cargoes of slaves admitted to Virginia and sold to a remote and obscure planter in Nottoway county, a region at that time in the backwoods and destitute particularly as to religious life and instruction. He was converted under the occasional preaching of Rev. Dr. John Blair Smith, president of Hampden-Sidney College, and of Dr. Wm. Hill and Dr. Archibald Alexander of Princeton, then young theologues, and by hearing the scriptures read. Taught by his master's children to read, he became so full of the spirit and knowledge of the Bible that he was recognized among the whites as a powerful expounder of Christian doctrine, was licensed to preach by the Baptist Church, and preached from plantation to plantation within a radius of thirty miles, as he was invited by overseers or masters. His freedom was purchased by a subscription of whites, and he was given a home and a tract of land for his support. He organized a large and orderly Negro church, and exercised such a wonderful controlling influence over the private morals of his flock that masters, instead of punishing their slaves, often referred them to the discipline of their pastor, which they dreaded far more.

"He stopped a heresy among the Negro Christians of Southern Virginia, defeating in open argument a famous fanatical Negro preacher named Campbell, who advocated noise and "the spirit" against the Bible, winning over Campbell's adherents in a body. For over forty years, and until he was nearly a hundred years of age, he labored successfully in public and private among black and whites, voluntarily giving up his preaching in obedience to the law of 1832, the result of 'Old Nat's war.' . . . .

"The most refined and aristocratic people paid tribute to him, and he was instrumental in the conversion of many whites. Says his biographer, Rev. Dr. Wm. S. White: 'He was invited into their houses, sat with their families, took part in their social worship, sometimes leading the prayer at the family altar. Many of the most intelligent people attended upon his ministry and listened to his sermons with great delight. Indeed, previous to the year 1825, he was considered by the best judges to be the best preacher in that county. His opinions were respected, his advice followed, and yet he never betrayed the least symptoms of arrogance or self-conceit. His dwelling was a rude log cabin, his apparel of the plainest and coarsest materials.' This was because he wished to be fully identified with his class.

He refused gifts of better clothing, saying, 'These clothes are a great deal better than are generally worn by people of my color, and besides if I wear them I find I shall be obliged to think about them even at meeting."

---

* Ballagh, pp. 110–112. Cf. White: The African Preacher.

13

The Negro Church in 1890

(FROM THE ELEVENTH UNITED STATES CENSUS)

There were in the United States in 1890, 23,462 Negro churches. Outside of these there were numbers of Negroes who are members of white churches, but they are not distinguished from others:

SUMMARY OF COLORED ORGANIZATIONS

DENOMINATIONS.	Organizations.	Church Edifices.	Approximate Seating Capacity.	Halls, etc.	Seating Capacity.	Value of Church Property.	Communicants or Members.
Total	23,462	23,770	6,800,035	1358	114,644	$26,626,448	2,673,977
Denominations	18,835	19,631	5,791,384	940	78,719	20,389,714	2,303,151
Organizations in other denominations	4,627	4,139	1,008,651	418	35,925	6,236,734	370,826
Regular Baptists	12,533	11,987	3,440,970	663	45,570	$9,038,549	1,348,989
Union American Methodist Episcopal	42	35	11,500	7	250	187,600	2,279
African Methodist Episcopal	2,481	4,124	1,160,838	31	2,200	6,468,280	452,725
African Union Methodist Protestant	40	27	7,161	13	1,883	54,440	3,415
African Methodist Episcopal Zion	1,704	1,587	565,577	114	15,520	2,714,128	349,788
Congregational Methodist	9	5	585	4	450	525	319
Colored Methodist Episcopal	1,759	1,653	541,464	64	6,526	1,713,366	129,383
Zion Union Apostolic	32	27	10,100	1	100	15,000	2,346
Evangelist Missionary	11	3	1,050	9	2,650	2,000	951
Cumberland Presbyterian	224	183	52,139	34	3,570	195,826	12,956
Regular Baptists (North)	406	324	92,660	72	7,245	1,087,518	35,221

DENOMINATIONS.	Organizations.	Church Edifices.	Approximate Seating Capacity.	Halls, etc.	Seating Capacity.	Value of Church Property.	Communicants or Members.
Regular Baptists (South)	7	5	1,900	2	80	3,875	651
Freewill Baptists	5	3	800	2	200	13,300	271
Primitive Baptists	323	291	96,699	33	1,700	135,427	18,162
Old Two-Seed in the Spirit Predestinarian Baptists	15	4	1,025	11	825	930	265
Roman Catholic	31	27	8,370	3	60	237,400	14,517
Christians (Christian Connection)	63	54	16,495	7	800	23,500	4,989
Congregationalists	85	69	19,360	11	1,925	246,125	6,908
Disciples of Christ	277	183	41,590	75	5,850	176,795	18,578
Lutheran Synodical Conference	5	5	1,050	....	....	13,400	211
Lutheran United Synod in the South	5	3	550	2	250	1,750	94
Methodist Episcopal	2,984	2,800	635,252	165	12,925	3,630,093	246,249
Methodist Protestant	54	50	11,545	4	200	35,445	3,183
Independent Methodists	2	2	725	....	....	4,675	222
Presbyterian (Northern)	233	200	56,280	21	3,100	391,650	14,961
Presbyterian (Southern)	45	29	6,190	7	565	22,200	1,568
Reformed Presbyterian (Synod)	1	1	300	....	....	1,500	76
Protestant Episcopal	49	53	11,885	2	100	192,750	2,977
Reformed Episcopal	37	36	5,975	1	100	18,401	1,723

Organizations by States

STATES.	Organizations.	Church Edifices.	Approximate Seating Capacity.	Halls, etc.	Seating Capacity.	Value of Church Property.	Communicants or Members.
The United States	23,462	23,770	6,800,035	1,358	114,644	$26,626,448	2,673,977
Alabama	2,395	3,425	717,989	113	8,925	1,880,656	297,161
Arizona	2	2	450	....	....	8,000	155
Arkansas	1,375	1,432	378,058	94	6,835	962,149	106,445
California	29	23	5,879	8	2,000	65,300	3,720
Colorado	10	8	2,900	....	....	73,800	1,171
Connecticut	23	20	6,000	3	350	116,950	1,624
Delaware	82	91	21,310	7	570	187,825	6,595
District of Columbia	77	65	38,325	14	1,400	1,182,650	22,965
Florida	657	729	172,412	47	3,806	506,970	64,337
Georgia	2,878	3,134	953,873	102	7,035	2,171,267	341,433

STATES.	Organizations.	Church Edifices.	Approximate Seating Capacity.	Halls, etc.	Seating Capacity.	Value of Church Property.	Communicants or Members.
Illinois	192	207	53,744	14	2,075	566,835	15,635
Indiana	121	126	39,725	11	825	347,950	13,404
Indian Territory	27	31	4,530	....	....	5,593	780
Iowa	45	43	10,795	2	250	121,990	2,643
Kansas	149	136	32,699	21	1,675	270,145	9,750
Kentucky	816	734	212,795	84	6,880	1,143,380	92,768
Louisiana	1,340	1,343	323,311	27	2,525	1,228,617	108,872
Maine	1	....	....	1	150	....	45
Maryland	463	473	122,379	22	1,840	1,118,040	58,566
Massachusetts	34	30	12,050	5	950	285,700	3,638
Michigan	49	47	12,520	7	1,750	107,035	3,957
Minnesota	10	9	3,700	....	....	62,500	958
Mississippi	2,309	2,354	614,681	91	7,120	1,434,102	224,404
Missouri	549	515	133,809	72	4,700	919,427	42,452
Montana	3	2	350	1	100	14,000	32
Nebraska	4	4	1,350	....	....	62,000	399
New Jersey	136	140	40,076	10	1,448	405,490	12,720
New Mexico	3	3	550	....	....	3,300	62
New York	110	94	39,340	17	2,113	1,023,750	17,216
North Carolina	2,191	2,205	668,588	64	4,845	1,592,596	290,755
Ohio	250	214	66,515	31	1,750	576,425	19,827
Oklahoma	4	....	....	3	270	....	100
Oregon	3	2	300	....	....	20,000	291
Pennsylvania	228	234	77,865	25	3,025	1,156,408	26,753
Rhode Island	16	11	4,800	5	1,218	148,100	1,999
South Carolina	1,731	1,959	599,544	55	5,660	1,770,504	317,020
Tennessee	1,328	1,350	399,568	71	4,740	1,690,946	131,015
Texas	2,323	2,126	551,965	244	19,810	1,455,507	186,038
Utah	1	....	....	1	50	....	7
Virginia	1,360	1,346	449,972	52	4,139	1,735,873	238,617
Washington	2	1	400	....	....	4,000	66
West Virginia	27	96	24,045	31	3,415	154,768	7,160
Wisconsin	5	4	550	1	200	40,400	268
Wyoming	4	2	325	2	200	5,500	154

We may now consider these organizations by denominations:

Regular Baptists (Colored)

The colored Baptists of the South constitute the most numerous body of Regular Baptists. Not all colored Baptists are embraced in this division; only those who have separate churches, associations, and state conventions. There are many colored Baptists in Northern States, who are mostly counted as members of churches, belonging to white associations. None of them are included in the following tables.

The first state convention of colored Baptists was organized in North Carolina in 1866, the second in Alabama, and the third in Virginia in 1867, the fourth in Arkansas in 1868, and the fifth in Kentucky in 1869. There are colored conventions in fifteen states and the District of Columbia.

In addition to these organizations the colored Baptists of the United States have others more general in character: The American National Convention, the purpose of which is "to consider the moral, intellectual, and religious growth of the denomination," to deliberate upon questions of general concern, and to devise methods to bring the churches and members of the race closer together; the Consolidated American Missionary Convention, the General Association of the Western States and Territories, the Foreign Mission Convention of the United States, and the New England Missionary Convention. All except one are missionary in their purpose.

The Regular Baptists (colored) are represented in fifteen states, all in the South, or on the border, and the District of Columbia. In Virginia and Georgia they are very numerous, having in the latter 200,516, and in the former 199,871 communicants. In Alabama they have 142,437, in North Carolina 134,445, in Mississippi 136,647, in South Carolina 125,572, and in Texas 111,138 members. The aggregate is 1,348,989 members, who are embraced in 12,533 organizations, with 11,987 church edifices, and church property valued at $9,038,549. There are 414 associations, of which 68 are in Alabama, 63 in Georgia, 49 in Mississippi, and 39 in North Carolina.

Regular Baptists (Colored)

SUMMARY BY STATES AND TERRITORIES

STATES AND TERRITORIES	Organizations.	Church Edifices.	Approximate Seating Capacity.	Halls, etc.	Seating Capacity.	Value of Church Property.	Communicants or Members.
The United States	12,533	11,987	3,440,970	663	45,570	$9,038,549	1,348,989
Alabama............................	1,374	1,341	376,839	50	3,365	795,384	142,437
Arkansas..........................	923	870	243,395	51	3,310	585,947	63,786
District of Columbia........	43	33	18,600	10	1,150	383,150	12,717

STATES AND TERRITORIES	Organizations.	Church Edifices.	Approximate Seating Capacity.	Halls, etc.	Seating Capacity.	Value of Church Property.	Communicants or Members.
Florida............................	329	295	61,588	37	2,270	137,578	20,828
Georgia...........................	1,818	1,800	544,540	58	3,460	1,043,310	200,516
Kentucky.........................	378	359	109,030	26	2,025	406,949	50,245
Louisiana.........................	865	861	191,041	13	1,480	609,890	68,008
Maryland.........................	38	34	12,389	....	....	150,475	7,750
Mississippi......................	1,385	1,333	371,115	59	3,695	682,541	136,647
Missouri..........................	234	212	60,015	26	1,225	400,518	18,613
North Carolina................	1,173	1,164	362,946	14	750	705,512	134,445
South Carolina................	860	836	275,529	37	3,685	699,961	125,572
Tennessee........................	569	534	159,140	41	1,860	519,923	52,183
Texas...............................	1,464	1,288	282,590	180	12,000	664,286	111,138
Virginia...........................	1,001	977	358,032	32	1,955	1,192,035	199,871
West Virginia..................	79	50	14,175	29	3,340	50,090	4,233

African Methodist Episcopal

This branch of American Methodism was organized in Baltimore in 1816 by a number of colored members of the Methodist Episcopal Church. They withdrew from the parent body in order that they might have larger privileges and more freedom of action among themselves than they believed they could secure in continued association with their white brethren. The Rev. Richard Allen was elected the first bishop of the new church by the same convention that organized it. In the year 1787 Mr. Allen had been made the leader of a class of forty persons of his own color. A few years later he purchased a lot at the corner of Sixth and Lombard streets, Philadelphia, where the first church erected in this country for colored Methodists was occupied in 1794. This site is now covered by an edifice, dedicated in 1890, valued at $50,000.

In doctrine, government, and usage, the church does not essentially differ from the body from which it sprang. It has an itinerant and a local or non-itinerant ministry, and its territory is divided into annual conferences. It has a general conference, meeting once every four years; bishops or itinerant general superintendents, elected for life, who visit the annual conferences in the episcopal districts to which they are assigned, and presiding elders, who exercise sub-episcopal oversight in the districts into which the annual conferences are divided; and it has the probationary system for new members, with exhorters, class leaders, stewards, stewardesses, etc.

The church in its first half century grew slowly, chiefly in the Northern States, until the close of the war. At the end of the first decade of its existence it had two conferences and about 8,000 members. In 1856 it had seven conferences and about 20,000 members; in 1866, ten conferences and 75,000 members. Bishop B. W. Arnett, the ardent and industrious statistician of the church, in noting a decrease of 343 members in the decade ending in 1836, in the Baltimore conference, explains that it was due to the numerous sales of members as slaves. According to elaborate figures furnished by him the increase in the value of church property owned by the denomination was not less than $400,000 in the decade closing in 1866, or nearly fifty percent. In the succeeding ten years the increase was from $825,000 to $3,064,000, not including parsonages, which seem to have been embraced in the total for 1866. According to the returns for 1890, given herewith, the valuation is $6,468,280, indicating an increase of $3,404,280 in the last fourteen years, or 111.11 percent.

The church is widely distributed, having congregations in forty-one states and territories. The states in which it is not represented are the two Dakotas, Idaho, Maine, Nevada, New Hampshire, and Vermont, the territories being Alaska, Oklahoma, and Arizona. Its members are most numerous in South Carolina, where there are 88,172. Georgia comes second, with 73,248; Alabama third, with 30,781; Arkansas fourth, with 27,956; Mississippi fifth, with 25,439. Tennessee has 23,718, Texas 23,392, and Florida 22,463. In no other state does the number reach 17,000. The eight Southern States above given report 315,169 members, or considerably more than two-thirds of the entire membership of the church. It will be observed that of the 2,481 organizations only thirty-one worship in halls, school-houses, etc. All the rest, 2,450, own the edifices in which their meetings are held.

African Methodist Episcopal

SUMMARY BY STATES AND TERRITORIES

STATES AND TERRITORIES.	Organizations.	Church Edifices.	Approximate Seating Capacity.	Halls, etc.	Seating Capacity.	Value of Church Property.	Communicants or Members.
The United States	2,481	4,124	1,160,838	31	2,200	$6,468,280	452,725
Alabama	145	274	77,600	4	200	$242,765	30,781
Arkansas..........................	173	333	77,585	....	....	233,425	27,956
California........................	13	15	2,929	....	....	24,300	772
Colorado	8	6	2,300	....	....	63,500	788
Connecticut.....................	4	4	1,275	....	....	16,000	158
Delaware..........................	16	33	7,025	....	....	39,500	2,603
District of Columbia	6	7	5,500	....	....	117,500	1,479
Florida.............................	152	269	63,445	....	....	168,473	22,463

STATES AND TERRITORIES.	Organizations.	Church Edifices.	Approximate Seating Capacity.	Halls, etc.	Seating Capacity.	Value of Church Property.	Communicants or Members.
Georgia	334	654	181,592	7	250	601,287	73,248
Illinois	74	105	23,799	....	....	310,985	6,383
					....		
Indiana	36	51	16,450	....	....	138,280	4,435
Indian Territory	14	22	1,680	....	....	2,618	489
Iowa	29	29	7,115	....		87,365	1,820
Kansas	48	58	14,309	....	....	153,530	4,678
Kentucky	90	106	39,100	....	....	181,201	13,972
Louisiana	81	115	36,150	....	....	193,115	13,631
Maryland	58	93	29,881	....	....	266,370	12,359
Massachusetts	12	11	5,950	1	75	119,200	1,342
Michigan	21	26	7,155	....	....	72,185	1,836
Minnesota	6	6	2,350	....	....	30,000	489
Mississippi	122	255	59,833	1	50	226,242	25,439
Missouri	87	126	27,870	....	....	281,289	9,589
Montana	3	2	350	1	100	14,000	32
Nebraska	4	4	1,350	....	....	62,000	399
New Jersey	54	68	19,510	1	300	159,850	5,851
New Mexico	3	3	550	....	....	3,300	62
New York	34	29	12,900	6	325	231,500	3,124
North Carolina	61	147	42,350	....	....	112,998	16,156
Ohio	111	113	40,965	1	50	318,250	10,025
Oregon	1	....	....	......	....	....	16
Pennsylvania	87	112	39,900	5	600	605,000	11,613
Rhode Island	4	3	2,050	1	....	95,000	595
South Carolina	229	491	125,945	....	....	356,362	88,172
Tennessee	144	236	61,800	....	....	461,305	23,718
Texas	138	208	82,850	....	....	233,340	23,392
Utah	1	....	....	1	50	....	7
Virginia	67	102	34,375	....	....	187,245	12,314
Washington	2	1	400	......	....	4,000	66
West Virginia	3	3	1,050	......	....	11,000	216
Wisconsin	3	3	400	......	....	40,000	118
Wyoming	3	1	200	2	200	4,000	139

African Union Methodist Protestant

This body, which has a few congregations divided among eight states, came into existence at about the same time the African Methodist Episcopal Church was organized (1816), differing from the latter chiefly in <u>objection to the itinerancy, to a paid ministry, and to the episcopacy.</u>

SUMMARY BY STATES

STATES.	Organizations.	Church Edifices.	Approximate Seating Capacity.	Halls, etc.	Seating Capacity.	Value of Church Property.	Communicants or Members.
The United States..................	40	27	7,161	13	1,883	$54,440	3,415
Delaware......................................	6	4	1,250	2	270	$9,600	368
Maine...	1	....	....	1	150	....	45
Maryland.....................................	8	7	2,255	1	240	5,600	1,546
New Jersey..................................	8	6	836	2	108	5,940	281
New York....................................	3	....	....	3	568	....	60
Pennsylvania..............................	8	8	2,140	....	....	32,100	852
Rhode Island..............................	1	....	....	1	148	....	49
Virginia.......................................	5	2	680	3	399	1,200	214

Congregational Methodist (Colored)

Dissatisfaction with certain features of the system of polity led a number of ministers and members of the Methodist Episcopal Church, South, to withdraw and organize a body in which laymen should have an equal voice in church government, and local preachers should become pastors.

This body consists of congregations of colored members organized into conferences by presidents of the Congregational Methodist Church, to which it corresponds in all particulars of doctrine, polity, usage. The only difference between the churches of the two bodies is, that they are composed of white and colored persons, respectively.

SUMMARY BY STATES

STATES.	Organizations.	Church Edifices.	Approximate Seating Capacity.	Halls, etc.	Seating Capacity.	Value of Church Property.	Communicants or Members.
The United States.............................	9	5	585	4	450	$525	319
Alabama	7	5	585	2	250	525	215
Texas..	2	....	......	2	200	......	104

African Methodist Episcopal Zion

A congregation of colored people, organized in New York city, in 1796, was the nucleus of the African Methodist Episcopal Zion Church. This congregation originated in a desire of colored members of the Methodist Episcopal Church to hold separate meetings in which they "might have an opportunity to exercise their spiritual gifts among themselves, and thereby be more useful to one another." They built a church, which was dedicated in 1800, the full name of the denomination subsequently organized being given to it.

The church entered into an agreement in 1801 by which it was to receive certain pastoral supervision from the Methodist Episcopal Church. It had preachers of its own, who supplied its pulpit in part. In 1820 this arrangement terminated, and in the same year a union of colored churches in New York, New Haven, Long Island, and Philadelphia was formed, and rules of government adopted. Thus was the African Methodist Episcopal Zion Church formally organized.

The first annual conference was held in 1821. It was attended by nineteen preachers, representing six churches and 1,426 members. Next year James Varick was chosen superintendent of the denomination, which was extended over the states of the North chiefly, until the close of the civil war, when it entered the South to organize many churches.

In its polity lay representation has long been a prominent feature. Laymen are in its annual conferences as well as in its general conference, and there is no bar to the ordination of women. Until 1880 its superintendents or bishops were elected for a term of four years. In that year the term of the office was made for life or during good behavior. Its system is almost identical with that of the Methodist Episcopal Church, except the presence of laymen in the annual conference, the election of presiding elders on the nomination of the presiding bishop, instead of their appointment by the bishop alone, and other small divergences. Its general conference meets quadrennially. Its territory is divided into seven Episcopal districts, to each of which a bishop is assigned by the general conference.

The church is represented in twenty-eight states and the District of Columbia. It is strongest in North Carolina, where it has 111,949 communicants. Alabama comes next, with 79,231 communicants; South Carolina third, with 45, 880, and Florida fourth, with 14,791. There are in all 1,704 organizations, 1,587 church edifices, church property valued at $2,714,128, and 349,788 communicants.

African Methodist Episcopal Zion

SUMMARY BY STATES AND TERRITORIES

STATES AND TERRITORIES.	Organizations.	Church Edifices.	Approximate Seating Capacity.	Halls, etc.	Seating Capacity	Value of Church Property.	Communicants or Members.
The United States	1,704	1,587	565,577	114	15,520	$2,714,128	349,788
Alabama	336	315	118,800	17	2,500	$305,350	79,231
Arkansas...........................	29	23	8,800	6	750	17,250	3,601
California.........................	13	6	2,600	7	1,950	37,200	2,627
Connecticut......................	12	10	2,900	2	150	79,350	1,012
Delaware...........................	2	1	115	1	200	500	158
District of Columbia.........	6	6	3,400	......	......	298,800	2,495
Florida	61	61	23,589	......	......	90,745	14,791
Georgia	70	62	19,775	9	200	52,360	12,705
Illinois.............................	5	5	2,000	......	......	13,400	434
Indiana.............................	5	5	2,400	......	......	54,700	1,339
Kentucky..........................	55	52	13,075	3	250	86,830	7,217
Louisiana	21	19	5,200	2	350	12,920	2,747
Maryland..........................	13	10	2,375	3	400	17,350	1,211
Massachusetts	7	6	2,050	1	75	58,800	724
Michigan..........................	6	4	650	2	500	3,200	702
Mississippi.......................	64	50	22,350	14	2,375	22,975	8,519
Missouri...........................	6	6	3,900	....	......	6,000	2,037
New Jersey........................	25	24	7,400	1	150	107,700	2,954
New York	47	47	17,000	......	......	371,400	6,668
North Carolina.................	541	527	171,430	14	1,300	485,711	111,949
Ohio	8	5	1,160	3	......	13,000	194
Oregon.............................	2	2	300	......	......	20,000	275
Pennsylvania	62	55	17,625	7	275	256,150	8,689
Rhode Island	3	1	400	2	870	2,000	401
South Carolina	130	128	66,770	2	250	126,395	45,880
Tennessee	55	52	21,093	3	250	78,813	12,434
Texas	47	38	11,500	9	1,775	26,450	6,927
Virginia............................	72	66	16,770	6	950	68,449	11,765
Wisconsin.........................	1	1	150	......	......	400	102

Colored Methodist Episcopal

The Colored Methodist Episcopal Church was organized in 1870 of colored members and ministers of the Methodist Episcopal Church, South.

Before the late civil war the Methodist Episcopal Church, South, did a large evangelistic work among the Negroes. Bishop McTyeire, of that body, in his "History of Methodism," says:

"As a general rule Negro slaves received the gospel by Methodism from the same preachers and in the same churches with their masters, the galleries or a portion of the body of the house being assigned to them. If a separate building was provided, the Negro congregation was an appendage to the white, the pastor usually preaching once on Sunday for them, holding separate official meetings with their leaders, exhorters, and preachers, and administering discipline, and making return of members for the annual minutes." For the Negroes on plantations, who were not privileged to attend organized churches, special missions were begun as early as 1829. In 1845, the year which marks the beginning of the separate existence of the Methodist Episcopal Church, South, there were in the Southern conferences of Methodism, according to Bishop McTyeire, 124,000 members of the slave population, and in 1860 about 207,000.

In 1866, after the opening of the South to Northern churches had given the Negro members opportunity to join the African Methodist Episcopal, the African Methodist Episcopal Zion, and other Methodist bodies, it was found that of the 207,742 colored members which the church, South, had in 1860 only 78,742 remained. The general conference of 1866 authorized these colored members, with their preachers, to be organized into separate congregations and annual conferences, and the general conference of 1870 appointed two bishops to organize the colored conferences into a separate and independent church. This was done in December, 1870, the new body taking the name "Colored Methodist Episcopal Church." Its rules limited the privilege of membership to Negroes. The Colored Methodist Episcopal Church has the same articles of religion, the same form of government, and the same discipline as its parent body. Its bishops are elected for life. One of them, Bishop L. H. Holsey, says that for some years the body encountered strong opposition from colored people because of its relation to the Methodist Episcopal Church, South, but that this prejudice has now almost entirely disappeared.

Colored Methodist Episcopal

SUMMARY BY STATES AND TERRITORIES

STATES AND TERRITORIES.	Organizations.	Church Edifices.	Approximate Seating Capacity.	Halls, etc.	Seating Capacity.	Value of Church Property.	Communicants or Members.
The United States	1,759	1,653	541,464	64	6,526	$1,713,366	129,383
Alabama	222	220	69,200	......	......	$264,625	18,940
Arkansas	116	104	31,059	13	1,200	60,277	5,888
Delaware	6	3	430	3	100	1,125	187
District of Columbia	5	4	3,500	1	100	123,800	939
Florida	36	26	7,000	5	1,236	14,709	1,461
Georgia	266	256	100,495	7	1,075	167,145	22,840
Illinois	2	2	800	......	......	1,250	56
Indian Territory	13	9	2,850	......	......	2,975	291
Kansas	17	15	3,625	....	......	14,400	713
Kentucky	91	63	16,000	12	1,225	140,330	6,908
Louisiana	138	131	43,220	2	100	134,135	8,075
Maryland	2	2	205	......	......	475	44
Mississippi	293	292	72,150	......	......	230,490	20,107
Missouri	35	31	5,554	3	100	22,140	953
New Jersey	5	3	625	2	140	7,500	266
North Carolina	26	20	7,725	6	......	23,120	2,786
Pennsylvania	6	2	310	4	1,050	1,400	247
South Carolina	34	33	15,045	1	100	65,325	3,468
Tennessee	206	205	67,900	......	......	258,120	18,968
Texas	222	216	88,330	3	......	147,075	14,895
Virginia	18	16	4,850	2	100	33,150	1,351

Cumberland Presbyterian (Colored)

This body was organized in May, 1869, at Murfreesboro, Tenn., under the direction of the General Assembly of the Cumberland Presbyterian Church. It was constituted of colored ministers and members who had been connected with that church. Its first synod, the Tennessee, was organized in 1871, and its general assembly in 1874. It has the same doctrinal symbol as the parent body and the same system of government and discipline, differing only in race. It has twenty-three presbyteries, and is represented in nine states and one territory. It has 224 organizations, 183 church edifices, 12,956 communicants, and church property valued at $195, 826.

Cumberland Presbyterian (Colored)

SUMMARY BY STATES AND TERRITORIES

STATES AND TERRITORIES.	Organizations.	Church Edifices.	Approximate Seating Capacity.	Halls, etc.	Seating Capacity.	Value of Church Property.	Communicants or Members.
The United States	224	183	52,139	34	3,570	$195,826	12,956
Alabama	44	38	9,574	7	475	$26,200	3,104
Arkansas	2	......	......	2	300	......	255
Illinois	7	4	1,300	2	75	5,375	195
Kansas	6	3	650	3	150	15,000	190
Kentucky	36	31	7,730	2	......	31,645	1,421
Mississippi	4	4	950	......	......	1,825	278
Missouri	10	9	1,650	1	50	17,900	471
Oklahoma	4	......	......	3	270	......	100
Tennessee	81	72	24,125	7	825	88,660	5,202
Texas	30	22	6,160	7	1,425	9,221	1,740

14

Local Studies, 1902–3

To realize the present condition of churches and the changes in the last thirteen years, the Conference of 1903 arranged for a number of local studies of churches: one in a black belt county of Georgia, another in a county of southern Ohio, a third in the city of Chicago and the state of Illinois, a fourth in Virginia, and a fifth in Atlanta, Ga. To these studies were added the results of previous investigations in DeLand, Fla., Farmville, Va., and Philadelphia, Pa. The study in Thomas county, Ga., was made by a colored Congregational minister, the Rev. W. H. Holloway, a graduate of Talladega College. The study in Greene county, Ohio, was made by the Rev. R. R. Wright, Jr., who later made a more comprehensive study for the United States Bureau of Labor. Mr. Monroe N. Work, of the University of Chicago, studied Illinois, and the investigations in Atlanta were by senior students in Atlanta University. Dr. Annie M. MacLean kindly furnished the study of Deland, Fla. The students of Virginia Union University, under the direction of Professor B. F. Williams, made the investigations in Virginia.

To realize just the change in moral conditions it is instructive to preface these studies with several verbatim paragraphs taken from the work of an apologist for slavery, but one who strove manfully for the uplift of the slaves.* The period referred to is generally the decade, 1830–1840:

> "Persons live and die in the midst of Negroes and know comparatively little of their real character. They have not the immediate management of them. They have to do with them in the ordinary discharge of their duty as servants, further than this they institute no inquiries; they give themselves no trouble. The Negroes are a distinct class in the community, and keep themselves very much to themselves. They are one thing before the white and another before their own color. Deception before the for-

* C.C. Jones: Religious Instruction of Negroes, pp. 89–176, *passim*.

mer is characteristic of them, whether bond or free, throughout the whole United States. It is habit, a long established custom, which descends from generation to generation. There is an upper and an under current. Some are contented with the appearance on the surface; others dive beneath. Hence the diversity of impressions and representations of the moral and religious condition of the Negroes. Hence the disposition of some to deny the darker pictures of their more searching and knowing friends. . . . . .

"Their general mode of living is coarse and vulgar. Many Negro houses are small, low to the ground, blackened with smoke, often with dirt floors, and the furniture of the plainest kind. On some estates the houses are framed, weather-boarded, neatly whitewashed, and made sufficiently large and comfortable in every respect. . . . . .

"It is a matter of thankfulness that the owners are few in number, indeed, who forbid religious meetings on their plantations, held either by their servants themselves, or by competent and approved white instructors or ministers. 'All men have not faith.' I have never known servants forbidden to attend the worship of God on the Sabbath day, except as a restraint temporarily laid, for some flagrant misconduct. . . . . .

"Nor can the adult Negro acquaint himself with duty and the way of salvation through the reading of the scriptures any more than the child. Of those that do read, but few read well enough for the edification of the hearers. Not all the colored preachers read. . . . . .

"Such, then, are the circumstances of the slave population, which have an unfavorable influence upon their moral and religious condition. Those circumstances only have been referred to which prominently assist us in our inquiry. In conclusion, it may be added that servants have neither intellectual nor moral intercourse with their masters generally, sufficient to redeem them from the adverse influence of the circumstances alluded to; for the two classes are distinct in their association, and it cannot well be otherwise. Nor have servants any redeeming intercourse with any other persons. On the contrary, in certain situations there is intercourse had with them, and many temptations laid before them against which they have little or no defense, and the effect is deplorable."

"To know the extent of their ignorance, even where they have been accustomed to the sound of the gospel in white churches, a man should make investigation for himself. The result will frequently surprise and fill him with grief. They scarcely feel shame for their ignorance on the subject of religion, although they may have had abundant opportunity of becoming wiser. Ignorance, they seem to feel, is their lot; and that feeling is intimately associated with another every way congenial to the natural man, namely, a feeling of irresponsibility—ignorance is a cloak and excuse for crime. Some white ministers and teachers, in their simplicity, beholding their attention to the preaching of the gospel, adapted to their comprehen-

sion, and hearing the expressions of their thankfulness for the pains taken for their instruction, come to the conclusion that they are an unsophisticated race; that they form one of the easiest and pleasantest fields of labor in the world; and that they are a people 'made ready, prepared for the Lord,' nothing more being necessary than to carry them the gospel and converts will be multiplied as drops of morning dew: yea, a nation will be born in a day. Experiment shortly dissipates these visions, and well is it if the sober reality does not frighten the laborer away in disgust and disappointment.
. . . . .

"But a brief view of the prevailing vices of the Negroes will best reveal their moral and religious condition.

"*Violations of the Marriage Contract.* The divine institution of marriage depends for its perpetuity, sacredness, and value, largely upon the protection given it by the law of the land. Negro marriages are neither recognized nor protected by law. The Negroes receive no instruction on the nature, sacredness, and perpetuity of the institution; at any rate they are far from being duly impressed with these things. They are not required to be married in any particular form, nor by any particular persons. Their ceremonies are performed by their own watchmen or teachers, by some white minister, or as it frequently happens, not at all; the consent of owners and of the parties immediately interested, and a public acknowledgement of each other, being deemed sufficient.

"There is no special disgrace nor punishment visited upon those who criminally violate their marriage vows, except where they may be inflicted by owners, or if the parties be members, by the church in the way of suspension and excommunication.

"Families are, and may be, divided for improper conduct on the part of either husband or wife, or by necessity, as in cases of the death of owners, division of estates, debt, sale, or removals, for they are subject to all the changes and vicissitudes of property. Such divisions are, however, carefully guarded against and prevented, as far as possible, by owners, on the score of interest, as well as of religion and humanity. Hence, as may well be imagined, the marriage relation loses much of the sacredness and perpetuity of its character. It is a contract of convenience, profit, or pleasure, that may be entered into and dissolved at the will of the parties, and that without heinous sin, or the injury of the property or interests of any one. That which they possess in common is speedily divided, and the support of the wife and children falls not upon the husband, but upon the master. Protracted sickness, want of industrial habits, of congeniality of disposition, or disparity of age, are sufficient grounds for a separation. While there are creditable instances of conjugal fidelity for a long series of years and until death, yet infidelity in the marriage relation and dissolution of marriage ties are not uncommon.

"On account of the changes, interruptions and interferences in families, there are quarrellings and fightings, and a considerable item in the management of plantations is the settlement of family troubles. Some owners become disgusted and worried out, and finally leave their people to do their own way; while others cease from the strife ere it be meddled with, and give it as an opinion that the less the interference on the part of the master the better. A few conscientious masters persevere in attempts at reformation, and with some good degree of success.

Polygamy is practiced, both secretly and openly. In some sections, where the people have been well instructed, it is scarcely known; in others, the crime has diminished and is diminishing; it is to be hoped universally so. It is a crime which, among all people and under all circumstances, carries, in its perpetration, vast inconveniences and endless divisions and troubles, and they are felt by the Negroes as well as by others, and operate as a great preventive. Polygamy is also discountenanced and checked by the majority of owners, and by the churches of all denominations.

"*Uncleanness.* This sin may be considered universal. The declaration will be sufficient for those who have any acquaintance with this people in the slave-holding states or in the free states; indeed, with the ignorant laboring classes of people wherever they may be found. It is not my object to institute comparisons. If it were, I could point to many tongues and people, in civilized governments, upon the same level of depravity with the Negroes. The sin is not viewed by them as by those of higher intelligence and virtue, so that they do not consider character as lost by it, not personal degradation as necessarily connected with it. A view which, however it may spring from vitiated principle, preserved the guilty from entire prostration."

"Intimately connected with this view is the crime of

"*Infanticide.* A crime restrained in good measure by the provision made for the support of the child on the part of the owner, by the punishment in case of detection, and by the moral degradation of the people that takes away the disgrace of bastardy.

"*Theft.* They are proverbially thieves. They bear this character in Africa; they have borne it in all countries whither they have been carried; it has been the character of slaves in all ages, whatever their nation or color. They steal from each other, from their masters, from anybody. Cows, sheep, hogs, poultry, clothing; yea, nothing goes amiss to which they take a fancy; while corn, rice, cotton, or the staple productions, whatever they may be, are standing temptations, provided a market be at hand, and they can sell or barter them with impunity. Locks, bolts, and bars secure articles desirable to them, from the dwelling of the master to that of the servant, and the keys must always be carried.

"*Falsehood.* Their veracity is nominal. Duplicity is one of the most prominent traits of their character, practiced between themselves, but more especially towards their masters and managers. Their frequent cases of feigned sickness are vexatious. When criminal acts are under investigation, the sober, strenuous falsehood, sometimes the direct and awful appeal to God, of the transgressor, averts the suspicion, and by his own tact and collusion with others, perhaps fixes the guilt upon some innocent person. The number, the variety, and ingenuity of falsehoods that can be told by them in a few brief moments is astonishing. Where opportunity is given they will practice imposition. Servants, however, who will neither steal nor lie, may be found, and in no inconsiderable numbers.

"*Quarreling and Fighting.* The Negroes are settled in some quarter of the plantation, in houses near each other, built in rows, forming a street. The custom is to give each family a house of its own. The houses sometimes have a partition in the middle and accommodate a family in each end. These are called double houses. Living so near each other, and every day working together, causes of differences must necessarily arise. Families grow jealous and envious of their neighbors; some essay to be leading families; they overhear conversations and domestic disagreements; become privy to improper conduct; they deprecate upon each other; a fruitful source of tumult is the pilfering and quarreling of children, which involve their parents. The women quarrel more than the men, and fight oftener. Where no decisive measures are taken to suppress these practices, plantations sometimes become intolerable, might is right; the strong oppress the weak. Every master or manager has the evil under his own control.

"They come to open breaches, too, with their neighbors on adjoining plantations, or lots, if they live in towns. The Sabbath is considered a very suitable day for the settlement of their difficulties. However, with truth it may be said, there are fewer personal injuries, and manslaughters, and murders, among the Negroes in the South, than among the same amount of population in any part of the United States; or perhaps, in the world.

"*Insensibility of Heart.* An ignorant and degraded people are not wont to exhibit much of the milk of human kindness.

"Unless the Negroes are carefully watched and made accountable for power lodged in their hands, it will be abused. Parents will beat their children, husbands their wives, master mechanics their apprentices, and drivers the people. In sickness, parents will neglect their children, children their parents; and so with the other social relations. They cannot be trusted as nurses. Hence they must be made to attend upon the sick, and then watched lest they neglect them; which ultimately brings the whole care of the sick upon the master or manager. It is a saying of their own, "that white people care more for them than their own color,' and again, 'that black people have not the same feeling for each other that white people have.' It is an indisputable fact that when Negroes become owners of slaves they are generally cruel masters. They will overload, work down, bruise and beat, and starve all working animals committed to their care, with careless indifference. . . . . .

"The moral and religious condition of town and city Negroes, may be disposed of in a few lines.

"They admit of division into four classes: family servants, or those who belong to the families which they serve; hired servants, or those who are hired out by their owners to wait in families, or to any other service; servants who hire their own time, and work at various employments and pay their owners so much per day or month; and watermen, embracing fishermen, sailors and boatmen.

"Town and city Negroes are more intelligent and sprightly than country Negroes, owing to a difference in circumstances, employments, and opportunities of improvement. Their physical condition is somewhat improved; and they enjoy greater access to religious privileges.

"On the other hand, they are exposed to greater temptations and vices; their opportunities of attending upon places of pleasure and dissipation are increased; they have stronger temptations to theft, and idleness, and drunkenness, and lewdness; and the tendency to Sabbath breaking is equally great. Their moral and religious condition is precisely that of plantation Negroes, modified in some respects by peculiarities of circumstances. They are more intelligent, but less subordinate; better provided for in certain particulars, but not more healthy; enjoy greater advantages for religious improvement, but are thrown more directly in the way of temptation; and, on the whole, in point of moral character, if there be any pre-eminence it is in favor of the country Negroes; but it is a difficult point to decide. . . . . .

"The Honorable Charles Cotesworth Pinckney, in an 'Address before the Agricultural Society of South Carolina,' (Charleston, 1829, second edition, pp. 10–12), said:

"There needs no stronger illustration of the doctrine of human depravity than the state of morals on plantations in general. Besides the mischievous tendency of bad example in parents and elders, the little Negro is often taught by these natural instructors, that he may commit any vice that he can conceal from his superiors, and thus falsehood and deception are among the earliest lessons they imbibe. Their advance in years is but a progression to the higher grades of iniquity. The violation of the seventh commandment is viewed in a more venial light than in fashionable European circles. Their depredations of rice have been estimated to amount to twenty-five per cent on the gross average of crops, and this calculation was made after fifty years of experience, by one whose liberal provision for their wants left no excuse for their ingratitude." . . . .

"The Honorable Whitemarsh B. Seabrook, in an 'Essay on the Management of Slaves,' Charleston, (1836, pp. 7, 8, 12, etc.), says: 'As human beings, however slaves are liable to all the infirmities of our nature. Ignorant and fanatical, none are more easily excited. Incendiaries might readily embitter their enjoyments and render them a curse to themselves and the community. The prominent offences of the slaves are to be traced in most instances to the use of intoxicating liquors. This is one of the main sources of every insurrectionary movement which has occurred in the United States, and we are, therefore, bound by interest, as well as the common feeling of humanity, to arrest the contagious disease of our colored population. What have become of the millions of freemen who once inhabited our widely-spread country? Ask the untiring votaries of Bacchus. Can there be a doubt, but that the authority of the master alone prevents his slaves from experiencing the fate of the aborigines of America? At one time polygamy was a common crime; it is of now of rare occurrence. Between slaves on the same plantation there is a deep sympathy of feeling which binds them so closely together that a crime committed by one of their number is seldom discovered through their instrumentality. This is an obstacle to the establishment of an efficient police, which the domestic legislator can with difficulty surmount.'

"The executive committee of the Kentucky Union for the moral and religious improvement of the colored race, in their 'Circular to the ministers of Kentucky,' 1834, say: 'We desire not to represent their condition worse than it is. Doubtless the light that shines around them, more or less illuminates their minds and moralizes their character. We hope and believe that some of them, though poor in this world's goods, will be found rich in spiritual possessions in the day when the King of Zion shall make up his jewels. We know that many of them are included in the visible church, and frequently exhibit great zeal; but it is to be feared that it is often 'a zeal without knowledge,' and of the majority it must be confessed that 'the light shineth in darkness and the darkness comprehendeth it not.' After making all reasonable allowances, our colored population can be considered, at the most, but semi-heathen.' . . .

"C.W. Gooch, Esq., Henrico country, Virginia, in a Prize Essay on Agriculture in Virginia, said:

"'The slave feels no inducement to execute his work with effect. He has a particular art of slighting it and seeming to be busy, when in fact he is doing little or nothing. Nor can he be made to take proper care of stock, tools, or anything else. He will rarely take care of his clothes or his own health, much less of his companion's when sick and requiring his aid and kindness. There is perhaps not in nature a more heedless, thoughtless human being than a Virginia field Negro. With no care upon his mind, with warm clothing and plenty of food under a good master, is far the happier man of two. His maxim is 'come day, go day, God send Sunday!' His abhorrence of the poor white man is very great. He may sometimes feel a reflected respect for him, in consequence of the confidence and esteem of his master and others. But this trait is remarkable in the white, as in the black man. All despise poverty and seem to worship wealth. To the losses which arise from the dispositions of our slaves, must be added those which are occasioned by their habits. There seems to be an almost entire absence of moral principle among the mass of our colored population. But details upon this subject would be here misplaced. To steal and not to be detected is a merit among them, as it was with certain people in ancient times, and is at this day, with some unenlightened portions of mankind. And the vice which they hold in the greatest abhorrence is that of telling upon one another. There are many exceptions it is true, but this description embraces more than the majority. The numerous free Negroes and worthless, dissipated whites, who have no visible means of support, and who are rarely seen at work, derive their chief subsistence from the slaves. These thefts amount to a good deal in the course of a year, and operate like leeches on the fair income of agriculture. They vary, however, in every country and neighborhood in exact proportion as the market for the plunder varies. In the vicinities of towns and villages they are most serious. Besides the actual loss of property occasioned by them, they involve the riding of their horses at night, the corruption of the habits and the injury of the health of the slaves; for whiskey is the price generally received for them.'

"These extracts, selected at random, are sufficient. A multiplication of them would be but a tiresome repetition. After all, the best testimony is the observation and experience of all persons who are intimately acquainted with them. That the Negroes are in a degraded state is a fact, so far as my knowledge extends, universally conceded. It makes no difference if it be shown, as it might be, that they are less degraded, and it is with this fact which we have to do . . . .

"All approaches to them [the slaves] from abroad are rigidly guarded against, and no ministers are allowed to break to them the bread of life, except such as have commended themselves to the affection and confidence of owners. I do not condemn this course of self-preservation on the part our citizens. I mention it only to show more fully the point in hand: the entire dependence of the Negroes upon ourselves for the gospel.

"While this step is taken another has already been taken, and that of a long time; namely, Negro preachers are discouraged, if not suppressed, on the ground of incompetency and liability to abuse their office and influence to the injury of the morals of the people and the infringement of the laws and peace of the country. I would not go all the lengths of many on this point, for from my own observation, Negro preachers may be employed and confided in, and so regulated as to do their own color great good, and community no harm; nor do I see, if we take the word of God for our guide, how we can consistently exclude an entire people from access to the gospel ministry, as it may please Almighty God from time to time, as he unquestionably does, to call some of them to it 'as Aaron was.' The discouragement of this class of preachers, throws the body of the people still more in their dependence upon ourselves, who indeed cannot secure ministers in sufficient numbers to supply our own wants.

"Nor have the Negroes any church organizations different from or independent from our own. Such independent organizations are, indeed, not on the whole advisable. But the fact binds them to us with still stronger dependence. And, to add more, we may, according to the power lodged in our hands, forbid religious meetings, and religious instruction on our plantations; we may forbid our servants going to church at all, or only to such churches as we may select for them; we may literally shut up the kingdom of heaven against men, and suffer not them that are entering to go in?' . . . .

"The celebrated John Randolph, on a visit to a female friend, found her surrounded with her seamstress, making up a quantity of clothing. 'What work have you in hand?' 'O, sir, I am preparing this clothing to send to the poor Greeks.' On taking leave at the steps of the mansion, he saw some of her servants in need of the very clothing which their tender-hearted mistress was sending abroad. He exclaimed: 'Madam, madam, the Greeks are at your door!' . . . . .

"We have colored ministers and exhorters, but their numbers are wholly inadequate to the supply of the Negroes; and while their ministrations are infrequent and conducted in great weakness, there are some of them whose moral character is justly suspected and who may be considered blind leaders of the blind."

Finally, a word must be added on the church and slave marriages in ante-bellum days. The sale of a slave away from his home and family "was a virtual decree of divorce and so recognized, not only by usage, but by the deliberate decree of the churches."

"The time will come when this statement will seem almost incredible. The usage, considered as a barbarism for which no religious defense would be possible, is bad enough. But to give it the sanction of religion, the religion of Jesus Christ, and to invoke the divine blessing upon a marriage which was no marriage at all, but simply a concubinage which the master's word might at any moment invalidate, seems at first beyond all manner of excuse. Yet it was done, and that not only by individual ministers of Christ, but by authority of ecclesiastical conventions, the resolutions to that effect went upon record in Methodist, Baptist, Presbyterian churches, declaring that the separation of husband and wife under slavery, by the removal of either party, was to be regarded as 'civil death,' sundering the bonds, and leaving both parties free to make another marriage contract. Slavery, by necessity of the case, abolished all family ties, of husband and wife, of parents and children, of brothers and sisters, except so far as the convenience of the master might be suited by recognition. Legal sanction there was none. But the sham service which the law scorned to recognize was rendered by the ministers of the gospel of Christ. I have witnessed it, but could never bring myself to take part in such pretence.

"And yet I feel compelled by truth to say that, among all the allevia-tions of slavery, there was none greater than this. While the nominal rela-tion continued at all, it was made sacred to the slave husband and wife, and the affectionate African nature was comforted and sustained by it. It was a strong motive to good behavior, it promoted decency in social intercourse, it tended towards keeping the slave-family together, and was some restraint upon masters—a great restraint upon the better class of them—against arbitrary separation by sale; in short, it was one of the fear-ful anomalies of a brutal and barbarous social system existing among a civilized, Christian people.

"The question was fully discussed by the Savannah River Baptist Association of Ministers in 1835; and the decision was, 'that such separa-tion, among persons situated as slaves are, is civilly a separation by death, and that in the sight of God it would so viewed. To forbid second mar-riages in such case would be to expose the parties to church censure for disobedience to their masters, and to the spirit of the command which regulates marriages among Christians. The slaves are not free agents, and dissolution by death is not more entirely without their consent and beyond their control than by such separation.'

"Truly the logic of slavery was the destruction of humanity."[*]

---

[*] Eliot: Story of Archer Alexander.

15

A Black Belt County, Georgia

(BY THE REV. W. H. HOLLOWAY)

Thomas county is situated in extreme southwest Georgia, within twenty miles of the northern boundary line of Florida. According to the census of 1900, the Negro population was 17,450. Among this population there are ninety-eight churches. These churches represent all denominations, Baptist predominating, there being only two Congregational and one Episcopal church. This number gives the actual churches which we have been able to learn of. It will be a safe estimate to affirm that about twenty per cent of this number may be added, of which we failed to learn.

This will give a church for every 150 persons, and here it might be said that, unlike much of our American population, the Negro is well-churched. It is his only institution and forms the center of his public life. He turns to it not only for his spiritual wants, but looks toward it as the center of his civilization. Here he learns the price of cotton or the date of the next circus; here is given the latest fashion plates or the announcement for candidates for justice of the peace. In fact, the white office seeker has long since learned that his campaign among the Negroes must be begun in the Negro church, and by a Negro preacher.

These ninety-eight institutions in Thomas county, like those of many other counties, have interesting histories. About half this number represent the churches whose beginning has been normal, the natural outgrowth of expansion. The other half's history is checkered. Their rise can almost invariably be traced to one or two methods. First, there is the proverbial "split." A careful study of the roll of membership in many of the churches will reveal the second method. Some brother is called to preach. This call is so thunderous, and the confidence that he can "make a better preach" than the present pastor so obtrusive, till he soon finds that there is little welcome in the sacred rostrum of the old church. He therefore takes his family and his nearest relatives and moves away. Study the rolls, therefore, of many of the churches and you will find that they are largely family churches, and that the first preacher was some venerable patriarch. I think one will be perfectly safe in concluding that two-thirds of the growth in churches of the various denominations has been made in this way; and that little has been accomplished by the church executives as the result of direct effort at church extension.

It will be readily seen that churches having their origin in this way merely duplicate the old institution; often it is not a creditable duplicate. I know of no rural church in Thomas county whose inception had the careful nursing of an educated, cultured leader. Others have labored and we have entered into their labors. The largest churches and the biggest preachers in Thomas county do little home missionary work and organize no new churches.

The result, therefore, must necessarily be a constant propagation of the old regime. Standards of slavery time and directly after still prevail. It is impossible that it should be otherwise. Like begets like.

The supreme element in the old system was emotionalism, and, while we hate to confess it, truth demands that we affirm it as the predominating element today. The church which does not have its shouting, the church which does not measure the abilities of a preacher by the "rousement" of his sermons, and indeed which does not tacitly demand of its minister the shout-producing discourse, is an exception to the rule. This is true of the towns as well as the country. Of course we all understand that it has always occupied first place in the worship of the Negro church; it is a heritage of the past. In the absence of clearly defined doctrines, the great shout, accompanied with weird cries and shrieks and contortions and followed by a multi-varied "experience" which takes the candidate through the most heart-rending scenes—this today in Thomas county is accepted by the majority of the churches as unmistakable evidence of regeneration.

Now, the preachers who have had some advantages of study, who have come into contact with the learning of the schools, and have in their intelligence gotten above the ignorant preacher of the country, know that the old order of things is wrong. Talk with them and they all confess it. Confront them with the truth that it prevails in their own churches, and their reply puts the question upon the basis of supply and demand. They say: "My people have been used to it, my predecessor was thought to be the embodiment of perfection, and this was his standard; therefore, if I would succeed, if I would hold my people, I must supply this demand; and if I would make the record of my success more enduring than my predecessor I must supply this demand in greater quantities and more acceptable quality than he."

The spirit of rivalry also has much to do with the continuance of this emotional feature. Two churches in the same community—one presided over by an educated minister, with lofty ideals and correct standards, and to whose better nature the old order is repulsive, and the other presided over by a typical representative of the old school: the educated minister will often preach unseen and waste his eloquence of the desert air. He soon finds that not only is his church losing its pristine prominence, not only is his own reputation as a representative clergyman waning, but that there is soon a very perceptible diminution in the loaves and fishes. It is a problem and it is forcing young preachers who would otherwise do good work in the ministry into the old rut which, while their better natures condemn it, they have not the power to resist. Any system which robs the man of his individuality and makes him less than a man, finds itself early bereft of its power for the highest service. Another effect is, that it is driving out of the work the young men of ability whom the work most needs. I know one promising young man in my county who is driven to desperation and vows, for none other cause than this of which we have been speaking, that he will leave the work at the next annual conference. And, too, the young men in our schools turn their faces toward other vocations.

Under this old system, which prevails in Thomas county, the question arises, is the moral condition of the people being raised?

Of the blanks which we had returned, while some said openly "No," the majority left the question in doubt.

We would conclude, however, that the moral standard of the Negroes in Thomas county is being bettered; but I seriously raise the question whether the church is the great factor in this improvement. Speaking especially now of the towns, whose condition has been studied more carefully and at first hand, the conclusion is almost inevitable that there are other factors equally potent, doubtless more so, than the church.

This question of better morals must affect not so much the older generation, who still occupy a large place in the church, as it does the newer and younger people.

If this is true, then we find certain conditions in many of the churches which give credence to the foregoing assertion.

I beg you to note that I am giving what is true of the majority of the churches of Thomas county as insinuated in the answers to the questions sent out, supplemented by my own knowledge upon the subject.

The first condition I would speak of is the relation of the church to the popular amusements. The supreme end of the church is spiritual: the bringing of the individual up to the higher ideals as exemplified in the life and teachings of Christ. When, therefore, the institution subordinates, even for a moment, this supreme end to a lower one, there can but be a perceptible lessening of the moral force of the institution. Now this is just what the church is doing. They vie with each other so strongly, the rivalry in new inventions and performances is so intense, till it has lead them into the realm of the questionable.

To a great extent the church has so entered into this business that the young people look to it more as a bureau whose object is to provide amusement than they do toward it as a holy institution whose high privilege it is to deal with eternal realities and interpret the weightier matters of the law.

Inordinate rivalries among the denomination is another condition. Rivalry is no mean motive and to its stimulating influence is traceable much of the world's progress; but when the church, in its ambition to excel, stoops to petty meannesses, then she need not complain if her moral dynamic becomes a doubtful quantity. We shall not mention examples here, for this is a condition which prevails in other churches than the Negro's.

The prominent place in church circles taken by characters whose lives in the community are a constant contradiction to the creed prescribed to when they entered the church, is another condition which lessens the moral force of the church.

True, as a race, we have had neither time nor training to establish that caste which marks the higher development in the moral code, and whose logical sequence is closer moral discrimination and segregation; yet the church, whose very motto is separation from the world, should have itself on record as being the most discriminating in this respect.

The fact is, however, that some of the churches are too lax in this matter. It is true in Thomas county that some of the secret societies, especially among women, are more vigilant as to their constituencies than the church. I am personally acquainted with people who occupy first place in all the affairs in the church whose applications to the societies have been repeatedly turned down.

The fact that their monied connections and their popularity are sufficient guarantees for the success of any church enterprise, seem to make their fitness for church membership unquestioned. Their lives may be black but no notice is paid to it.

Now what is the effect of all this? Nothing other than that the young people, and the older people who do their own thinking, lose regard for the moral standards of the church. The preacher may discourse frequently on purity of life, but if he shuts his eyes to the impurity of some of his own members, and seems to insist that they be placed at the forefront of the church's activities, then his precepts become sounding brass and tinkling cymbals; and his example, weightier by far than his precepts, becomes a barrier to the highest usefulness of his institution as a moulder of the community's morality.

Another condition which gives rise to our assertion that the church is not exercising its highest moral influence, is seen in its lax business methods. Let us give one example, which we dare assert is true of nine-tenths of the churches in Thomas county and in the South: A contract is made with every incoming minister. They promise him a stipulated sum for his year's service and when the year ends, he goes to conference with only about two-thirds of the pledge fulfilled. If he is sent back to the same field, the second year finds the church still deeper on the debit side of the ledger. If he is sent to another field the debt is considered settled, a new contract is made with the new preacher, and the same form is gone through.

As far as I have been able to learn fully 75 percent of the churches in the county are in debt to their former preachers, and what is worse, there seems never to arise a question as to the honesty of the religious body.

Now, this may seem a too minute selection of ecclesiastical faults, but when it is remembered that the simple virtues of honesty, truthfulness, and business promptness are the qualities most needed by the race, then that institution which represents the embodiment of all that is perfect in its precepts loses its moral force by the laxity of its example, and this laxity which is characteristic of the body must find counterpart in the individuals who compose the body.

We ventured the assertion that the church in this county is not too potent a factor in the moral betterment of the race; and we went further and raised the question as to whether there were not other factors equally potent, perhaps more so than the church.

You will notice that I have not said that the church is doing nothing toward this betterment. Some of them are, and some of the denominations more than others; but what we are talking about is the weight of the combined influence of all the churches; and we still claim that its power is small, smaller to be sure than it should be, when it has such exalted example of all that is good to draw from in the enforcement of its teachings.

We have been able to learn of about 120 preachers in the county. Of this number fully seventy-five are either ordained or licensed. The most of their names appear in the minutes of the various denominations. Now this number may be almost doubled if we search for all those who call themselves preachers and fill the function of interpreters of the word of God. This number moulds as great a sentiment for or against the church as those who hold license.

You will get some idea of the vast host who belong to this class when I tell you that the records of the last conference of the Southwest Georgia District of the African Methodist Episcopal Church show that there were forty-three applicants for admission to the conference. Note that this is only one of the four or five conferences of this church in the state. Be it said to the lasting credit of the conference that it in unmistakable terms put the stamp of condemnation upon the presumption of about thirty-five of them and sent them back to their homes disappointed men. And yet, while it sent them back home unadmitted, it did not make them less determined to preach, for in their several communities you will find them still exercising themselves in the holy calling.

Now of this vast number, so far as I have been able to learn, only four of them hold diplomas from any institution giving record of previous fitness. Only about one percent of them can point to any considerable time spent in school.

The course of study prescribed in the African Methodist Episcopal Church has helped some, but after all this, it can be truthfully said that for real fitness, fitness in the truest sense of the word, there is little to be found among the ministers of the county.

Putting this another way is to say, that the majority of the ministers are unlearned or ignorant men, ignorant in the sense of fitness for leadership; for, learned or unlearned, the Negro preacher is today the leader of the race. If they are ignorant, then this ignorance manifests itself in any number of ways:

1st. His home life as a general rule is on no higher level than that of his neighbor. In most cases he married before he began to preach and his wife is ignorant. Here, then, is no toning example for the community which he serves. I beg you to note that the pulpit is not the only place where the minister is to do powerful and eloquent preaching.

2d. In morality he has much to learn. Morality as it affects: (1) Temperance; (2) debt paying and business honesty; (3) sexual morality.

I have presented a gloomy picture. I have one consolation, however, that it is true, if it is black.

Your criticism will be that I have not brightened the picture a particle. But your conclusion will be erroneous if you decide that there is no brightness in it.

First. The greatest hope lies in the young people who go out to these darkened *optimism* places and sacrifice themselves for the betterment of the people. Thomas county is dotted with these young people from the schools.

Second. Young men are seeing the need and are responding to it by entering the ministry.

Third. In every community there is a body of older men, men indeed of the old school; but during the years their ideas of the function of the church, the qualifications and requirements of the minister have all undergone a very radical change. They are thoroughly disgusted with the old order of things and besides withdrawing their own support they give their children no encouragement to support it.

Fourth. There is also a strong tendency in my county toward the newer denominations. This tendency will have two results: These newer denominations will continue to draw the young people and will continue to push the crusade for religious education. Second, this growth and popularity of the newer denominations will stimulate the older ones to greater efforts and to more intelligent worship.

In these and other ways the race is gradually coming out of the darkness into the light, and the next generation will see all of the denominations of the South exerting a stronger religious and moral influence upon the Negro than they are today doing.

Statistics of Three Churches, Thomas County

	C.M.E	A.M.E	Episcopal
Membership	120	72	149
Active Membership	110	28	22
Value of Church	$800.00	$700.00	$2,500.00
Expenses			
Salaries	240.00	259.10	....
On debt	.00	.00	....
Running expenses	12.00	23.80	....
Charity, etc	2.00	4.90	....
Missions	2.50	6.00	....
Support of connection	50.00	31.00	....
Other expenses	10.00	3.20	....
Total	$316.50	$328.00	....

Negro Baptist Churches, Thomas County, Ga.

NAME.	Membership.		Value of Church Property.	
	1901.	1902.	1901.	1902.
Spring Hill	95	95	$ 750	$ 500
St. Mary	17	25	250	125
Evergreen	28	28	100	200
Ocklochnee	125	80	100	150
St.Paul	161	157	1,000	150
N.O. Grove	240	250	1,000	1,500
Centennial	35	30	322	275
Bethel	329	325	500	350
Paradise	51	54	100	100
Walnut Hill	109	112	....	....
New Hope	....	38	....	75
Aucilla	202	169	1,000	500
Centenary	150	159	....	100
A.B.C.,Thomasville	500	500	10,000	12,000

NAME.	Membership.		Value of Church Property.	
Richland	38	37	150	200
Mt. Pilgrim	43	48	....	200
Friendship	150	140	....	200
Antioch	83	75	85	100
St. Luke	10	15	100	100
Beulah Road	13	14	100	100
Piney Grove	65	70	500	250
Silver Hill	87	88	250	250
Mt. Olive	80	80	350	380
Mt. Calvary	113	68	600	600
Magnolia	16	19	30	600
Shady Grove	77	65	700	250
Mt. Moriah	50	44	1,500	300
Midway	50	48	250	300
Rebecca	....	38	....	150
County Line	30	30	200	200
Oaky Grove	19	22	50	50
Turner Grove	....	12	....	75
Jerusalem	120	....	150	...
Total	3,086	3,035	$17,465	$20,320

Opinions of Intelligent Colored Laymen on Thomas County Churches

1. Condition of the churches.

   "Well attended." "More centers for amusement than for worship." "Little spiritual life." "Half are in debt." "Not what they should be." "Lack competent leaders."

2. Influence of Churches.

   "Influence good." "Influence bad." "Good on the whole." "Ten percent of the membership is honest, pure, and upright." "Influence is bad, but there are some earnest folks."

3. Are the ministers good?

   "No." "Out of ten, three are sexually immoral, one drinks, three are careless in money matters." "Weak in morals." "One is sexually impure and frequents disreputable places." "Lack intellect." "They fairly represent those whom they lead." "Some of them are good men."

4. Charity work.

"Nine-tenths believe there is but one object of charity—the minister; give all you've got to the minister and if any one is sick or in prison, give him one-half of what is left."

5. The young people.

"The church amuses the young people, and they pay for the amusement." "Young people join slowly." "Church support comes largely from non-members."

6. Are moral standards being raised?

"Cannot say; much laxity." "Standard never lower." "Raised by presence of a score or more of graduates of city schools." "Being raised." "In six years I note a change for the better." "Reaching high moral standards." "In some cases standards are being raised, in others, not." "There are fewer separations of man and wife, and fewer illegitimate children."

16

A Town in Florida

(BY ANNIE MARION MACLEAN, A.M., PH.D.)

The Negro is always an interesting subject for study in a Southern town, and one feels amply repaid for any effort made to understand his life. The town of Deland appealed to me as being an excellent place to make a study of the Negro population, both on account of its character and size. The town is largely Northern in population and sentiment, and it is small so that city problems do not need to be considered.

There are three regularly organized Negro churches in Deland. In and around these the religious life of the colored inhabitants centers, and we may study these in order of importance.

1. Missionary Baptist Church

This church, the largest and most flourishing in the community, is located on the outskirts of the town, in the best Negro district. Its founding dates back to 1883, when one of the prominent white citizens gave a lot of land and erected a small house of worship. The membership has constantly increased since that time, and in 1895 a new site was purchased and the present structure put up at a cost of about $1,000. A parsonage was bought immediately adjoining the church at a cost of $300, the necessary money for these improvements being raised by the members themselves. The church building is kept in good repair and is provided with a small organ, good, comfortable pews, and has carpeted aisles and plain stained glass windows. The seating capacity is 250, the membership 109—forty-six male and sixty-three female. The average attendance is about one-quarter of the total membership, and contrary to the usual state of affairs in white churches, men are always in the majority at the meetings. The minister's explanation of this is that the women work very hard during the week, and when Sunday comes they are too tired to leave their homes. He says that it is much easier for the women to get steady employment than for the men. No children are received into membership under the age of twelve years. The Sunday-school is well attended, and there are two fully organized missionary societies—one to aid home and the other to aid foreign missions. The other societies are a Young People's Society of Christian Endeavor and a Baptist Young People's Union, both of which meet in the church weekly, with fair attendance. The minister is a man of average intelligence, his early education having been obtained in the public schools. He is elected by the congregation, and preaches three Sundays in the month at morning and evening service. The fourth Sunday he preaches in a small country church. His regular salary is $300 a year, and from his country charge he receives $125. In addition to this he has the use of the parsonage and its furnishings. When he was called, two years ago, the church was $250 in debt. It now owes but $50.

2. Bethel Church (African Methodist Episcopal)

This is the second largest church in the community, and is located on the opposite side of the town from the one just described. It was organized in 1882, and has now its second building. The church and the parsonage immediately adjoining are valued at $800 and $400, respectively. The church has not always been self-supporting, having from time to time received aid from the Extension Board of the denomination. The building is kept in very good repair, and a large belfry has been added during the past year. Inside is a very good small organ, good, plain pews, and other necessary furniture. The seating capacity is 235, the membership ninety-three, one-quarter of which is men; and the average attendance is one-third the total membership. Children are baptized and received at any age, and later, upon confession of faith, are confirmed.

Among flourishing church organizations may be mentioned the Young People's Society of Christian Endeavor, a Christian Willing Working Club, which corresponds to a missionary society, and a Stewardesses' Board, composed of the most intelligent women in the church. This last named society has charge of all charities, church furnishings, and the like. The two former meet once a week, and are well attended. There is a well organized Sunday-school. A prayer service is held on Thursday of each week.

The pastor is a remarkable Negro in many respects. He is a little past middle age; never attended school, and yet is by all odds the most intelligent of his race in the community. He was born of slave parents, and early in life was seized with a desire to learn. As a boy he had no advantages. He educated himself, "after whistle time," to use his own words. This is his first year in his present pastorate. He was for eight consecutive years presiding elder of this, the eleventh, district, which includes the entire state of Florida. He is a good conversationalist, being well posted on the topics of the day. He spends his whole time in the work of this one church and in looking after his business interests. He pays taxes on $16,000 worth of property, and has an income of $102 per month on rentals. The church pays him about $300 per year salary, and gives him the use of the parsonage. He gave his son a college education, and sent him through a medical course of four years. The son is now a physician of large practice in St. Augustine. Under the African Methodist Episcopal form of church government the ministers are appointed to their charges at the annual conference.

There are two regular Sunday services—one in the morning and one in the evening. The debt at present amounts to about $228, which the pastor expects to pay in the near future at a "rally."

The church has a mission about two miles distant, at a Negro settlement called Yamassee. This mission has but eight members and holds services once a month, at which time communion is given. The preacher comes from a town about thirty miles distant, and is said to be a man of but average ability. There are no activities within the church, except the monthly services. The building is extremely rough and is valued at $400.

3. St. Annis' Primitive Baptist (Primitive Orthodox Zion Baptist Church)

This church is the most interesting of the three, from the standpoint of the student of sociology. It is the principal church of Yamassee, the only other being the mission just mentioned. Yamassee is the largest of the Negro settlements and lies about a mile and a half from the center of the town, but within the town limits.

Facts concerning the origin and history of the church are hard to obtain. Indeed neither the minister nor any of the members seem to know just when or how it had its beginning. The building is valued at $1,800 and it has never been painted, and is not kept in good repair. The floors are uncarpeted, the interior is finished in wood, the windows plain, and there is no musical instrument. The seating capacity is 300, the membership fifty-six, twenty of whom are male. The average attendance is two-thirds of the membership, and the men and women are about evenly divided. No children under twelve years are admitted to membership. There is an organized Sunday-school, which is fairly attended, and also a weekly prayer meeting. This is led by some member of the church. There is a society called "The Young People's Band," which corresponds to the "Young People's Society of Christian Endeavor." It meets in the church once a week, but is poorly attended and not strongly organized.

This church asserts, with much vigor, that it is the original Baptist Church; that the so-called "Missionary Baptist" (of the type described above) is a false body, which withdrew from the mother church in 1832. It points with pride to the list of the great men who were "Primitive Baptists." Its members believe in the scriptures of the Old and New Testaments, in predestination, in the fall of man, in the covenant of redemption, in justification, regeneration, in the resurrection and general judgment, baptism, the Lord's supper, and foot-washing. This last (foot-washing) is, of course, the main distinguishing characteristic. The regular communion service is held on the second Sunday of each month and after the sermon the members turn their benches so as to form two large squares on each side of the pulpit, the men on one side and the women on the other. They then wash each other's feet in turn, the preacher taking the lead. This, they say, is merely carrying out the example of Christ. The service generally ends with a kind of a dance, which they call "Rocking Daniel." No information could be gained as to the origin of this most peculiar custom. A leader stands in the center of a circle, which the members form in front of the pulpit. They begin with singing the lines:

> "Rock Daniel, rock Daniel,
> Rock Daniel till I die."

Gradually they move round in the circle, single file, then begin to clap hands and fall into a regular step or motion, which is hard to describe. Finally, when they have become worked up to a high state of excitement, and almost exhausted, the leader gives a signal, and they disperse. This ceremony reminds one quite strongly of an Indian war dance, except that it is on a somewhat tamer plan.

The songs sung by the church are extremely interesting, as they embody so many strange and original sentiments. These people seem to believe thoroughly in a noisy religion. They frequently interrupt the speaker with shouts of approval or disapproval and songs. The prayers are long and earnest in the extreme. The churches spoken of above are much more conventional in their services.

The minister preaches one Sunday in a month at a country church; the remainder of the time he spends with his own congregation. He was educated in the public schools of Jacksonville, Fla., and in Cookman College, and is a graduate of the Correspondence Bible College, and of the Christian University, Canton, Mo., having taken the degree of M. A. L. (Master of Ancient Literature) at the last named institution. Bethaney College of North Carolina conferred upon him the honorary degree of D. D. In 1895 he delivered the annual address to the literary societies of the Southern

University of New Orleans, La. He is the author of several pamphlets, and was the general secretary of the Eleventh Annual Sunday-school and Ministers' Convention of the Eastern and Southern District of his church in 1901. He is considered to be a man of unusual ability and attainments by the residents of his community.

Generally speaking, the ministers are men of good character and of fair education. They are highly respected by their congregations and others. They all agree that the Negro was given citizenship long before he was ready for it; that his only salvation lies in education. They try to impress upon their people the real extent and meaning of the ignorance which is so prevalent among them, and also the fact that they must look to the white inhabitants for encouragement and help.

There is very little sectarian animosity between the different denominations; union meetings and efforts are common, and much good often results from them. The church members play almost no part in the politics of the community, although most of them are property holders.

There is comparatively little moral or religious training in the homes or in the schools. Family worship is not observed. The churches are the center of social life and activity, but one finds the meetings of the morning poorly attended, while those of the evening are full, and are generally very lengthy.

Just how deep the every-day lives of the members are affected by their religion it is difficult to say, but the pastors agree that it has a decided tendency to keep them "in the straight path."

To sum up, the following brief table may be presented as an indication of the present condition of the Negro churches in the town under consideration:

CHURCH.	Founded.	Value of Property.	Seating Capacity.	Members.
Missionary Baptist	1883	$1,900	250	106
	1882	1,200	255	93
Bethel Church (African M.E.)...........................	?	1,800	300	56
Primitive Baptist				

17

A Southern City[*]

There are in the city of Atlanta, Ga., the following Negro churches:

DENOMINATION.	No. Churches.	Membership Claimed.	Active Membership.	Value of Property.	Income, 1902.
Baptist...	29	10,363	5,274	$61,273	$23,259.30
Methodist	21	5,015	2,571	149,235	23,101.75
Other denominations	4	883	578	42,000	5,451.79
Total	54	16,261	8,423	$252,508	$51,812.84

The Negro population of Atlanta (1900) was 35,727. This means one church to every 662 men, women, and children, or one to every 130 families. Half the total population is enrolled in the church, and probably nearly two-thirds of the adult population. The active paying membership is much smaller.

There are 29 Baptist churches, with an active membership of over 5,000 and $60,000 worth of real estate. The $23,000 raised by them annually is expended as follows:

For salaries......................................	$10,811.00	.....46.4%
Running expenses, etc............................	4,629.70	.....19.9
Debt and interest	4,493.40	.....19.3
Charities and missions............................	2,751.60	.....11.9
Support of Connectional Boards.............	573.60	.... 2.5
Total	$23,259.30	100.0%

The Baptist churches may be tabulated as follows:

* The data in this section were gathered by students in the senior and junior college classes in Atlanta University in 1902–3.

Baptist Churches

Serial No.	Membership Claimed.	Active Members.	Value of Buildings.	Income.
1	79	12	$ 125	178.20
2	874	350	2,500	750.00
3	85	50	....	162.00
4	400	150	1,500	310.00
5	20	14	....	87.00
6	150	60	1,000	263.00
7	30	20	800	112.00
8	37	20	700	791.00
9	600	300	7,000	1,148.50
10	387	200	4,000	2,405.00
11	34	32	200	120.00
12	125	75	1,000	582.00
13	120	80	500	300.00
14	12	7	85	57.00
15	22	18	200	101.00
16	500	200	4,000	2,408.00
17	750	150	6,000	1,960.00
18	800	200	2,500	2,400.00
19	200	125	2,000	392.25
20	62	40	800	....
21	50	20	800	106.00
22	500	250	4,500	1,200.00
23	15	6	13	25.50
24	60	30	1,000	....
25	13	10	900	55.00
26	265	165	1,200	514.60
27	2,598	1,560	2,700	4,040.00
28	1,500	1,100	15,000	2,774.00
29	75	30	250	17.25
All.	10,363	5,274	$ 61,273	$ 23,259.30

The twenty-one Methodist churches are divided as follows:

Methodist Churches

DENOMINATIONS.	No.	Membership Claimed.	Active Members.	Real Estate.	Income.
African Methodist Episcopal	14	3,242	1,461	$ 90,200	$13,831.10
Methodist Episcopal..........................	4	1,333	910	48,500	6,927.00
Colored Methodist Episcopal	3	440	200	10,535	2,343.65
Total..	21	5,015	2,571	$149,235	$23,101.75

Annual expenditures of these churches are approximately as follows:

Salaries..............................	$ 9,174.53	........39.7%
Debt and Interest	7,510.02	........32.5
Charities, etc..................................	1,137.50	.... 4.9
Support of connection......................	1,694.00	.... 7.4
Other expenses..............................	3,585.75	........15.5
Total..............................	$ 23,101.80	100.0%

The churches in detail are:

African Methodist Episcopal Churches

Serial No.	Membership Claimed.	Active Members.	Real Estate.	Income.
37	340	110	$ 9,200	$1,420.00
38	30	20	200	125.00
39	40	32	150	120.00
40	20	6	1,200	233.00
41	35	20	600	307.00
42	400	600	50,000	4,864.86
43	100	70	2,000	585.00
44	506	200	20,000	5,274.00
45	370	135	3,500	3,058.67
46	16	8	500	....
47	90	50	250	740.02
48	110	100	300	587.55
49	135	85	2,000	135.00
50	50	25	300	140.00
All.	3,242	1,461	$90,200	$17,590.10

Methodist Episcopal Churches

Serial No.	Membership Claimed.	Active Members.	Real Estate.	Income.
33	740	500	$40,000	$3,235.00
34	227	115	1,000	$542.00
35	166	100	2,500	1,425.00
36	200	195	5,000	1,725.00
All.	1,333	910	$48,500	$6,927.00

Colored Methodist Churches

Serial No.	Membership Claimed.	Active Members.	Real Estate.	Income.
30	100	50	$4,000	$1,543.05
31	75	25	35	20.65
32	265	125	6,500	780.00
All.	440	200	$10,535	$2,343.65

The remaining churches are four in number, one each of the Congregational, Episcopal, Christian, and Presbyterian denominations. Figures for them are:

Serial No.	Membership Claimed.	Active Members.	Real Estate.	Income.
51	485	400	$25,000	$2,225.00
52	180	80	10,000	$1,494.00
53	68	....	4,000	1,296.79
54	150	30	3,000	436.00
All.	4,125	1,971	$42,000	$5,451.79

The expenditures of three of these deserve to be given in detail:

	51	52	53
Salaries..................................	$1,200	$ 214	$ 950.00
Debt and interest..................	0	495	44.08
Charities	300	75	5.80
Connection...........................	25	....	....
Other expenses.....................	700	180	296.91
Total	$2,225	* $ 994	** $1,296.79

Three extracts, from the reports of first-hand young investigators, throw some general light on the general character of these churches:

> From an old colored citizen of Atlanta, I learned of the marked advancement he has witnessed in the erection of church edifices and in the character of worship. Just after the war, when the colored people were in their bitter struggle for the necessities of life, he says the race worshipped in box cars frequently, for they could not always obtain houses. As conditions changed the churches were moved to better quarters. The people generally supported the church very well until finally the Negro began to pattern his churches after the white churches, building structures which were far too costly for the Negro's financial status at the time. It seemed very sad to this old man that the "worship of the good, old time" was not what it used to be.

> The character of the pastors of the seven Methodist churches in my district seems, in every case, to be good. Such phrases as "you could not find any one to say anything against his character," express the sentiments of the members of these churches. The education of the pastors is fair, although there are exceptions. Among the schools represented by the different pastors, are: Bennet College, Clark University, Turner Theological

* To this the general church adds $500 for salaries.

** Only partially raised by members themselves.

Seminary (Morris Brown Theological Department), and Gammon Theological Seminary.

The education of the members seems to vary from fair to very poor. In the case of my largest church (membership 740) a large number of the members were graduates of Clark University, and nearly all have a fair education. However, in the smaller churches, having from 16 to 277 members, the education of the congregation was very meager.

A great majority of the members of the smaller churches are common laborers and are quite poor. The members of the larger churches are in moderate circumstances, and although most of them are laborers, there is a fair per cent of artisans and business men among them.

The total expenses for the respective churches for last year varied from $6 to $5,274. The salaries paid by churches varied from $500 to $1,240, not considering a case where there was no fixed salary and one where the church had no preacher last year, the pulpit being supplied by "local" preachers.

Four of the seven churches are in debt. The debts ranged from $35 to $600, the latter of which was incurred by the building of a new church.

Most of the churches have relief societies to look after the charity and relief work. Some churches did no special relief work. One church, however, has a deaconess, who devotes her time to such work. The money expended in such work varied from nothing to $100 in the different churches. That spent for missions varied from nothing to $200.

The government of all Baptist churches is extremely democratic. Each member has the power of taking part in any of the general meetings and of voting. The financial and business matters of the church are attended to by the deacons' board. The power of the pastor varies somewhat according to the different congregations, and the difference of esteem in which the pastor is held sometimes governs his influence and sway over them.

All Baptists agree that each church is complete in itself and has the power, therefore, to choose its own ministers and to make such rules as it deems to be most in accordance with the advancement of its best interest and the purpose of its existence. The time that a pastor is to serve is not fixed but varies according to the wishes of the people. If the people like the pastor, he is kept as long as he desires to remain, but if they do not, he is put out immediately.

The general condition of the ten Baptist churches in this part of the city shows that on a whole their work is not progressing very fast. Over half of them are very small, with very small memberships, and very ignorant and illiterate pastors. And certainly where there are ignorant leaders of ignorant people not very much progress or good influence can be expected to follow. The places of meeting are not comfortable, being poorly lighted and unclean most of the time, and in some cases the church was situated in an unhealthy place. These, however, represent the worst half; and on the other hand, the larger churches are progressing very fast and their influence is gradually but surely spreading far and wide, and includes all grades of society. Many of the most influential and wealthy Negro churches of the city are Baptist.

The pastors of the Congregational, Episcopal, and Presbyterian churches have excellent characters, and are doing much towards lifting the moral standard and religious life of the people. Not only are they earnest workers, but they are also well equipped for their work. They are well educated, one being a graduate of Fisk and Yale Universities, another is a graduate of St. Augustine College, Raleigh, N.C., and took a post graduate course at Howard University, Washington, D. C., and one is a graduate of Lincoln University, who completed both the college and theological courses. They have excellent reputations, and are held in high esteem by their Alma Maters. The Yale graduate is well known North and South. The character of the members of these churches is good. They are quiet and intelligent, and there is no emotionalism in the churches. Most of the members of these churches are at least high school graduates, and a large per cent is composed of business and professional men and women.

The best picture of Atlanta churches can be obtained by studying certain typical congregations now existing in the city. The primitive Negro congregation as it emerged from slavery was of two types: the large group, lead by a masterful personality; the small democratic group, led by one of their own number. This latter group is of interest as approximating conditions in the early Christian Church. In the case of the Negro, however, the communicants were ignorant people, with largely perverted, half-mystical ideals, and liable to become the victims of mountebanks and rascals. A few such groups still survive, although they are dying out rapidly. Here is an example:

No. 24. Primitive Baptist—Active members thirty.

The pastor can read and write, but is not well educated. His character is good, but he will not do laborious work, which the members think he ought to do outside his church work. Most of the members were slaves, and the church is about twenty-eight years old. It has no influence except among its members and it began where it now stands, and was organized by most of the present members. No collection is taken except on communion day. The building is an old wooden one of rough lumber, raised about five feet from the ground. I looked through one of the cracks to get a view of the interior. Its seating capacity is about seventy-five. The benches are of rough lumber. The lamps (four oil lamps) are hanging from the shabby ceiling. I saw a large Bible upon an altar of dressed lumber. One of the oldest members told me that he gave all the coal and oil used this year. He said that the church had a meeting once a month, and every three months communion and washing of feet. They believed in having no music, save singing. They believed in the pastor's working for his living just as the members did, and because the present pastor would not do this they were going to let him go. I could not find the pastor nor could they tell where he or any of the other members lived.

This is an example of church communion among lowly ignorant and old people—survival from the past. Such groups tend to change—to absorption into some larger group or to degenerate through bad leaders and bad members. Two other specimens of this type follow:

No. 5. Baptist—Fourteen active members.

The old store, which is used for church purposes, is a very shabby building. A few chairs, two lamps, and a small table and a Bible make up the furniture. All of the members are old and ignorant. There is no Sunday-school connected with the church. The church government is a pure democracy, the pastor and the active members governing the church. The members are ignorant and of questionable character. The pastor is an old and ignorant man, but is fairly good. He went away two years ago and left his flock because they did not give him the proper support. The church did not split but degenerated. Very little charitable work is done. When one of the members is sick he is given aid if he asks to be aided. There are several ignorant Negroes living in the vicinity of the church.

No. 25. Baptist—Six active members.

The pastor has a fairly good education, but there seem to be some serious doubts as to his character. In the church there seem to be three classes of members: some with good character, some with questionable character, and some about whose character there is no question. There is no charitable and rescue work done. The building is simply a small room house which is not used regularly for worship, but is used sometimes when the people in the neighborhood desire to meet there and can get the pastor to attend. They hold no regular meetings.

The other type of church, with a strong leader and a number of followers, is a more effective organization, but its character depends largely on its pastor. Here is one:

No. 26. Baptist (Missionary)—165 active members.

The education of the pastor is fair, but his character is not good. He has the reputation of being very immoral. He is, however, a good speaker. There are a few intelligent members, but the larger portion of the members are very illiterate. There is connected with the church an organized body of women (Woman's Mission) which looks after the poor, the old, and the sick. The church was organized in 1878, in the old barracks of this city. It has had eight pastors since its organization, and it is very influential over a large number of people in the vicinity. The church building is large and was once a beautiful wooden structure, but at present it is very much in need of repairs. It is furnished fairly well on the inside, and is situated in one of the black belts of Atlanta. There is an official board appointed by or elected by the church. This official board attends to the affairs of the church. The pastor presides over the meetings. The pastor now in charge was once forced to give up his charge and leave the city, so the general report goes, because of his immorality. There were seven preachers called during his absence and two church splits, brought about through the pastors who were leading. Then the first pastor was recalled. While many of the members and the pastor bear the reputation of being immoral, they are also said to be very good to the poor. The entire collection of every fifth Sunday goes to the poor. There is a fairly good Sunday-school connected with the church, and this Sunday-school has recently purchased an organ for the church. The church debt is $400.

To reform a perverted group like this is extremely difficult, and yet the work is slowly going on. If the reform is attempted through a change in the type of pastor the result at first is likely to be the substitution of a less forceful personality and the consequent loss of enthusiasm and interest among the mass of members.

No. 8. Baptist—Twenty-five active members.

The pastor, from the report of the clerk and two or three other members, is an upright man. He attended the Atlanta Baptist College, but did not graduate. He is a tailor, with a place of business on Edgewood Avenue, near Ivy Street. He does not depend on the church to support him, but is supported entirely by his business. The majority of the members are hard-working people. The men are employed as day laborers and the women do house-work. There is a lack of interest among the members. The Sunday-school is held at 3 o'clock each Sunday afternoon, and is composed of about ten or twelve children. The pastor is planning an organization, a B.Y.P.U., to meet each Sunday afternoon after Sunday-school. There is now being carried on a revival at the church. This church building is one story, and has about twenty-five or thirty benches in it. There are four windows on each side and a seating capacity for about 150 or 175. It has a small organ, and is lighted by one large kerosene lamp with a few lamps on the walls. It is situated in an unhealthy spot, but the pastor is contemplating changing the locality. As soon as the debt is paid he says that he and the deacons intend to sell and move to a more desirable locality, where they can do more effective work.

No. 49. African Methodist Episcopal—Eighty-five active members.

The church was built about fourteen years ago. It was organized in a small house, where the meetings were held for about three years. The present building was then erected and a pastor called, but the church was so poor that after a few years there was no pastor sent. In January of this year the present minister was sent, but he is pastor of two other small churches. The influence of the church depends largely on the activity of the minister, yet its location would restrict its influence in any case. It is bounded on one side by Oakland cemetery and all others by a small settlement of Negro hovels, while back of these for a long way extend only white residences. The building is a wooden structure, with basement, fairly large. It is kept fairly clean on the inside, and was recently whitewashed. Outside the woodwork is unpainted.

When, however, inspiration comes from without through the larger churches or the church connection these small groups often show renewed activity and grow into influential churches.

No. 30. Colored Methodist Episcopal—Fifty active members.

The church was first begun with one family, at the old barracks, in a one-room cabin. From there it was moved to Peters street, to Shell hall, where it was joined by a second family. Then it was moved to Markham street, where it was joined by others; then to Hunter street, in a white church, where it was burned. It was then re-established at Taylor street, in a store house, from hence it was moved to its present site. It now has a fair brick building, which cost about $3,000, and is fairly well furnished inside. The present building and parsonage were built largely by the co-operative labor of it own members. The pastors are noisy, but of pretty good education.

No. 34. Methodist Episcopal—115 active members.

The pastor has attended Clark University, and is a graduate of Gammon. He is well liked by his parishioners. The church recruits it members from the railroad hands and their families, who are for the greater part uneducated. Some charitable work is done by different societies in the church. Such, for instance, as aiding paupers. The church is nineteen years old. It is not in debt, and has a large membership. Its influence is wide-spread, being one of the largest churches in this particular section. The church has connected with a Woman's Home Missionary Society and an Epworth

League. Through the missionary society, and through the help department of the league, much charitable work is being done in the community. I am told that during this year a poor woman was taken and given a decent burial, whereas otherwise the county would have had it to do. There is also a parsonage adjoining the church, which, together with the church, is estimated to be worth $1,500.

The services in churches of this type are calculated to draw the crowd, and are loud and emotional. A student thus describes a sermon in a large Baptist church of 500 active members on the occasion of the annual sermon before the Knights of Pythias. "He began by telling the history of the Knights of Pythias. This was interesting and I could understand him; but when he shut the Bible and began to preach I could not understand him at first. As soon as I could distinguish between the words and the peculiar sound made by the intaking of his breath, I found myself listening to what the people called 'a good sermont.' During his talk he spit behind the altar many times, and often raised his voice to a veritable yell. I could not keep any record of his exact words. After the sermon there were speeches by several laymen and then the deacons, gathering around the table in front of the pulpit, began to call for the collection. The choir then sang, but the calls of the deacons so interrupted that I could not hear the singing well. Twenty-three dollars were finally collected, each bringing forward his collection and placing it on the table."

Such churches grow into large and influential organizations, losing many of their unconventional features and becoming very much like churches in any part of the land.

No. 42. African Methodist Episcopal–600 active members.

The pastor is of good character and education, a graduate of Howard University Theological School. The members vary from the old, poor, and respectable, to the young and well educated. In 1866 this church was organized by Rev. J. J. Wood; the membership increased steadily until 1868. The church moved into a new building. This old structure itself is yet sufficiently well preserved to show what a nice building it was. In 1891 the present structure was begun. In a short while the building went up, but owing to poor workmanship it was condemned. For this reason one wall had to be torn away at a loss of about $5,000. This meant a great blow to the congregation for the edifice was constructed at a great cost and as a result of much sacrifice on the part of many people. This left the people under the burden of a heavy debt, and the ministers who have succeeded have worked hard to pay it. The present structure is a handsome one, with a beautiful interior. The building is granite and is finished inside in yellow pine. Beautiful glass windows adorn the church and there are electric light fixtures and theatre chairs in the auditorium, while a $2,500 pipe organ also adds to the beauty. The church is very large, having a seating capacity of 3,000. The total membership is about 1,400, and is composed of some of the most influential and cultured colored people of the city, a considerable number being school teachers and property owners and respected people. The church is valued at $50,000 and a statement of the money paid out during the previous year shows a total of $4,964.86, which includes $984.86 for salary to the pastor and $3,020 for the church debt. This church does a great deal of relief work among the indigent members. Last year the amount expended was $200 for such work and $360 for missions; $500 was given to the general connections.

The growth of such great Negro institutions involves much effort and genius for organization. The greatest danger is that of the "split;" that is, the withdrawal of a dissatisfied minority and the formation of a new church. The government of the Methodist churches hinders this, but the Baptist churches are peculiarly liable to it. A case in the Methodist church follows:

No. 37. African Methodist Episcopal—110 active members.

The pastor is educated and respected and the grade of membership is fairly high. The church property, building and parsonage, is worth about $9,200. On this there is a debt of $2,800, but as this was loaned by one of the church members, no interest is charged on it. The church is a nice brick structure, with stained glass windows, galleries, choir, and organ. In the basement is a Sunday-school room. The church was founded in 1870 by members of No. 44, who had moved too far from their own church to attend services. As the church grew a cleft appeared between the richer and poorer members and the result was that some thirty or more members of the poor class withdrew and formed:

No. 54. Christian—Thirty active members.

The leader and pastor is a man of questionable character. The members are mainly the middle working classes of average intelligence. Very little charitable and relief work is done because the church has a hard time to keep on its feet. The church drew out of No. 37 in 1897 and established this church, and since that time the young church has been struggling for existence. The church building is a large barn-like structure, roughly finished on the outside and rather crudely furnished on the inside. It will accommodate about 400 people.

Such splits in the Negro church have been numerous in the past, but as the churches grow stronger this method of protest is less effective. Of the present fifty-four churches, eleven represent withdrawals from older churches. In some cases this represents only natural growth; in others the establishment of more convenient local churches; in others quarrels and differences. Since splits are so easy in the democratic Baptist churches a large church of this denomination is evidence of great cohesion and skilled leadership:

No. 57. Baptist—1,560 active members.

The character of the pastor is good and he is educated. The membership includes some of the best people of the city, less than 100 are illiterate; there are many business men, property owners and steady laborers and servants. The church supports two missions, and has a committee for charitable work and general relief. The organization dates back to 1870, when a few members of No. 28 formed a small church. Today the church is out of debt and has a bank account; has the largest Sunday-school in the state and one of the largest congregations in the city. It occupies a large plain building, furnished comfortably but not elaborately. It has two organs and a piano. It has had but three pastors, the second retiring on account of age, with a pension paid by the church.

Another type of church is the Negro church which is an organization in one of the great white denominations. The Episcopal Church, for instance, has had Negro communicants from early times, but while it helps them there is the feeling that the church wants them to keep in their "place," and their churches are not growing.

No. 53. Protestant Episcopal—Sixty-eight communicants.

The character of the rector is excellent. He was educated at St. Augustine College, Raleigh, N.C., and at Howard University, Washington, D.C. The membership is small, quiet, and intelligent. Charity and relief work is done by distributing clothing to the needy; periodicals are also distributed and visits made to the sick. The present structure was erected in 1893. It is a frame building, painted, of moderate size, and neatly but plainly furnished on the interior. There is under the auspices of the church and in an adjoining building a primary school with an enrollment of 120 students and three teachers.

The Methodist Church has treated its Negro members with much consideration and sympathy and has in consequence many large and influential churches. One of the best of these in Atlanta is:

No. 33. Methodist Episcopal—500 active members.

The pastor is a "gentleman and honest man." The membership is composed of the best class of working people with a large number of educated people and graduates of the schools. The church supports a salaried deaconess to take charge of its charitable work and spends nearly $300 a year on this work outside of salaries. The church was organized in 1870 with thirty members. The present building was owned by white Methodists, but they gave it up after the war and it was turned over to the Negroes, and has become the leading church of this denomination in the South. The church is especially noted for its harmonious work and lack of "splits." It does much for its young people, having a large Sunday-school besides classes in cooking and sewing and a week-day class in religious training.

The Congregational Church is virtually independent and its growth and influence is due almost entirely to Negroes.

No. 51. Congregational—400 active members.

The membership presents the highest average of intelligence of any colored church in the city. The charitable work is regularly and efficiently organized and a mission is maintained in the slums. The church was founded thirty-eight years ago by two white missionaries. The church became self-supporting under its present pastor and exerts a wide-spread influences in the city. The building is plain but substantial and well located. The church raises $2,225 a year and has no debt. Three hundred dollars is given in charity annually.

A word may be added here as to the character of pastors and the finances of churches. In several of the smaller churches the pastors are ignorant and immoral men, who are doing great harm. In the larger churches there is not in the city a man of notoriously immoral life. Against a few ministers there are rumors of lapses here and there, but it is difficult to say how far such gossip is trustworthy and how far it is the careless talk of a people so long used to a low standard among ministers that they hardly realize that there has been any change. That there has been a change, however, is certain. The older type of minister who built up the great churches of twenty years ago had a magnetic personality, great eloquence, and a power of handling men. In private life he varied in all degrees from an austere recluse to a drunkard and moral leper. This type of man has passed away and his place has been gradually taken by a quiet, methodical man, who can organize men and raise money. Such men are usually of good average character and are executive officers of organizations strong enough to hold together with or without a pastor. They, however, fall behind the present demand in two particulars: they are not usually highly educated men, although they are by no means illiterate, and their goodness is the average goodness of every day men and not the ideal goodness of a priest, who is to revivify and reinspire the religious feelings of a rapidly developing group.

While the salaries paid ministers are still small, there has been a great improvement in recent years. The ministers of the fifty-four Atlanta churches are paid as follows per annum:

$1,000 and over	7
750-1,000	3
500-750	10
300-500	7
100-300	8
50-100	6
Under $50	5
No fixed salary	8
Total	54

The greatest change in the last decade has come in the forming of the church groups. Ability to organize and systematize, arrange a regular income and spend it effectively is demanded more and more of ministers and church officials. There is still much looseness and waste in money matters and some dishonesty in the smaller churches. Over $12,500 was paid out in interest and principal of debts last year. This probably represents a total indebtedness of $50,000 to $75,000 on a quarter of a million dollars worth of property.

18

Virginia.[*]

There are twenty-four Negro churches in Richmond,[†] nineteen of which are Baptist. The active membership of these churches is nearly the same as that of the fifty-four churches in Atlanta. As the Negro population of the two cities is nearly the same, this shows a striking concentration in church fellowship and is probably the result of longer growth in the older city, eliminating the smaller churches. The statistics of membership and expenses are:

DENOMINATION.	No. of Churches.	Membership Claimed.	Active Members.	Value of Church Property.	Expenses of Last Year.
African Methodist Episcopal	1	236	78	$25,000	$3,810.00
Methodist Episcopal	1	97	50	3,500	1,490.00
Baptist	19	14,802	6,949	291,400	40,653.29
Presbyterian..	1	83	60	11,000	732.00
Episcopal..	2	143	138	10,800	1,210.70
Totals	24	15,361	7,275	$341,700	$47,895.99

The expenditures of these churches are distributed as follows:

[*] The data on which this paragraph is based were collected by students of Virginia Union University.

[†] Including Manchester.

ITEMIZED EXPENSES.

DENOMINATION.	For Salaries.	For Interest and Principal Debt.	For Running Expenses.	For Charity and Relief Work.	For Missions.	For Support of the Connection.	For other Expenses
African Methodist Episcopal.........	$ 600.00	$ 4,100.00	$ 1,500.00	$90.00	$ 20.00	$...........	$ 500.00
Methodist Episcopal.........	500.00	750.00	100.00	20.00	20.00	30.00	70.00
Baptist..................	15,278.22	14,843.79	5,859.94	1,607.02	1,042.46	446.81	4,616.08
Presbyterian........	570.00	....	150.60	....	12.00	....	....
Episcopal............	600.00	360.00	190.00	54.20	0.50	....	6.00
Total................	$17,548.22	$14,053.79	$7,699.91	$1,831.22	$1,094.96	$476.81	$5,191.08

Richmond is noted for its large Baptist Churches. If we divide the twenty-four churches according to active membership, we have:

Over 1,000 active members...	2
750-1,000 active members	1
500-750 active members	3
250-500 active members	2
100-250 active members	8
Under 100 active members	8

The three largest churches claim a total membership of 6,169 persons, and an active membership of 3,134. They are all Baptist churches with interesting histories. Over one the noted John J. Jasper was stationed for years. The largest church has a total membership of 2,553, of which one-half are active. This church raises $5,229 a year and spends nearly $700 in charity and mission work. It has no debt. Ninety-four persons joined the church last year, of whom sixty-two were under twenty years of age. The pastor is a college graduate. Another church has 1,058 active members. It raises $5,000 a year and spends $270 in charities. It paid nearly $3,000 on its debt last year. A third church, with 800 active members, raises $3,250 a year. They paid off the last indebtedness on a $3,000 church last year. The Protestant Episcopal Church has 133 communicants and raises $1,200 a year. It spends $243 a year in charity.

The present condition of Richmond churches seems, on the whole, to be good. While the standard of the ministry is not yet satisfactory, the proportion of upright and moral men is increasing. There is considerable work among the sick and the poor, and this kind of work is increasing.

For a picture of the condition of churches in Farmville, Va., in 1898, we may quote the following:[*]

> "The church is much more than a religious organization: it is the chief organ of social and intellectual intercourse. As such it naturally finds the free democratic organizations of the Baptists and Methodists better suited to its purpose than the strict bonds of the Presbyterians or the more aristocratic and ceremonious Episcopalians. Of the 262 families of Farmville, only one is Episcopalian and three are Presbyterian; of the rest, twenty-six are Methodist and 218 Baptist. In the town of Farmville there are three colored church edifices, and in the surrounding country there are three or four others.
>
> "The chief and overshadowing organization is the First Baptist Church of Farmville. It owns a large brick edifice on Main Street. The auditorium, which seats about 500 people, is tastefully finished in light wood, with carpet, small organ, and stained glass windows. Beneath this is a large assembly room with benches. This building is really the central club-house of the community, and in greater degree than is true of the country church in New England or the West. Various organizations meet here, entertainments and lectures take place here, the church collects and distributes considerable sums of money, and the whole social life of the town centers here. The unifying and directing force is, however, religious exercises of some sort. The result of this is not so much that recreation and social life have become stiff and austere, but rather that religious exercises have acquired a free and easy expression and in some respects serve as amusement-giving agencies. For instance, the camp-meeting is simply a picnic, with incidental sermon and singing; the rally of the country churches, called the 'big meeting,' is the occasion of the pleasantest social intercourse, with a free barbecue; the Sunday-school convention and the various preachers' conventions are occasions of reunions and festivities. Even the weekly Sunday service serves as a pleasant meeting and greeting place for working people, who find little time for visiting during the week.
>
> "From such facts, however, one must not hastily form the conclusion that the religion of such churches is hollow or their spiritual influence bad. While under present circumstances the Negro church can not be simply a spiritual agency, but must also be a social, intellectual, and economic center, it nevertheless is a spiritual center of wide influence: and in Farmville its influence carries nothing immoral or baneful. The sermons are apt to be fervent repetitions of an orthodox Calvanism, in which, however, hell has lost something of its terrors through endless repetition; and joined to this

[*] Bulletin of the United States Department of Labor, No.14, pp. 34–35.

is advice against the grosser excesses of drunkenness, gambling, and other forms disguised under the general term 'pleasure' and against the anti-social peccadillos of gossip, 'meanness,' and undue pride of position. Very often a distinctly selfish tone inculcating something very like sordid greed and covetousness is, perhaps, unconsciously used; on the other hand, kindliness, charity, and sacrifice are often taught. In the midst of all, the most determined, energetic, and searching means are taken to keep up and increase the membership of the church, and 'revivals,' long continued and loud, although looked upon by most of the community as necessary evils, are annually instituted in the August vacation time. Revivals in Farmville have few of the wild scenes of excitement which used to be the rule; some excitement and screaming, however, are encouraged, and as a result nearly all the youth are 'converted' before they are of age. Certainly such crude conversions and the joining of the church are far better than no efforts to curb and guide the young.

"The Methodist Church, with a small membership, is the second social center of Farmville, and there is also a second Baptist Church, with some habitual noise and shouting."

Outside the city of Richmond, we have returns from thirty-five churches. Thirty-two of these are Baptist, one is Christian, and two Presbyterian:

Total churches	35
Total membership	18,727
Total actual membership	10,842
Total value property	$ 114,810.00
Total expenses	21,155.54
Total expenses	$ 21,155.54
Salaries	$9,738.28
Debt and interest	862.00
Running expenses	3,821.68
Charity, etc	1,247.66
Missions	1,475.09
Support and connection	437.68
Other expenses	4,335.15

The condition of the Methodist churches can be judged by the reports of the African Methodist Episcopal Churches in the Norfolk, Portsmouth, Richmond, and Roanoke districts-108 churches in all:

Ministers	77
Members	9,126
Churches	108
Parsonages	38
Value churches and parsonages	$168,114.09
Present indebtedness	64,739.61
Money raised for—	
Pastors' support	18,578.62
Missionary money	1,177.46
Charitable purposes	1,162.53
Educational purposes	512.40
Building and repairs	8,489.40
Current expenses	38,284.22
For all purposes	70,584.67

19

The Middle West, Illinois

in Chicago?

(By Monroe N. Work, A. M., and the Editor)

There are approximately about 250 Negro churches in the state with a total membership of 15,177. The Negro population of the state was 85,078 for 1900. This gives about 22½ percent of Negro population of the state as members of the church. There is a large number of persons who have moved into the state that in their native homes were members of churches. These would raise the actual number of church communicants considerably, for they commune, etc., and to all intents and purposes are members of the churches where they happen to reside. These would in a census be returned as members and counted in the state where residing.

By denominations the membership is as follows:

largest

African Methodist Episcopal	8,375	Episcopal	380
Baptist	8,812	Presbyterian	210
African Methodist Episcopal		Cumberland Presbyterian	65
Zion	100	Christian	50
Methodist Episcopal........................	360	Catholics (not ascertained) → *Why?*	
Old Time Methodist Episcopal	100	Adventists (estimated)	25

The total amount of church property owned in the state was about...................... $445,000

The total expenses for 1902 were about... 133,000

Of the above amount about $70,000 was for pastors' salaries about $20,000 on church debt.

The following conclusions are based on my own observations and the replies to questions sent out:

The Negro church, as a result of slavery, emphasized the emotional side of mentality and the future life. Freedom, with its changed environments and opportunities, has modified these two aspects. It is found in the study of churches of this state, that there is a decided tendency away from the emotional and the emphasizing of the future life. This is especially noticeable in both Baptist and Methodist churches, which contain the bulk of the Negro communicants. In the churches of these denominations in the city of Chicago there are only a few where the emphasis is on the emotional and the future life. There are some churches where the emphasis is placed sometimes on the emotional, the future life, and sometimes on the intellectual and this present life. There is a large number of churches in which the emphasis is almost entirely on the intellectual and the things of this life. It may be said, therefore, that in general the farther the people have moved from slavery conditions the less emotional and unpractical they are religiously; the more effort there is to make religion a rule of conduct for every day life.

Historically the Negro ministry has had three distinct stages of development and appears to be passing into a fourth stage. The minister of slavery days and early freedom, for the most part ignorant, was the leader of the people along all lines—religiously, intellectually, politically, etc. The emancipated Negro had few or no church buildings. This, with the additional fact of a large emigration to the cities, caused a demand for ministers who could build large church buildings and control large congregations. The church-building, congregation-managing minister was the result. It was not necessary that he should be intellectual or morally upright if he could meet with the demands, hence the development of this type of ministry. The need of church buildings was largely met, but almost every church had a debt upon it. There arose a demand for ministers who could raise money to pay these debts and keep the church doors from being closed. This, the third type, has more business ability than his predecessors. He is stronger intellectually and better morally. There is arising a demand for still another type of ministry, viz.: the man strong intellectually and sound morally. This demand is, as yet, not very strong, mainly because there are not many churches out of debt, and the energies of the people are largely expended in raising money to pay on church debts. It is more than probable that as the people progress in intelligence and the churches are freed from debt, thus permitting them to pay more attention to internal aspects of religion, the intellectual and moral man will become more and more the leader in the churches.

The above is not intended as a full or adequate explanation of the churches in Illinois, especially in Chicago, but rather as one of the main causes in producing the present conditions of the churches in the state.

The present conditions of the churches seem to be about as follows: they are for the most part deeply in debt. Hence the energies of the people are expended in raising money to pay interest, etc., of debt, thereby causing the emphasis to be laid on the incidentals instead of upon the essentials of the religious life. The people live for the church instead of the church existing for the people. There is not as much attention given to teaching the essentials of religion as should be, but the tendency seems to be more toward this phase as the churches are freed from debt. This is best illustrated by the institution of pastors having for their purpose the ministering to the social needs of the people. The Institutional Church, established in Chicago by the African Methodist Episcopal denomination, is the most advanced step in the direction of making the church exist for the people rather than the people for the church. Because of the financial needs and other things this church has been compelled to modify its efforts to minister to the people and lay emphasis on the incidental features.

The church appears to be occupying a somewhat less prominent place in the social life of the people than it once did, although it is yet probably the most influential factor, or one of the most influential, in their social life.

The ministry has probably improved, both intellectually and morally. It is, however, not meeting the needs of the people in the best possible manner, because there are few ministers with college and theological training, and the debt-ridden conditions of the churches call for men with ability to raise money rather than for men intellectually and morally strong.

The morals of the people are probably being raised. This is best evidenced by the wide-spread dissatisfaction that is found to exist among church members and the criticism of present conditions which they make; also the increasing demand for a better ministry. This criticism is:

(1) One of the ministry.
    a. It lacks edification.
    b. It lacks morality.
    c. It lacks business ability.

(2) Of the members.

    a. Of the officers of the church who are often dishonest and lacking in business ability.

    b. The members lack moral sense and appreciation, i.e., the ethical standards are bad.

The church is probably losing its influence on the young people because of the scarcity of ministers able to meet the intellectual needs of the times and the emphasis which the church is compelled to place on eternal things. The conditions of the churches in this state, while far from being good, are probably being improved.

1. A better type of ministry is appearing (very few).

2. The business affairs of the church are being better managed. This is notably true in Chicago.

3. The people are demanding better ministers and higher morals (demand very weak and uncertain as yet).

4. Tendency appears to be toward more honest and upright living among the members.

how were they identified / selected?

The opinions of seventy-five intelligent colored laymen throughout the state are as follows:

The majority think that the present condition of the churches is bad. The churches' influence is, on the whole, toward better and more upright life, but there is great room for improvement. The ministers are said not usually to be the right sort of men, their faults being ignorance and immorality, and in some cases, drunkenness. Opinions are divided as to the efficiency of Sunday-schools. Not much charitable work is done and the church is not attracting young people.

The great needs of the church in Illinois are better ministers, better business management, a high standard of living among members, a larger income, and more practical work.

The standards of morality among Negroes are being slowly raised.

Detailed returns as to churches have been received directly from sixty-one Negro churches having an enrolled membership of 10,144 and an active membership of 6,172. Of this active membership, 4,969 is in the thirty-two churches in the city of Chicago. The twenty-nine churches outside of Chicago report the following statistics:

Twenty-nine Churches in Illinois

Total membership	2,143
Active membership	1,093
Cost of churches	$72,660.00
Salaries	$8,200.91
Debt and interest	3,206.49
Running expense	2,388.23
Charity	481.66
Missions	310.03
Support of connection	698.26
Other expenses	3,176.10
Total	$ 18,461.68

For southern Illinois we have reports of seventy-four African Methodist Episcopal Churches as follows:

Ministers	52
Members	4,085
Churches	74
Parsonages	35
Value churches and parsonages	$83,190.00
Present indebtedness	23,304.44
School houses	3
Money raised for-	
Pastors' support	$17,964.11
Missionary money	481.35
Charitable purposes	650.08
Educational purposes	243.75
Building and repairs	8,215.74
Current expenses	4,161.98
For all expenses	33,207.58

There are in Chicago thirty-two colored churches and missions. Sixteen of these own the places where they worship. There are no returns from four of them. The figures are:

The Negro Churches in Chicago

DENOMINATION.	No. Reporting.	Membership.	Active Membership.	Valuation of Church Property.	Expenses Last Year.
African Methodist Episcopal	9	3,549	2,080	$ *125,800	$39,372.95
Baptist	11	3,097	2,140	16,500	12,674.74
African Methodist Episcopal Zion	1	500	300	20,000	....
Presbyterian	2	215	134	8,000	2,640.60
Christian	1	50	40	....	....
Episcopal	1	280	125	5,000	1,811.25
Methodist Episcopal	2	310	150	3,500	1,909.00
Adventist	1	....	....	....	....
Total	28	8,001	4,969	$178,800	$58,408.50

[N.B.] These totals are smaller than they really should be owing to the fact that some churches were only partially reported, while the "Adventist Church" has *no* report of statistics.

* One of the African Methodist Episcopal Churches does not own property, but uses a rented building.

Four of the Baptist Churches do not own property, but use rented buildings.

One of the Presbyterian Churches owns no property.

The Christian Church uses a rented building.

One of the Methodist Episcopal Churches uses a rented building.

The active membership of the churches varies as follows:

750–1,000	2
500–750	2
300–500	1
100–300	7
Under 100	14
Unknown	6
Total	32

The pastors of these churches may be classified as follows: Of the five larger churches (300–1,000 members) the pastors are reported:

No. 1. "Reputation fair."

No. 2. "Charged with drunkenness and immorality; but charges not confirmed."

No. 3. "Charged with misuse of church funds."

No. 4. "No especial charges."

No. 5. "Character not good—immoral."

Of the pastors of churches with 100–300 members:

Nos. 6, 7, 8, 9,10 and 12. "Character good."

No. 11. "Character not good—given to drink."

Of the pastors of the smaller churches nine are of good character. The others are:

No. 14. "Reputation not good."

No. 26. "Charged with misuse of funds."

Nos. 15 and 17. ?

No. 20. Has no pastor at present.

In the larger churches four are composed largely of ignorant or lower middle class people. One has a pretty intelligent class of people. Of the seven medium churches three have intelligent congregations of the upper class and four congregations of fair intelligence. The smaller churches consist of three rather intelligent congregations, seven of fair or medium intelligence, and five ignorant bodies.

Only one of the large churches does much charitable work. It spent last year nearly $400. One other church claims to spend considerable, but does not do very effective work. Two of the medium sized churches do charitable work of some importance. One of these was originally organized as a social settlement, but for lack of proper guidance has had but partial success. Nevertheless, it is a significant movement and indicates a drift in the right direction. It has done some good work, among other things co-operating with Atlanta University in this study. One of the smaller churches has a day nursery and kindergarten, and two others do some institutional work among the young people. The oldest of the Negro church was established in 1850. It was for some time a station on the underground railroad. It is today a center of social and religious life and also of the political life of the Negroes. President McKinley spoke in the church on his last public visit to Chicago. The second oldest church was established in 1853.

The actual services in these churches can best be judged by recording the results of a series of visits. In four of the large churches we have the following results:

African Methodist Episcopal Church—700 active members.

11 a.m. Sunday service. There was a long ritualistic introduction. The singing was good and effort was put forth to make strangers feel at home. The sermon was preached especially to converts and there was much emotion prevalent. The emphasis was laid on the after life. The house was well filled and the ventilation bad.

African Methodist Episcopal Zion Church—300 active members.

Morning service. The attendance was poor and much emotion was displayed. The Sermon was on "God's love." There was much insistence on money. The ventilation was bad.

African Methodist Episcopal Church—800 active members.

Special afternoon service. Discussion of the decrease consumption by colored physicians of the city. Talks on care of the body.

Baptist Church—1,000 active members.

Evening service. The house was crowded and the sermon emotional. The service was, running forty-five minutes over time. Sermon had some practical bearing at the close. Ventilation was good.

Ten other church services in the medium and smaller churches are reported. In nine of these there was no evidence of emotion—in some cases for lack of interest, in other cases from custom. In one case the church had white and colored members and a colored pastor. They showed much emotion at the service, but were very sincere and earnest people. The sermons varied: one was on the "Future life:" another took the theme "Get ready to leave this world," but ended with practical advice on home-owning. Another spoke of the "Blessed life," putting emphasis on both this and the future life. Another sermon was on "Self-control."

The expenditures of Chicago churches were as follows:

very different from my Catholic experience!

Thirty-two Churches in Chicago

Total membership............	6,811
Active membership...........	4,329
Valuation of Churches.......	$199,300.00
Salaries........................	17,895.13
Debt and interest.............	17,617.39
Running expenses............	12,869.32
Charity.........................	2,760.98
Missions........................	609.10
Support of connection.......	1,550.95
Other expenses...............	4,267.10
Total.......................	$57,569.97

The comments of intelligent Negroes and some of the pastors on the condition of the churches are worth listening to. As to the condition of the churches there is much complaint of the debts due largely to the erection of imposing edifices:

"As a rule, they are marked with inefficiency and a lack of proper regard for the moral development of the people. The emphasis placed on the financial condition is so great that the church is lacking in that which works for the moral development of the people in honesty, in sexual purity, etc."

"I have been informed that all but two of the churches in this city carry large debts. These debts range from $5,000 to $27,000. In appearance and appointments the church structures compare favorably with the edifices of the white population. One was built and completed at a cost of nearly $50,000. The Institutional Church was bought from the First Presbyterian Church for $33,000, of which sum $9,000 has been paid. The Bethel African Methodist Episcopal Church and the Olivet Baptist Church cost in the neighborhood of $30,000 each. They each owe about $15,000."

"The majority are in debt. The larger churches are largely attended by fashionably dressed people. The smaller ones have a hard struggle to exist. There is a constant demand for money at every service in all of them."

The influence of these churches is criticized:

"The thought of right doing and right living seems to be secondary. The primary idea seems to be to get the most good-paying members."

"We have many loyal and faithful members in our churches, and, I may add, altogether too many bad ones."

The ministers are especially taken to task:

"As a rule, I think the ministers are good men. There are dangerous exceptions, however."

"I know some good, pure, and upright men in the ministry, but I know some who are not good, pure, and upright. In my observations, I have noticed drunkenness, poor paymasters, lack of interest in their families, and very much tainted with sexual impurity."

"The ministers of . . . . . churches are excellent Christian gentlemen, and doing all in their power to raise the standard of Christian citizenship."

"So far as my personal knowledge goes, the ministers are good men. I can not deny that I have heard some ugly and persistent rumors concerning the life and character of several of the local staff of preachers. Sexual immorality and drunkenness are the offenses charged. I do not know of this from personal knowledge, however. In making this statement I am not attempting to evade whatever responsibility may rest with me in this matter. I simply do not know of my own knowledge of the correctness of these charges."

"I do not know of any specific cases of immorality such as you make mention of here. I can only judge by what I hear and that not too harshly. If I should judge strictly according to what I hear, I should not believe that there were any Christians among our ministers. This I am unwilling to accede."

"I regret to say some of those in our larger churches have not conducted themselves as Christian ministers should, numerous scandals having arisen about them. Whether false or true, it has a tendency to destroy their influence for good."

"Common rumor charges the ministers of our largest churches in this community with gross immorality—sexual impropriety and drunkenness. The ministers of three larges Methodist churches are charged with drunkenness, and the one at another church with gross sexual immorality. According to persistent rumor, one church was robbed by a former pastor who still has a charge here."

"Several ministers whom I know have had the above charges laid at their door. I cannot say whether they are guilty or not. I know, however, that a great deal of money passes through their hands and still the churches groan under the heavy weight of debt. Some I know are positively immoral."

Several pastors write of their especial difficulties, enumerating them as follows:

"How to secure sufficient means to prosecute the work in my district, which is the 'Slum District,' and how to treat and deal with the influx now migrating here from the South."

"One is poverty. Another is to have my message received for its own sake. A third is the utter lack of moral stamina in the community, extending to everything."

"The pastor's greatest difficulty is to meet his financial obligations because of his meager salary."

"The one great difficulty of the Negro pastor is to overcome the persistent, well nigh peremptory demand for something which appeals to the animal rather than to the human—that rouses the excitable rather than convicts the judgment."

"Lack of competent officials in a business way."

The greatest needs of the churches, according to the pastors, are:

"More intelligence and more piety, as well as an infinitely greater degree of purified refinement."

"(1) New methods of giving, i.e., from principle: (2) harmony between inner and external life; (3) promptness in attendance; (4) true conception of the meaning of worship; (5) to keep the church out of politics." *interesting*

"The greatest need is money."

The laymen think the needs are:

"I think the greatest need of our churches is good business management of funds, honest, intelligent and industrious business men on our trustee and deacon boards."

"More earnestness, higher moral tone, particularly in pulpit. To reform methods of raising money so as to preserve the quiet calm that should prevent devotional meetings from degenerating into a bargain counter session. The building of large and imposing edifices without previous monetary arrangements or its spiritual value being thought of, makes morals and religion serve as bell-ringer merely to call the congregation in order to cajole, importune or brow-beat interest money and pastor's salary."

And above all, *"Better ministers."*

Yet, that there is some good work done in matters of charity and reform by the churches, all admit.

"Yes, we have Sunday Clubs, as for instance, the Ladies' Aid of Berean Church, which did noble work during the severe cold weather just passed. They meet from house to house and sew for the poor."

"The Institutional Church and Social Settlement does the most of this kind of work. The other churches confine their charitable and reformatory work to their membership. I think this is accounted for in the small and moderate means of the membership."

"No specialized charity, but particularly generous and open-hearted in request cases."

"The Institutional, Quinn Chapel, Bethel, and others in Chicago. Special collections are lifted to bury some poor unfortunate or to relieve the wants of the destitute."

The churches are not attracting young people as they should.

"Owing to present conditions, as I see them, the young people of the intellectual class are not attracted to the church. They give very little for the support of the church."

"Not in large numbers. A few are scattered throughout all of the churches, but the vast majority seems to have no inclination toward the church."

"Taking Chicago as a whole, No! In the community of which I write, Yes! One of the largest Negro churches in the city until recently actually set a premium on ignorance, and drove the younger element from the church."

"I am sorry to have to answer No. Our young people are being educated away from the church. A very small percentage of our professional men and women are regular in their church attendance."

In spite of all drawbacks the weight of opinion is that moral standards in Chicago are being slowly raised despite the influx of the new colored immigrants.

"It is my firm belief that the standards are being raised in these particulars. The accumulations in property holdings and homes, the increase in bank accounts, the visible improvement in the matter of good taste in dress, are signs which, in my opinion, confirm the belief that the standards included in this question are being raised."

"I do not think the standards are being raised by any means."

"Through the efforts of the church, Woman's Clubs, and Sunday Clubs, there seems to be an improvement in morals."

"Lowered, as viewed from large numbers of marriages, which are not held in such sacredness as such tie demands and in careless rearing of children."

"I think the standard of morality is being raised. Marriages are common, every-day occurrences, and illicit and illegal cohabitation is no longer common but is very rare. The chief agencies in this work are church and school."

20

The Middle West, Ohio

(By R. R. Wright, Jr. *)

Green County is situated in the southwestern portion of the states of Ohio, about midway between Cincinnati and Columbus. Its area is 453 square miles and its population is 31,613, of whom 4,055 are Negroes. Greene County is a typical county for the study of the Negro problem, as it refers to the Northern Negro of the country and small town, for it not only has a very varied population of Negroes, but also the largest proportion of Negroes to whites in the state; and among these Negroes are some of the oldest inhabitants of the state as well as some of the most recent immigrants from the South.

Negro Church in Ohio

Ohio has a population of 4,157,545 persons, of whom 96,901 are Negroes. Of these about 28,000 or twenty-nine per cent, are reported as church members.

Early in the last century the Negro church had its rise in this state. In 1815, when there were but few Negroes here, the first Negro church was established at Cincinnati. This was under the Methodist Episcopal church. Rev. B. W. Arnett, now bishop of the African Methodist Episcopal Church, gives the following account in his "Proceedings of the Semi-Centenary Celebration of the African Methodist Episcopal Church of Cincinnati, 1874:" "The first religious society organized in Cincinnati by colored people was the Deer Creek Church, organized in 1815, under the auspices of the Methodist Episcopal Church. This was one year before the organization of the African Methodist Episcopal denomination in Philadelphia by

* Cf. Mr. Wright's longer study, Bulletin United States Bureau of Labor, No. 48.

Richard Allen and others. What Negroes there were in Cincinnati had been attending Old Stone Church, or 'Wesley Chapel' Methodist Episcopal Church; but on account of the shouting habit they were not very much desired at this white church. They were all crowded into one section of the church, where with much effort they tried not to disturb their white brethren by their frequent outbursts of praise to God. The whites tolerated them as long as they were successful in suppressing this inclination to shout. The crisis came, however, in 1815, when a brother, striving to suppress his shout by muffling his mouth with a handkerchief, burst one of his blood vessels in the attempt. After this the whites themselves took serious steps to have a separate church for Negroes. The result was the Deer Creek Church, whose pastor for a long while was a slave who came over from Kentucky from time to time. This new church was under the Methodist Episcopal connection until 1823, when, on account of alleged discrimination and unbrotherly action on the part of white brethren toward the colored, many of the latter withdrew and went over to the African Methodist Episcopal Church. Those who remained continued in the Methodist Episcopal Church, known later as Union Chapel. Thus began the Negro church in Ohio. Its mother was the Methodist Episcopal Church. The first African Methodist Episcopal Church was at Steubenville. In 1823, according to Bishop D. A. Payne's History of the African Methodist Episcopal Church, there were churches of this denomination at Cincinnati, Steubenville, and Chillicothe. When the Chillicothe and Steubenville churches were founded is not exactly known. In 1824 the report for the African Methodist Episcopal churches was as follows: Jefferson County Circuit (composed of Steubenville, with forty-five members, Cape Belmont, six members, Mount Pleasant, twelve members)—total sixty-three members; Chillicothe Circuit (composed of Chillicothe, Zanesville, Lancaster, and Cincinnati), only thirty-three members were reported on these charges. In 1833 there were churches at twenty different points with a membership of 690. In 1836 the membership of the African Methodist Episcopal Church was 1,131, and in 1838 it was 1,817. It has steadily increased until today it is more than 6,000."

When the separate Negro church was established, in 1815, nearly all the Negroes of the town joined or attended it regardless of what denomination they had before belonged to. It was not until 1835 that the first Baptist organization was begun—"Union Baptist Church" of Cincinnati.

There are now in the state seven denominations maintaining separate churches for Negroes, with a membership as follows:

Baptists..................................... 16,213

      Western Association.............. 6,885

      Eastern Association.............. 3,704

      Zion Association................ *3,500

      Providence Association............. 2,124

African Methodist Episcopal Church..... 6,308

      Ohio Conference.................. 3,179

    North Ohio Conference....... 3,129

Methodist Episcopal Church, North........ 1,645

      Wesleyan Methodists................. 557

      Christian (Disciples).................. *1,000

      Episcopal and Presbyterian............. 2,000

      Total....................... 27,723

These with the number of Negroes who are members of white congregations among Presbyterians, Catholics, Congregationalists, Zionists (Dowieites), would make the total about 28,000, or about twenty-nine percent of the total Negro population of the state. Of the population over fifteen years of age—70,032—forty percent are church members. In 1890 there were 250 organizations in the state among Negroes, having 19,827 communicants. This was 22.8 percent of the total population of 87,113 Negroes, much less than in 1902. The number of church members in the country at large in 1890 was 2,673,977 or 35.7 percent of the total Negro population. By this we see that Ohio is now still somewhat behind what the country at large was in 1890. The following table is taken from the United States census of 1890:

STATE.	Organizations.	Edifices.	Seating Capacity.	Halls.	Seating Capacity.	Value.	Communicants.	Population.
Total for United States.	23,462	23,770	6,800,035	1,358	114,644	$26,626,488	2,673,977	7,488,788
Ohio....................	250	214	66,516	34	1,750	576,425	19,827	87,113

There are now over 300 organizations distributed among over 200 cities and towns in the state.

Greene County

Greene County has a population of 31,613, of whom 4,055 are Negroes. The county is favorably situated for farming, and outside of Xenia many Negroes engage in this

* Estimated by Secretary

occupation, chiefly as "hands" at odd labor, however, as the census of 1900 gave only ninety farmers among the colored population of the county. The county is one of the oldest in the State, constituted in 1802, and named for General Nathaniel Greene. From its earliest days it has had Negroes among its population, as the following table will show:

POPULATION OF GREENE COUNTY BY UNITED STATES CENSUS, 1810–1900

Year.	White.	Colored.	Total.
1810................	5,834	36	5,870
1820................	10,468	61	10,521
1830................	14,639	162	14,801
1840................	17,184	344	17,528
1850................	21,292	654	21,946
1860................	24,722	1,475	26,197
1870................	24,199	3,839a	28,038
1880................	26,774	4,575b	31,349
1890................	25,950	4,060c	29,820
1900................	27,554	4,055d	31,613

a. Includes 24 Indians.
b. Includes 6 Chinese and 19 Indians.
c. Does not include 3 Chinese and 7 Indians.
d. Negroes only. Does not include 4 Chinese and Japanese.

The following table gives a partial exhibit of the general financial condition of the churches of the State:

CHURCHES.	Value of Property.	Indebtedness.	Salary of Pastor.	Paid on Debt.	Total Raised.
M. E. Church...........	a$79,050.09	$10,439.00	$8,430.00	b$9,074.00	......
A. M. E.–					
N. O. Conference.........	242,375.00	17,055.25	14,692.01	14,898.29	$37,878.57
Ohio Conference.........	108,570.00	10,364.53	13,116.28	10,806.64	28,522.43
Baptist { Eastern Association......	......	......	......	......	......
Western Association...	......	......	13,380.00	d13,510.00	......
Zion Association.........	......	......	......	......	......
Providence Association	31,350.00	......	c1,414.40	......	......
Wesleyan......	9,400.00	......	1,954.99	......	3,296.52

a $12,200 for parsonages.
b $5,628 for improvements, $3,466 on debt.

c For six pastors only.
d The total valuation of church property of the Baptists is estimated at $259,200.

Greene County is noted for its many small towns, among a score of which the most prominent are Xenia, with a population of 8,696; Jamestown, 1,205; Yellow Springs, 1,371; Cedarville, 1,189; Osborn, 948; Bowersville, 370; Springvalley, 522; and Bellbrook, 352. In five of these, viz: Xenia, Jamestown, Yellow Springs, Cedarville, and Wilberforce, we find the Negro church. To describe one of these is to describe all save Xenia and Wilberforce, the latter a college community, where Wilberforce University is located.

One rides into one of the other of these little towns and here he finds two more or less neat little church buildings, with seating capacity, on an average, of about 150 to 200 persons; sometimes of brick, sometimes frame. At Yellow Springs, the seat of Antioch College, where once the great Horace Mann presided, both churches are of brick and neat. One of these churches is an African Methodist Episcopal, and the other a Baptist Church. Almost invariably you will find that the younger and more intelligent class of Negroes is at the Methodist Church, while the older contingent generally constitutes the membership of the Baptist Church. At the Baptist Church one will find more fervency of speech and a more sanctimonious look on the part of both pastor and people, more of heaven and the future is talked of; at the Methodist churches there is all of this but less in proportion. The sermons one very probably will hear at the Baptist Church will abound in much good thought, ending generally in the same way, with something foreign more or less to the text. While the Methodist pastor may not be free from digressions, yet he is in every case the more logical speaker, and now and then gives his people something out of the "same old way." This is natural, when we know that the pastor of the Baptist Church is generally a middle-aged man * of but meager English and no theological training, while the pulpit of the Methodist Church is occupied by a student in the Theological Seminary at Wilberforce, who is also generally the equivalent of a high school graduate. These circumstances account for the above-named facts that the more intelligent class attends the Methodist Church. This comparison is somewhat abnormal when the whole state is considered, because the Methodist pastors are students who, were they engaged solely in preaching, would have much better churches, and leave these smaller churches to more poorly equipped men, as is the case with the Baptists now. The Baptist churches are, however, generally larger than the Methodist chiefly because they receive more time from their pastors. This was the case up to two years ago. Still there is no friction, but the most cordial feeling between both pastors and both flocks. Indeed many of the members of the Methodist Church take active parts in affairs of the Baptist Church and *vice versa*. The pastors even change their pulpits,

* The pulpit of Cedarville Baptist Church has been recently given to a young man—student at Wilberforce.

which once was not common. During the winter of 1902, when the revival fever had taken vigorous hold of Greene County, in order that there be no disadvantage in fighting Satan occasioned by a division of the hosts of the Lord, an agreement was made in Cedarville to the effect that one of the denominations would hold its revival and that all the members of the other church would give aid. After this first re-vival, then all, regardless of denomination, should combine their forces at the other church. This worked well for both. On the day that the Methodist Church was visited by the writer, he found the pastor of the Baptist Church present to preach.

In all of these churches the chief stress is put upon "saving souls;" that is, in persuading people to forsake sin and accept the Christian religion as the guiding force of their lives. And the method is quite rational. Usually in the middle of the winter, i.e., the first thing in the new year, the churches begin their revivals. This first work of the year lasts from two to eight weeks and many come to be saved, and are converted. Some of these see visions or dream dreams, some spend weeks in mourning, and still others are converted in a few minutes. In the revivals the sermons are chiefly on hell and its terrors, the love of Christ and God as shown in the suffering and death of Christ, Christ seeking sinners, the awful doom of those rejecting Him, etc. They abound in pathetic stories, which are related with great feeling, and which seldom fail in the desired result. This result is a large number of conversions and accessions to the churches. These are in due time baptized and admitted to full membership. Then the revival has closed, not only having been of great benefit to those converted, but also a positive moral help to the community at large. The remaining nine or ten months of the year are used for strengthening and teaching the members in the Christian religion and in the doctrines of the church. The Baptists take in their members directly. The Methodists require six months of probation, during which the candidate is supposed to receive instruction in his duty as a Christian and church member by the pastor, beside the regular instruction given from the pulpit. In none of the Methodist churches of Greene County is this carried out fully, but in those where it is attempted with anything like success, the results show well in the character of the members.

If there is any criticism as to method in arousing and directing the religious consciousness it should be more severe as regards post-revival methods than revival methods. Experienced revivalists, and some men of much intelligence living in the county, state that for the average Negro congregation their method, though accom-panied by much of the spectacular, is best suited for those to whom they appeal, but that after the "revival" is over the proper oversight is seldom given the young Christian and, as is quite natural, the life is far from the ideal.

WILBERFORCE.—The value of the Wilberforce church consists in the fact that many students are interested in Christian work, and are trained for larger service after leaving school. The pastor of the church is the instructor in science and a very devout man. Under his preaching from forty to eighty students are converted every year. Of these some take an active interest in the local Christian work, and of these latter some enter the ministry. In many states of the Union there are men and women earnestly engaged in church, Sunday-school, Young Men's Christian Association work, now leaders and pastors, who were converted in the Wilberforce revival and got their first interest and training here. For the training of the newly converted there is a class led by one of the instructors. Beside this the Bible classes of the Y. M. C. A and Y. W. C. A., taught by professors in the University, have in the past year been successful in imparting systematic knowledge of the Scriptures more than at any previous time,

Payne Theological Seminary is at Wilberforce, and its students and teachers are local preachers in the church. Its dean is superintendent of the Sunday-school. In the Seminary are forty-five students, representing South America, South Africa, West Africa, and various states in the Union. The class of 1903 numbers eleven members.

XENIA.—Xenia is the county seat of Greene County and one of the oldest towns in the state. Its population by the census of 1900 was 8,696, of whom 1,988, or 21.7 percent, were Negroes. These Negroes are made up of about half natives of the state of Ohio and about half immigrants from Kentucky, Virginia, North Carolina, Tennessee and other Southern states. In general the immigrants make up the lower class, being the poorer and more illiterate. The illiteracy of Xenia Negroes is 13.42 percent for all above ten years, and 1.57 percent for those between ten years and forty years. About 63 percent of Xenia Negroes own their homes and they pay taxes on $116,828 worth of property. The school advantages, through high school, are far above ordinary. Yet Xenia is a town of but little thrift compared with the advantages offered. The chief businesses are barbers, small groceries and an undertaking establishment. While the Negroes are not extraordinarily thrifty, they are not, on the other hand, very vicious. Composing 21.7 percent of the population, they furnish 29.9 percent of the arrests. The number for 1901-2 was ninety-eight. Among these cases were: Drunk, ten; loitering, three; disorderly, twenty; drunk and disorderly, seven; assault and battery, seven; suspicion, five; safe keeping, eleven; stealing ride, seven; petit larceny, one; lunacy, two; burglary, fugitive from justice, murder in another state, larceny, threatening, execution, one each; gambling, seven; horse stealing, two.

Xenia, then, is a slow, not good, not bad, conservative, somewhat conceited sort of a town, whose people live, in the main, comfortably, i.e., according to the general standard for Negroes.

Negroes have lived in the county ever since it has been established. The first count made in the county, in 1803, took a record only of white males over twenty-one years of age, but United States census gives the colored population of Xenia only since 1830, as follows:

Year.	White.	Colored.	Total.
1830	902	17	919
1850	2,694	330	3,024
1860	3,856	802	4,658
1870	4,687	1,690	6,377
1880	5,077	1,949a	7,026
1890	5,424	1,877b	7,301
1900	6,705	1,991c	8,696

a Includes 3 Chinese and Japanese and 3 Indians.
b Includes 3 Chinese and 6 civilized Indians.
c Includes 3 Chinese.

There are seven churches in Xenia, viz: Three Baptist, one African Methodist Episcopal, one Methodist Episcopal, one Wesleyan Methodist, and one Christian Church.

The first church in Xenia was established by the African Methodist Episcopal connection in 1833. Nothing is known of it save that it was on the Hillsboro Circuit, and Rev. Thomas Lawrence was its pastor. In 1836 Rev. William Paul Quinn, afterwards bishop of the African Methodist Episcopal Church, was pastor. In 1842 the church was called the "Greene County Mission," had twenty-five members and paid its pastor the neat sum of $7.91. The first Baptist Church was established in 1848. Henry Howe's first "History of Ohio," published in 1852, says that then Xenia contained one German Church, one Lutheran Church, one Methodist Episcopal Church, one Seceders' Church, one Associated Reformed Church, one Baptist Church, and two churches for colored people.

Membership.—The seven churches of Xenia report a total membership of 1,068, or 53.4 percent of the entire Negro population. The membership is as follows:

Church	Membership
Baptist.	640
Zion.	370
Middle Run.	140
Third.	130
African Methodist Episcopal.	240
Methodist Episcopal.	54
Wesleyan.	9
Christian.	125
Total	1,068

By a personal count of 1,832 persons made by the writer during May-June, 1902, 976, or 53.6 percent, reported themselves as church members. These members were all persons over ten years of age. The number of persons counted who were over ten years of age was 1,505. Hence 64.8 percent of these were church members. The following table will show the membership as reported by the persons themselves:

AGE PERIOD.	Church Members			Total Population.			Percent of Members.
	Males.	Females.	Total.	Males.	Females.	Total.	
10 to 19 years.......	46	102	148	142	189	331	44.7
20 to 29 years.......	52	124	176	149	168	317	55.5
30 to 39 years.......	44	106	150	104	133	237	63.3
40 to 49 years.......	73	119	192	112	125	237	81.0
50 to 59 years.......	64	93	157	82	103	185	84.8
60 to 69 years.......	53	47	100	73	51	124	80.7
70 to 79 years.......	17	15	32	25	18	43	74.4
80 years and over	4	12	16	5	12	17	94.1
Unknown age........	4	1	5	9	5	14	35.7
Total........	357	619	976	701	804	1,505	64.8

This table shows very strikingly that the young people are not forsaking the church to such an extent as to discard membership. More than half for every age period above twenty years are members, and in the first period more than half from fifteen to nineteen years of age are church members. The excess is of women over men. These persons are distributed throughout all occupations, but almost invariably those in the most lucrative positions or employments are church members. As to culture, as indicated by scholastic training, it appears from a personal count by the writer that out of ninety-five high school graduates 80 or 84.2 percent are church members—fifty-nine out of sixty-seven women, and twenty-one out of twenty-eight men. In the African Methodist Church the principal of the high school is superintendent of the Sunday-school, and the principal of the elementary school, although a woman, is a class leader. The only college graduate in the city is also an ordained minister connected with the local African Methodist Episcopal Church. As to material standing of the church members it is noted that of the 318 families who own their homes, 288, or 90.6 percent, were connected with the church by some members of the family, and 237 of them were connected by the head of the family.

This chief means of increasing the membership is through the revival, which is substantially the same as conducted in other parts of the county. Last year there were

THE NEGRO CHURCH

175 conversions, of whom the sixty-nine were under twenty years of age, and eleven were over forty years, according to the report of the pastor. (See table, page 00).

Activities.—These churches make some attempt to satisfy all the legitimate social desires of their members. There are sick benefit societies, educational societies, Home and Foreign Missionary Societies, Christian Endeavor Societies, Baptist Young People's Unions, sewing circles, besides various temporary organizations for raising money and other purposes. These are in addition to the organizations fundamental to the church government, such as the Methodist Church, the various conferences, boards of trustees, stewards, spiritual officers, Sunday-school, etc.

As before stated, the chief activity is to preach and teach Christian doctrine and morality. The method for this is preaching in all the churches two or three times on Sunday, once or twice during the week, prayer meeting on Wednesday night, class-meeting once a week in the Methodist Church and pastoral visiting, beside monthly love feasts or covenant meetings. As a means to this end is the material side of the church life to be looked after, and this is chiefly in regard to raising funds for the pastor's salary, current expenses, the debt, improvements, general purposes, etc. This is done by way of the Sunday and weekly collections and by organizing the members into clubs to solicit subscriptions or to raise funds by concerts and other entertainments. In this way the African Methodist Episcopal Church paid its debt of some $400 last year.

The next function of the church is the purely social. This is carried forward in other organizations and as a part of the more religious and financial activity. At church service old friends are met and new ones often made, but as no part of the special program. To raise money socials are given, etc., so that as secondary through all the activity there is the purely social. Along literary and musical lines, in spite of the fact that Negroes have free access to the theatre, the University Extension Courses, and the Y. M. C. A. lecture courses, the church is still the most powerful factor in Xenia life. Here the local talent finds the best opportunity for expression and development, and here the best available talent is brought from afar. In the Baptist Church last year there were ten lectures and two high class concerts. Among the lecturers was Rev. M. C. B. Mason, one of the most distinguished Negro orators. The Methodist (African) Church had during this year Miss Flora Batson, the noted singer, and a few weeks later the Canadian Jubilee Singers to entertain the people. In this way the church fulfills a social need which neither the extension courses or the theatre would fulfill—that of bringing the Negroes into touch with some of the best of their own race.

128

The table below will show that there is not much charity work done in Xenia by the churches, chiefly because there is not much need for such. Last year the churches gave as follows:

Zion Baptist............................	$ 25.00
Middle Run Baptist......................	7.00
St. John African Methodist Episcopal	50.00
Total............................	$ 82.00

Eighty-two dollars are reported, but the amount of charity work is more. By this it is seen that Middle Run Baptist Church reports $7, but Middle Run takes care of an old woman of eighty years, granting her free rent of a small house owned by the church and furnishing her, from time to time, with other necessities. In times of sickness, in many ways the church influences charity, though it does not get credit for it. On the first Sunday of each month most of the churches take an offering called the "Poor Saints' Collection." Beside this there are connected with several of the churches sick benefit societies. For instance, connected with Zion Baptist there are two: The Ladies' Home Aid and the Ladies' Auxiliary, both of which are especially designed to help the sick. There is practically no prison work undertaken by the churches of Xenia, except an occasional visit to the workhouse or jail by one of the pastors.

Pastors.—The pastors of Xenia are all men of high moral character, as is the universal testimony of those who have given opinions. They are all men of zeal for their work, intelligent, though none are college graduates. (See table, page 105.) It seems that Xenia has always had as ministers men of good reputations and high character. A historian * of Greene County, writing in 1881, speaking of the different Negro ministers of the city, said of one: "He has always been an upright Christian man;" of another: "By his gentlemanly deportment and Christian walk, he has gained many warm friends;" of another: "A congenial, attractive man, he shows from his fruits that he practices what he preaches;" of another: "The people of this county will find it a hard matter to fill his place should he be called to some other locality."

* Dill's History of Greene County

Value of Church Properties, Indebtedness, Pastor's Salary and Total Amount Raised by Churches of Greene County

CHURCH.	Value of Property.	Indebtedness.	Pastor's Salary.	Total Raised.
Baptist-				
Zion......................	$ 12,000	$3,400.00	$500.00	$1,025.00
Middle Run............	1,000	00	170.00	....
Third....................	8,000	....	500.09	....
Yellow Springs............	3,000	....	210.00	....
Cedarville.................	1,000	....	170.00	223.25
Jamestown...............	2,000	....	350.00	505.00
Massies' Cresek............	700	....	....	....
Methodist Episcopal.........	1,500	266.00	640.00	....
Wesleyan Methodist.........	500	....	25.59	42.49
Christian....................	3,000	....	300.00	600.00
A.M.E-				
Jamestown....................	2,000	00	300.00	956.71
Cedarville....................	1,200	00	167.50	316.80
Yellow Spring...............	3,000	00	250.00	495.85
St. John, Xenia............	6,000	00	768.00	1,178.00
Wilberforce............}	Use Chapel of Wilberforce University.	0	250.00	624.75

Incomplete.

General Financial Statistics

CHURCH.	Current Expenses.	For Connection.	Interest on Debt and Principal.	Charity.	Missions.	Education and Other Purposes.	Salary.	Total.
Baptist								
Zion	100.00	....	400.00	25.00	....	....	500.00	1,025.00
Middle Run.....	100.00	32.60	475.00	7.00	14.00	....	170.00	....
Third.........	....	....	....	....	....	....	500.09	....
Yellow Springs ...	....	3.83	210.00	....	22.00	54.17	....	280.00
Cedarville......	2.60	....	40.00	1.50	6.75	2.40	170.00	....

CHURCH.	Current Expenses.	For Connection.	Interest on Debt and Principal.	Charity.	Missions.	Education and Other Purposes.	Salary.	Total.
Jamestown......	75.00	10.00	0.00	30.00	25.00	15.00	350.00	505.00
Massies' Creek ..	...	....	....	....	....	....	....	....
Methodist Episcopal	72.00	....	10.00	....	2.00	....	640.00	....
Wesleyan	7.40	7.00	....	....	....	9.50	25.59	42.49
Christian	92.00	....	208.00	....	....	....	300.00	600.00
A.M.E-.........								
Jamestown	89.00	37.50	448.71	12.50	9.00	60.00	300.00	956.71
Cedarville	37.20	11.50	0.00	19.60	27.58	53.42	167.50	316.80
Yellow Springs ...	18.78	33.30	125.00	....	8.77	....	2.50	495.85
Xenia.........	200.00	120.00	400.00	50.00	40.00	....	768.00	1,178.00
Wilberforce......	113.72	65.75	....	49.68	60.00	127.00	250.00	665.65

Incomplete.

The questions on the schedules for "Data from Negro Churches" were answered as follows by the pastors of Greene County:

I.

What do the churches need most?

Preachers that study the Bible and teach it in its purity.................... 1

Educated ministers on fire with glory of God and uplift of the people... 1

Leaders, pure, courageous, with executive ability.......................... 1

Educated, experienced, courageous, and honest men as preachers........ 1

Religion and good sense... 1

Religion and faithful ministers, and refinement............................ 1

Revival of religion and money... 1

More of the spirit of Christ.. 1

Better attendance and support from members.............................. 1

Union... 1

II.

What is the pastor's greatest difficulty?

Lack of conscientious Bible study on his part........................... 1

Minister too abusive and people too sensitive.......................... 1

Lack of courage and ability on part of minister....................... 1

Unconverted membership... 1

Irregular and desultory attendance of members........................ 2

Lack of cooperation on part of members............................... 1

Difficulty of getting people to live Christian lives after
joining the church... 1

Immorality and ignorance of the people........................ 1

III.

Are the morals of the people being raised or lowered in respect to sexual morals, honesty, home life, truth-telling, etc?

Raised.. 5

Raised by fifty per cent... 1

Doubtful... 1

Very little as to sexual morals, home life and truth-telling;
some as to honesty... 1

IV.

Is the Sunday-school effective?

Yes.. 8

How can it be improved?

By cooperation of parents.. 4

Systematic visiting through the week............................... 1

Gathering the little children...................................... 1

V.

How many persons joined the church last year?
How many of these were under 20 years of age?
How many were over 40 years of age?

CHURCH.	Accessions.		Total.	Total Members.	Total Active Members.
	Under 20 Years.	Over 40 Years.			
Baptist-					
Zion..........	19	....	38	370	250
Middle Run........	30	4	81	140	45
Third.......	0	0	2	130	27
Yellow Springs......	....	....	...	161	....
Cedarville.......	0	3	10	40	30
Jamestown.......	8	0	9	108	75
Massies' Creek......	0	0	0	25	14
Methodist Episcopal....	0	0	0	58	....
Wesleyan Methodist....	....	....	...	9	9
Christian..........	0	1	4	125	50
A. M. E.-					
Jamestown.......	18	1	20	124	85
Cedarville.......	24	0	24	47	35
Yellow Springs......	9	0	9	75	40
St. John, Xenia......	20	6	50	240	160
Wilberforce*.......	60†	2	80	108	55
Total..........	188	17	327	1,760	875

* 1901. Report for 1902 not available. † Estimated.

VI.

Is there much shouting or emotion?

Not very much.. 8

Considerable emotion, occasional shouting............................ 1

Yes.. 1

Too much for the good done... 1

VII.

Are the younger set of educated people joining the church and helping in its work?

Yes..	8
To some extent..	1
Slowly; they do a little......................................	1

VIII.

Sketches of Pastors of Greene County

(This includes also the A. M. E. and M. E. Presiding Elders.)

Church of Which Pastor.	Age	Birthplace.	Years of Experience.	Education.
Baptist–				
Zion............	45	Ohio.......	14	Normal.
Middle Run	25	Ohio.......	7	High School.
Third	48	South Carolina	18	Common Schools of South Carolina.
Cedarville	29	Ohio.......	1	Common School.
Jamestown	48	....	17	Common School.
Yellow Springs	50	....	...	Common School.
Massies' Creek	....	No pastor...	...	
Methodist Episcopal ...	....	....	...	
Wesleyan Methodist ...	....	No pastor...	...	
Christian	54	Kentucky ...	18	"Very Limited."
A.M.E–				
Xenia	34	Illinois	11	High School Graduate.
Cedarville.......	36	Florida.....	3	{Common School and Member of Class { '03 Theological Seminary.
Jamestown	31	Ohio.......	8	{Theological and High School Graduate.
Yellow Springs.....	30	Louisiana ...	5	{Grammar School and Graduate { Theological, '03.
Wilberforce.......	41	Ohio.......	7	College Graduate.
Presiding Elder A.M.E.	47	Ohio.......	25	Theological.
Presiding Elder M.E...	50	Indiana	20	College.

Opinions of Negro Church

These opinions are from people of long residence and good standing in Greene County. They are as to occupations as follows:

Pastors	6
Presiding Elders	2
Physicians	2
College Professors	3
Dean Theological Seminary	1
Principal High School	1
Principal Elementary School	1
Barbers	2
Grocer	1
Student	1
Total	20

I.

So far as you have observed, what is the present condition of the churches in your community?

Very gratifying	1
Improving	2
Embarrassed financially	2
Fair	3
Good	5

Some answered this question as follows:

Financially, poor	2
Financially, fair	1
Financially, good	1
Intellectually, fair	1
Intellectually, good	1
Spiritually, dull	1
Spiritually, fair	2

II.

Is their influence, on the whole, toward pure, honest living?

Yes... 12

Not as much as should be............................... 3

In part, but not all.. 2

Largely so.. 2

Generally so... 1

III.

(*a*) Are the ministers usually good men?

Yes.. 16

Usually, not universally............................. 2

(*b*) Their chief faults?

Whiskey and women................................. 2

(This does not apply to those in Greene County.)

Illiteracy and want of deep convictions.......... 1

(This also does not apply to those in Greene County.)

Desire to be popular................................. 1

Failure to study....................................... 1

IV.

Of the ministers whom you know, how many are notoriously immoral? What direction does their immorality take? Cite instances.

This question, like the third, was generally answered for the *general* condition and not as applying to Greene County in particular, as directed. One man of wide experience says he knows twenty-four notoriously immoral preachers, but there are only twenty-five in the county, including those who are idle and who preach outside of the county.

None... 11

A few.. 1

Two.. 2

Twenty-four.. 1

"Eighty-five percent are good men, five percent dishonest in money matters, ten percent tinctured with sexual impurity." —A Presiding Elder.

"I know a dozen who are immoral, basing my reply upon facts given by others." —A principal of city schools.

As to kinds of immorality, see above, and also—

Sexual impurity and drunkenness.....................................	1
Sexual impurity, dishonesty in money matters, and drunkenness...	3
Dishonesty in money matters...............................	1

V.

Is the Sunday-school effective in teaching children good manners and sound morals?

Yes...	10
In a large degree............................	1
Generally....................................	3
To some degree..............................	5
Not as much as might be......................	1

VI.

Do the churches with which you are acquainted do much charitable work?

Yes...	3
Some..	6
Not much....................................	7
Considerable among the poor..................	1
Yes, in large cities..........................	1

VII.

Do the young people join the church and support it?

Some do.....................................	4
Only a few..................................	2
Yes, but about one-fourth support it..........	2

Yes...	5
Yes, but do not support well................................	3
Not all, but a fair proportion..............................	3
Young women do, but not many young men..................	1

VIII.

What is the greatest need of our churches?

Pure gospel and money.......................................	1
More enforcement of spiritual duty of the church...............	2
Ministers of broader culture and deeper piety........................	3
Systematic business methods, trained men in pulpits, doctrinal preaching, and an earnest desire to persuade men to serve God from choice..	1
Religious enthusiasm, sound financial basis, respect for pastor.....	1
Higher ideals and deeper Christianity......................................	1
Educated and called ministry................................	1
Pure religion, money, and education................................	1
Fewer churches, better preachers, better religion.....................	1
More love for church and each other on part of members..............	2
Money, and instruction in race pride, and business....................	1
Good morals, home training, and piety................................	1

IX.

Are the standards of morality in your community being raised or lowered in respect to sexual morals, home life, honesty, etc.? Give instances.

Raised...	14
Inclined to think raised..............................	1
Raised very little.....................................	1
Raised to some extent.................................	1

"Twelve or thirteen years ago the patrol was constantly called to a class of resorts which have been wiped out."

"Xenia, Jamestown, Cedarville, Yellow Springs, are 'dry.'"

"Greater condemnation of men who deceive women."

21

An Eastern City. [*]

Philadelphia, Pa., gives an opportunity to study the growth of the Negro church for over a century. In 1800 there were in that county [†] 7,000 Negroes and three Negro churches, founded as follows:

1792—St. Thomas.........................Episcopal.

1794—Bethel.................African Methodist Episcopal.

1794—Zoar..........................Methodist Episcopal.

In 1813, when there were about 11,000 Negroes in the city, there were the following churches and members:

St Thomas, Protestant Episcopal.......................	560
Bethel, African Methodist Episcopal................	1,272
Zoar, Methodist Episcopal..............................	80
Union, African Methodist Episcopal....................	74
Baptist, Race and Vine Streets...........................	80
Presbyterian...	300
Total..	2,366

There were about 17,500 Negroes in 1838:

---

[*] From the more elaborate study on the Philadelphia Negro (Ginn).

[†] City and County are today co-terminous.

DENOMINATIONS.	No. Churches	Members.	Annual Expenses.	Value of Property.	Incumbrance.
Episcopalian......................	1	100	$1,000	$36,000	....
Lutheran.............................	1	10	120	3,000	$1,000
Methodist...........................	8	2,860	2,100	50,800	5,100
Presbyterian.......................	2	325	1,500	20,000	1,000
Baptist.............................	4	700	1,300	4,200	....
Total	16	3,995	$6,020	$114,000	$7,100

In 1847 the population had grown to 20,000. There were nineteen churches; twelve of these reported 3,974 members; the property of eleven cost $67,000. After the war the population had increased to 22,000. There were the following churches in 1867:

NAME	Founded.	No. of Members.	Value of Property.	Pastor's Salary.
Protestant Episcopal—				
St. Thomas.................	1792	....	....	....
Methodist—				
Bethel......................	1794	1,100	$50,000	$600
Union.......................	1827	467	40,000	850
Wesley.....................	1817	464	21,000	700
Zoar........................	1794	400	12,000	....
John Wesley.............	1814	42	3,000	No regular salary
Little Wesley.............	1821	310	11,000	500
Pisgah.....................	1831	116	4,600	430
Zion City Mission......	1858	90	4,500	....
Little Union..............	1837	200	....	....
Baptist—				
First Baptist.............	1809	360	5,000	....
Union Baptist............	....	400	7,000	600
Shiloh.....................	1812	405	16,000	600
Oak Street................	1827	137	....	....
Presbyterian—				
First Presbyterian...	1807	200	8,000	....
Second Presbyterian....	1824	....	....	....
Central Presbyterian.....	1814	240	16,000	....

By 1880 (population 30,000) there were twenty-five churches and missions. In 1897 there were about 60,000 Negroes in the city, and the following churches:

DENOMINATION.	Churches.	Members Claimed.	Value of Property.	Expenses.
African Methodist Episcopal....................	14	3,210	$202,229	$27,074
African Methodist Episcopal Zion.............	3	....	25,000	5,000
Union African Methodist Episcopal...........	1	....	....	....
Methodist Protestant............................	1	....	....	....
Methodist Episcopal............................	6	1,202	49,700	16,394
Baptist...	17	5,583	296,800	30,000
Presbyterian.....................................	3	633	150,000	4,473
Protestant Episcopal............................	6	791	130,000	6,613
Roman Catholic.................................	1	200?	....	....

There are three other small churches, making fifty-five churches in all, with 13,000 members, $910,000 worth of property, and an annual income of $95,000. In 1900 Philadelphia had 62,613 Negroes.

The general character of church life is thus set forth:

"Perhaps the pleasantest and most interesting social intercourse takes place on Sunday; the weary week's work is done, the people have slept late and have had a good breakfast, and sally forth to church well dressed and complacent. The usual hour of the morning service is eleven, but people stream in until after twelve. The sermon is usually short and stirring, but in the larger churches elicits little response other than an 'Amen' or two. After the sermon the social features begin; notices on the various meetings of the week are read, people talk with each other in subdued tones, take their contributions to the altar, and linger in the aisles and corridors after dismission to laugh and chat until one or two o'clock. Then they go home to good dinners. Sometimes there is some special three o'clock service, but usually nothing, save Sunday-school, until night. Then comes the chief meeting of the day; probably 10,000 Negroes gather every Sunday night in their churches. There is much music, much preaching, some short addresses; many strangers are there to be looked at; many beaus bring out their belles, and those who do not, gather in crowds at the church door and escort the young women home. The crowds are usually well-behaved and respectable, though rather more jolly than comports with a Puritan idea of church services.

"In this way the social life of the Negro centers in his church—baptism, wedding and burial, gossip and courtship, friendship and intrigue—all lie in these walls. What wonder that this central club-house tends to become more and more luxuriously furnished, costly in appointment and easy of access!

"It must not be inferred from all this that the Negro is hypocritical or irreligious. His church is, to be sure, a social institution first, and religious afterwards, but nevertheless, its religious activity is wide and sincere. In direct moral teaching and setting moral standards for the people, however, the church is timid, and naturally so, for its constitution is democracy tempered by custom. Negro preachers are condemned for poor leadership and empty sermons, and it is said that men with so much power and influence could make striking moral reforms. This is but partially true. The congregation does not follow the moral precepts of the preacher, but rather the preacher follows the standard of his flock, and only exceptional men dare seek to change this. And here it must be remembered that the Negro preacher is primarily an executive officer rather than a spiritual guide. If one goes into any great Negro church and hears the sermon and views the audience, one would say, either the sermon is far below the caliber of the audience, or the people are less sensible than they look. The former explanation is usually true. The preacher is sure to be a man of executive ability, a leader of men, a shrewd and affable president of a large and intricate corporation. In addition to this, he may be, and usually is, a striking elocutionist. He may also be a man of integrity, learning, and deep spiritual earnestness; but these last three are sometimes all lacking, and the last two in many cases. Some signs of advance are here manifest: no minister of notoriously immoral life, or even of bad reputation, could hold a large church in Philadelphia without eventual revolt. Most of the present pastors are decent, respectable men. There are perhaps one or two exceptions to this, but the exceptions are doubtful rather than notorious. On the whole, then, the average Negro preacher in this city is a shrewd manager, a respectable man, a good talker, a pleasant companion, but neither learned nor spiritual, nor a reformer.

"The moral standards are, therefore, set by the congregations, and vary, from church to church, in some degree. There has been a slow working toward a literal obeying of the Puritan and ascetic standard of morals which Methodism imposed on the freedmen, but condition and temperament have modified these. The grosser forms of immorality, together with theatre-going and dancing, are specifically denounced; nevertheless, the precepts against specific amusements are often violated by church members. The cleft between denominations is still wide, especially between Methodists and Baptists. The sermons are usually kept within the safe ground of a mild Calvinism, with much insistence on salvation, grace, fallen humanity, and the like." [*1]

* Philadelphia Negro, p. 204, ff.

22

Present Condition of Churches—The Baptists

"In the minutes of the old Savannah Association for 1812, is the following note: 'The Association is sensibly affected by the death of Rev. Andrew Bryan, a man of color and pastor of the first colored church in Savannah. This son of Africa, after suffering inexpressible persecutions in the cause of his Divine Master, was permitted to discharge the duties of his ministry among his colored friends in peace and quiet, hundreds of whom through his instrumentality were brought to a knowledge of the truth as it is in Jesus. He closes his useful and amazingly luminous course in the lively exercise of faith and in the joyful hope of a happy immortality.'

"The most of the colored Baptists were at this period identified with white churches, and in churches of mixed membership the whites were often in the minority. In the mixed churches of this period, the colored members had no voice in affairs, unless in the reception and discipline of members of their own race. After the emancipation of slaves, the Negro Baptists of the Southern states very generally separated from the white churches, and organized churches and Associations of their own. Other colored Baptist churches of that section, that were organized at an earlier period, besides the one at Savannah, above mentioned, are the Springfield Baptist Church, Augusta, Ga, 1790, and the one at Portsmouth, Va., 1841; the Nineteenth Street Baptist Church of Washington, D. C., 1832; one in Louisville, Ky., 1842; one in Baltimore, Md., 1836. In the Northern and Western states, the earliest organized colored Baptist churches are the Abyssinian of New York City, 1803; the Independent of Boston, 1805; the First of Philadelphia, 1809; Ebenezer of New York City, 1825; the Union of Cincinnati, 1827; the Union of Philadelphia, 1832; the Union of Alton, Ill., 1838.

"The Western states organized the first colored Baptist Association. The Providence Baptist Association of Ohio was organized in 1836, and the Wood River Baptist Association of Illinois in 1838. The number of colored Baptists in the United States in 1850 is reported but in part. In fifteen Southern states and four Northern states, 100 out of 336 Associations report 89,695 colored members. There is no report from 146 Southern Associations, but high authority puts the whole number of colored Baptists in this country in 1850 at 150,000. Then we have a numerical growth of Negro Baptists in America from 150,000 in 1850 to 1,604,310 in 1894; an increase of 1,454,310 in forty-four years, which is an increase of over 33,000 net each year. From one ordained preacher in 1777 to 10,119 in 1894; from one church in 1788 to 13,138 churches in 1894, or an average increase of 124 churches each year; increase in valuation of church property from nothing in 1788 to $11,271,651." [*]

The Baptist churches unite in Associations and State Conventions for missionary and educational work. For a long time, however, it seemed impossible to unite any large number of them in a National Convention, but this has at last been done.

The National Baptist Convention was organized at Atlanta, Ga., September 28, 1895. Its objects are missionary and educational work, and the publication of religious literature. The membership consists of representatives of churches, Sunday-schools, Associations, and State Conventions of Baptists, and of such individual Baptists as wish to join. The Convention meets annually, and has a president, vice-presidents from each state, a statistical secretary, and other officers. This Convention elects annually a Foreign Mission Board, a Home Mission Board, an Educational Board, and a Baptist Young People's Union Board. These boards all consist of one member from each state represented, and elect their own officers and executive committee so located as to be able to meet monthly. The Convention also collects statistics concerning the Negro Baptists throughout the United States. The Conventions of 1901 and 1902 follow.

These figures are not altogether accurate, but are probably understatements rather than exaggerations. [*]

[*] Growth of the Negro Baptists, by R. De Baptiste, 1896.

[*] A prominent church official writes:

"The statistics are not correct. For instance, you will notice New Jersey. At the time of getting the statistics from there we had only thirty-six churches. I have just returned from there, and know that they have sixty-seven. What is true of that state is true of many others.

"We have a very poor way of getting accurate statistics. We have had to depend upon the various minutes of the state meetings and, as you know, our people attend these meetings if they wish and let it alone if they please. There is no reason nor power to compel them to give statistics. A great number of our churches do not attend the Associations and a great number of our Associations do not attend the State Conventions and a number of the State Conventions are not represented in our National Convention. Therefore, you see that we only have to get such statistics as are in co-operation with us."

The most remarkable result of the united efforts of the Negro Baptists is the Home Mission department, including the publishing house:

"It has been the policy of our Board from its incipiency to do whatever missionary work that is done in any state in cooperation with the regular state authorities or state organizations in their organized capacity.

"We believe also that when this policy of our Board is better understood, the churches, Associations and Conventions will contribute more liberally to the advancement of the work of our Board. While we have not been able to do as much in this co-operative mission work as we had hoped, yet we have done what we could. We have gone as far as our limited means would allow. The following is a summary of the missionary work done by our Board and by its co-operative policy in the United States:

COMBINED REPORTS

Sermons preached.................	1,550	Homes visited............................	1,661
Sunday schools addressed......	905	Homes found without Bibles.............	84
Prayer-meetings attended...........	829	Churches visited............................	1,323
B.Y.P.U. meetings attended.....	478	Sunday-schools organized..............	7
Women's meetings addressed....	261	Missionary societies organized........	44
Other addresses made...........	1,495	Baptisms.....................................	70
Total number addresses made..	2,376	Miles traveled by railroad................	99,612
Conventions, Associations and women's meetings visited since last report..........................	253	Cost of Travel...............................	$1,493.64
Number of letters and cards written...............................	12,056	Miles traveled otherwise..................	5,491
Number of circulars and tracts distributed..........................	40,703	Cost of same..............................	$188.30
Number of books and tracts donated..............................	1,019	Total traveling expense...................	$1,681.94
Books sold........................	$1,774.83	Total amount of money sent to National Baptist Publishing Board...	$1,281.36
Money collected....................	$3,538.37	Amount of the money collected applied to salaries....................	$281.35
Total amount of money received from all sources...................	$5,114.02	Total amount of money collected and left with churches........................	79.80
Subscriptions to the Union........	256	Number of Missionary Conferences held............................	31
Money collected for same..	$57.20	Paid on salaries............................	$3,839.38
Days of services rendered........	2,223	Total paid on salaries	$4,174.73

"It has been our custom, from year to year, to call the attention of our Convention to the work of correspondence of our Board. This is done with a view of giving the members somewhat of an idea of the magnitude of this portion of our work. For the benefit of those who may be interested, we quote the following number of first-class letters received and disposed of by answers by the Corresponding Secretary and his assistants during the fiscal year:

September, 1901	4,303
October, 1901	6,255
November, 1901	2,243
December, 1901	3,355
January, 1902	5,968
February, 1902	2,709
March, 1902	6,432
April, 1902	9,607
May, 1902	4,866
June, 1902	8,576
July, 1902	7,922
August, 1902	2,720
Grand total for the year	64,956

General Summary of Baptists in the United States

	1901	1902
State Conventions	....	43
Associations	515	517
Churches	15,654	16,440
Ordained ministers	14,861	16,080
Present membership in the United States..	1,975,538	2,038,427
Meeting houses	7,576	11,069
Valuation	$11,605,891	$12,196,130
Sunday-schools	7,466	13,707
Teachers and officers	36,736	41,537
Pupils in Sunday-schools	473,271	544,505
Total in Sunday-schools	510,007	586,042

MONEY RAISED		
Church expenses................................	....	$3,090.190.71
Sunday-school expenses......................	....	107,054.00
State Missions...................................	....	9,954.00
Foreign Missions...............................	....	8,725.00
Home Mission and Publication...............	....	81,658.40
Education..	$115,809.55	127,941.00
Total raised during the year................	$1,816,442.72	$3,425,523.11

"The Publishing Board of the National Baptist Convention is acting as trustees of the Convention in holding and managing the publishing concern. It is composed of a committee of nine, and the vacancies are filled by three each year. These form the charter or corporate members and are incorporated under the laws of Tennessee, and hold and operate the property in trust for the National Baptist Association, and are amenable to our Home Board. They, under the authority of our Home Board, have their regular organization of chairman, secretary and treasurer. The secretary and treasurer is one and the same person, who is required to execute and file in the courts of Davidson County a suitable and sufficient, well secured bond. This has been the requirement since this board was inaugurated in 1808.

"In order to curtail the expenses and economize in our work, the Home Missionary Board has operated its missionary and Bible work under the management of the Publishing Board, together with its publication work. The experiment has proved a profitable one, and we find that the business has been operated with less than one-half the expense of other denominations doing similar work. In fact, the Corresponding Secretary of the Home Mission Board, upon a meager salary, has operated the missionary work, and has acted as secretary, treasurer and general manager of the National Baptist Publishing Board. By blending the four offices into one we have been able to save the salary of three other secretaries. This is one of the great causes or economical provisions that have enabled your board to give a dividend to missions each year.

"The publishing plant and offices are located at the corner of Market and Locust streets, one-half block from the Louisville and Nashville passenger depot. Market street, is one of the greatest business thoroughfares in the city of Nashville. This plant occupies four brick buildings, one one-story, two two-story, and one three-story building. The scattered condition of the plant makes it very inconvenient to operate the machinery in carrying on the great volume of manufacturing that is necessary to supply the increasing demands of this institution.

"This plant consists of a large first-class steam boiler, two engines, a complete electric plant, a complete system of telephones, with a well-regulated set of the most improved power printing presses, a well-regulated bindery, with all the machinery and equipment that is commonly attached to the most modern printing and publishing plant, together with a complete composing room, with all of the modern paraphernalia, including linotype machines. This plant, with its stock, is fully worth to the denomination $100,000 and if it were in a stock company its stock, if placed at $100,000 would sell in the market at par, and its income would pay a creditable dividend.

"The board has been compelled to purchase and exchange a considerable amount of its machinery. The authorities or managers were unable to foresee the large increase of work that would be necessary to supply the necessities. They, therefore, supplied themselves with machinery and material in proportion to then present needs of the institution, but so marvelous has been the increase that the machinery and quarters were found inadequate to meet the demands. They have, therefore, been compelled to exchange old machinery and buy new at a considerable loss in the dealings. They have been compelled to lease or rent other buildings. These increased demands have also created a demand for more and better skilled laborers, and they have, therefore, been compelled to increase the wages in each department in order to secure the help needed.

"The Book Department of our work is divided into three departments. First, books bought of other publishers and dealers and sold with or without profit to supply the needs of our patrons. Secondly, books manufactured by ourselves for the exclusive use of the denomination. Third, books manufactured for the author as job work, and, at the same time, bought and retailed by our board. These three features of the book work constitute the major portion of our actual work.

"The periodical and Sunday-school departments deal almost exclusively with the rising element of our denomination. In other words, in this department we are preparing the future church. In this periodical department we are sending fresh publications to the homes of our churches each quarter, month and week. We are thereby moulding the doctrines and opinions and shaping the destiny of the future church and race. The expression that we now put forth may be criticized by some, but we give it as our opinion that it is impossible for any race of people to keep their identity, sway their influence, keep pace with other races, hold the influence over their offspring, unless they provide themselves with literature and keep before their rising generation the great men that are passing from the stage of action. Artists and poets have done more to make the Caucasian great than has the writer of prose. The Negro Baptists of this country, therefore, will be compelled to cease talking or discussing cheap literature for their children, but they must discuss, produce or provide literature capable of keeping the identity and increasing race pride of the rising generation or they must be entirely overshadowed by the dominant race of this country, and each child born of Negro parents must be brought to feel that his God has made him inferior by nature to other races with whom he comes in contact. We, therefore, feel the value of the literature produced by the National Baptist Publishing Board cannot be measured by dollars and cents.

"The following is a list and number of periodicals published and circulated by our Board during the years 1900, 1901, and 1902:

PERIODICALS.	1900.	1901.	1902.
Teachers	84,800	136,000	139,000
Advanced Quarterlies	416,000	244,000	543,000
Intermediate Quarterlies	175,000	244,000	250,000
Primary Quarterlies	275,000	380,000	332,000
Leaflets and Gems	557,000	528,000	585,000
Picture Lesson Cards	1,560,000	2,340,000	2,500,000
Bible Lesson Pictures	33,800	41,600	50,000
National Baptist Concert Quarterly	259,000	800,000	850,000
Child's Gem	6,000	. . . . . .	. . . . . .
Davidson's Questions	. . . . . .	. . . . . .	85,000
Boyd's Questions	. . . . . .	. . . . . .	85,000
National Baptist Easy Lessons	. . . . . .	. . . . . .	90,000
Total	3,366,600	4,713,600	5,509,000

"These periodicals have been published and mailed to our Sunday-schools at such prices as in reality do not pay for the expense of producing them. In fact, our thirty-two paged magazines are retailed to our Sunday-schools, with the postage paid, cheaper than blank paper could be received through the mail. We call the attention of the Convention to this fact in order that they may see and know under what difficulties we are laboring.

"We are glad to call the attention again this year to the department of our work of issuing circulars and tracts. We still hold to the opinion that more people are influenced by tracts than by any other publications, and, as we have had occasion to say in the preface of the introductory of one of our little booklets, that the colored people, more than any other in this country, need the use of short and concise tracts; that is, they need Bible doctrine, true gospel teaching, put in plain, simple, concise form, and furnished to them in such a way that they can read it. A glance at the census of 1900 will show that the illiteracy in the South reaches over 50 percent, but as this may be overdrawn, it is perfectly safe to say that 40 percent, of the colored people are illiterate, and 20 percent of those who can read and write are not fluent readers. Sixty percent, of those who can read are youths—children. Therefore, it is very essential that reading matter for these people must not be in large and soggy books, but must be in small books, booklets, tracts and pamphlets. Our board has endeavored to turn some attention to raising a tract fund, but has done very little as yet.

"We are in need of both money and writers to produce these tracts. Addresses, papers and sermons read or delivered before the different annual gatherings, if they were put in print and circulated among the people, would do much toward elevating them. We have been able this year to publish a few tracts for free distribution. We have been able to print and distribute through our free distribution system something over 40,000 tracts. These the writers have contributed free of charge.

RECEIPTS

BUSINESS DEPARTMENT

Balance on hand	$ 1,054.09
Fourth quarter, 1901	12,119.01
First quarter, 1902	10,825.69
Second quarter, 1902	15,884.82
Third quarter, 1902	18,782.77
Total receipts from Business Department	$ 58,666.38

RECEIPTS FROM MISSIONARY DEPARTMENT

From Woman's Auxiliary Convention	$ 75.00	
From Home Mission Board of Southern Baptist Convention	1,800.00	
From Woman's Auxiliary of Southern Baptist Convention .	50.00	
By missionary collections.	(a)3,538.37	
By special missionary collections.	(b) 281.35	
By designated collections.	(c) 79.80	$ 5,824.52

SPECIAL DONATIONS FOR BIBLES AND COLPORTAGE WORK

From Sunday-school Board of Southern Baptist Convention . .	$ 121.25
By other donations.	119.00
For colportage and book work	2,100.94
From special periodical donations.	230.90
From special tract donations.	109.36

For special Bible work in Africa. 35.71

From general missionary and Bible donation. 432.48 $3,149.64

SPECIAL SUBSCRIPTION, ADVERTISING, NEGOTIABLE NOTES AND OUTSTANDING ACCOUNTS

From subscriptions to *Union*. . . . . $ 499.91

From advertisements 510.00

From negotiable notes. 738.26

From periodicals uncollected. 1,129.57

From printing uncollected accounts. 2,205.58

Remaining in hands of colporters and missionaries
unreported. 1,683.78 $6,767.10

  Grand total. $74,407.64

DISBURSEMENTS
BUSINESS DEPARTMENT

Wages, printing material and Editorial Department. . . . . . . $ 30,326.54

Merchandise, notes, machinery and other miscellaneous. . . . 17,073.84

Coal, ice, freight, drayage, boarding horses, etc. 2,842.54

Rents, water tax, gas, commission, insurance, traveling
  and special missions. 2,127.92

Stamps, postage, telephone, telegrams, electricity, etc. 5,360.54

To balance in hand. 934.94

  Total disbursements of Business Department. . . . . . . $ 58,666.38

MISSIONARY DEPARTMENT

In salaries of district secretaries, state and local missionaries,
  male and female. . . . . $ 5,824.52

In expenses, books, Bibles, tracts and periodicals donated
  by them. 3,149.64

Salary of secretary, advertising, special traveling expenses,
  uncollected accounts, negotiable notes, manuscripts, etc. . . 6,767.10 $ 15,741.26

  Grand total. . . . . $ 74,407.64

"Notwithstanding the failure of crops of 1901, by glancing over the report of the work done for the year it will be seen that this institution is not only self-supporting, but besides defraying its own expenses, has been able to spend on missionaries and their traveling expenses $11,683.19, and on machinery, notes, etc., which stand as a sinking fund, $5,352.48, making a dividend to the denomination of $17,035.67; and, if we add in the $1,601.09 deficit for running the denominational paper, and the $3,335.15 outstanding accounts for work and periodicals during the year, and $1,683.78 in the hands of agents, missionaries and colporters unreported, it will be seen that the denomination has a clear dividend arising from the work of these boards of $23,655.69."

The Negro Baptists support eighty schools, as follows:

List of Institutions by States

STATES.	INSTITUTIONS.	LOCATIONS.
Alabama	Baptist University..........	Selma.
"	Normal College	Anniston.
"	Eufala Academy..........	Eufala.
"	Marion Academy	Marion.
"	Opelika High School	Opelika.
"	Thomsonville Academy.......	Thomsonville.
Arkansas	Aouchita Academy	Camden.
"	Baptist College	Little Rock.
"	Arkadelphia Academy	Arkadelphia.
"	Brinkley Academy	Brinkley.
"	Magnolia Academy	Magnolia.
Florida	Florida Baptist College	Jacksonville.
"	Florida Institute	Live Oak.
"	West Florida Baptist Academy ...	Pensacola.
Georgia	Americus Institute	Americus.
"	Walker Academy	Augusta.
"	Jeruel Academy	Athens.
"	Central City College..........	Macon.
Illinois	Southern Illinois Polytechnic Institute	Cario.
Indiana	Indiana Colored Baptist University ..	Indianapolis.
Indian Territory	Dawes Academy..............	
"	Sango Baptist College........	Muskogee.

Kentucky	State University.................	Louisville.
"	Cadez Theological Institute......	Cadez.
"	Female High School..............	Frankfort.
"	Glasgow Normal Institute.........	Glasgow.
"	Western College....................	Weakly.
"	Danville Institute...........................	Danville.
"	Hopkinsville College..............	Hopkinsville.
"	Eckstein Norton University......	Cane Springs.
Louisiana...............	Leland Academy....................	Donaldsonville.
"	Baton Rouge Academy.................	Baton Rouge.
"	Houma Academy..................	Houma.
"	Morgan City Academy............	Morgan City.
"	Howe Institute.......................	New Iberia.
"	Opelousas Academy..............	Opelousas.
"	Central Louisiana Academy......	Alexandria.
"	Baptist Academy....................	Lake Providence.
"	Monroe High School..............	Monroe.
"	Ruston Academy....................	Ruston.
"	Shreveport Academy..............	Alexandria.
"	Mansfield Academy..............	Mansfield.
"	North Louisiana Industrial High School	Monroe.
"	Meridian High School..............	Meridian.
"	Ministerial Institute.................	West Point.
"	Nettleton High School...........	Nettleton.
"	Greenville High School...........	Greenville.
"	New Albany High School.........	New Albany.
Missouri...............	Western College....................	Macon.
North Carolina	Wharton Industrial School.........	Charlotte.
"	Latta University....................	Raleigh.
"	High School.......................	Wakefield.
"	Shiloh Industrial Institute.........	Warrenton.
"	Thomson's Institute..............	Lumberton.
"	Addie Norris' Institute...........	Winston.
"	Training School....................	Franklinton.
"	Roanoke Institute.................	Elizabeth.
"	Albemarle Training School.........	Edenton.
"	Bertie Academy....................	Windsor.

Ohio......................	Curry School.......................	Urbana.
South Carolina.........	Mather School.......................	Beaufort.
"	Peace Haven Institute..............	Broad River.
Tennessee	Howe Institute......................	Memphis.
"	Nelson Merry College..............	Jefferson City.
"	Lexington Normal School.........	Lexington.
Texas...................	Guadalupe College.................	Seguin.
"	Central Texas Academy...........	Waco.
"	Houston Academy..................	Houston.
"	Hearne Academy....................	Hearne.
Virginia.................	Virginia Seminary and College...	Lynchburg.
	Union Industrial Academy.........	Port Conway

Total number of schools 80   Valuation of property.....$564,000

Twenty of the above school reported last year as follows:

Teachers, males 75
Teachers, females . . . . . . _73_
Total   148

Students, males 1,833
Students, females . . . . . . _1,531_
Total students 3,364

Total in Home Missionary Society
Schools . . . . _6,198_

Total in schools heard from 9,562

The value of property owned by these schools is as follows:

Alabama..................................... $ 39,500
Louisiana................................... 45,000
Missouri.................................... 15,000
Georgia..................................... 10,000
Mississippi................................. 77,000
Ohio.. 5,000
Arkansas.................................... 70,000
Maryland.................................... 6,000
Kentucky.................................... 65,000

Florida..	20,000
Tennessee...................................	33,000
Texas..	80,000
North Carolina............................	16,000
South Carolina............................	19,000
Virginia......................................	60,000
Indian Territory...........................	3,700
Total..	$ 564,200

The total income of the schools for 1902 was:

Arkansas.....................................	$ 35,000.00
Alabama......................................	10,500.00
North Carolina............................	2,700.00
Louisiana....................................	15,000.00
Mississippi..................................	9,100.00
Tennessee...................................	4,300.00
Florida..	16,000.00
Georgia.......................................	12,000.00
Maryland.....................................	585.00
Virginia......................................	25,000.00
Texas..	23,000.00
Ohio...	3,500.00
Kentucky.....................................	20,000.00
Missouri......................................	8,041.02
District of Columbia......................	400.00
Pennsylvania................................	857.75
Miscellaneous sources....................	238.00
Total..	$ 186,221.97

The total number of pupils in all these schools is not given. Twenty of them report 148 teachers and 3,364 pupils. Probably there are at least 6,000 or 7,000 pupils in all the schools. The institutions are for the most part primary and secondary schools, despite their pretentious names, and supplement the public schools.

Beside, these Negro Baptists have contributed largely to the Baptist schools of higher denomination, supported by the Northern white Baptists, for Negro students. The chief schools of this class are:

Baptist Schools
(Report of the United States Commissioner of Education, 1900–1)

PLACE.	SCHOOL.	Teachers	Students	Value of Lands, Buildings, etc.
Richmond, Va..............	Hartshorn Memorial College...	11	120	$50,000
Richmond, Va...........	Virginia Union University..........	13	157	300,000
Raleigh, N.C..............	Shaw University.....................	27	511	90,000
Winton, N.C...........	Water's Normal Institute.........	5	272	12,000
Columbia, S.C...........	Benedict College....................	16	488	76,000
Athens, Ga..............	Jeruel Academy.....................	5	221	2,500
Atlanta, Ga..............	Atlanta Baptist College...........	13	165	75,000
Augusta, Ga...........	Walker Baptist Institute.........	6	121	4,500
Jackson, Miss...........	Jackson College....................	10	102	35,000
Marshall, Tex........	Bishop College.....................	16	337	100,000
Nashville, Tenn.........	Roger Williams University......	13	268	200,000
Little Rock, Ark........	Arkansas Baptist College.........	9	213	25,000
Atlanta, Ga..............	Spelman Seminary.................	.....	......	....
Harper's Ferry, W. Va...	Storer College.....................	7	142	50,000
Hampton, Va..............	Spiller Academy.....................	6	103	10,000
Windsor, N.C...........	Bertie Academy.....................	2	96	1,000
LaGrange, Ga...........	LaGrange Baptist Academy......	4	182	1,000
New Orleans, La........	Leland University...................	11	115	150,000

In the words of the late General Morgan, secretary of the American Baptist Home Missionary Society, this society "has already spent more than $3,000,000 in their (i.e., the Negroes') behalf; the value of school property used for their benefit is not less than $1,000,000; its expenditure in their interest at present exceeds $1,000,000 a year. It has aided in the erection of a good number of meeting-houses."

The other departments of the church are of less relative importance. The Baptist Young People's Union Board spent $7,000 for its work; the National Board spent $8,302.29 for missions, with the following results:

SIERRA LEONE, WEST COAST AFRICA—Churches, 2; pastors and workers, 3; members, 40.

LIBERIA, WEST COAST AFRICA—Churches, 52; pastors and workers, 86; members, 3,000.

LAGOS, SOUTHWEST COAST AFRICA—Churches, 21; pastors and workers, 56; members, 2000.

CAPE COLONY, SOUTH AFRICA—Churches, 23; pastors and workers, 80; members, 1750.

CHIRADZULU BLANTYRE, EAST COAST AFRICA—Churches, 3; pastors and workers, 5; members, 35.

GEORGETOWN DEMERARA, BRITISH GUIANA, SOUTH AMERICA—Churches, 3; pastors and workers, 11; members, 310.

LAGWAN, EAST COAST, BRITISH GUIANA, SOUTH AMERICA—Churches, 1; pastors and workers, 2; members, 10.

SURINAM, DUTCH GUIANA, SOUTH AMERICA—Churches, 1; pastors and workers, 3; members, 30.

BARBADOES, BRITISH WEST INDIES, BRIDGETOWN—Churches, 1; pastors and workers, 5; members, 62.

There are churches at St. George, St. John, Christ Church and St. Thomas, on the island, with pastors and workers, 7, and members, 42.

There is a Convention organized separately from the regular organization. It had in 1902:

State Conventions	22
Mission Societies	4,033
Children's Bands	1,380
Sewing Circles	420
Circles of King's Daughters	120
Money raised during 1902	$ 3,800

There are the following newspapers published by Negro Baptists in the interest of that denomination:

NAME	Where Published
American Baptist	Louisville, Ky.
Baptist Leader	Selma, Ala.
Baptist Magazine	Washington, D.C
The Pilot	Winston, N.C
The Sentinel	Raleigh, N.C
Christian Banner	Philadelphia, Pa.
Baptist Herald	Live Oak, Fla.
Florida Evangelist	Jacksonville, Fla.
Georgia Baptist	Augusta, Ga.
Western Messenger	Macon, Mo.
National Baptist Union	Nashville, Tenn.

Virginia Baptist..	Richmond, Va.
Baptist Vanguard...	Little Rock, Ark.
The Western Star...	Houston, Tex.
The Baptist Truth...	Savannah, Ga.
The Baptist Truth...	Cairo, Ill.
The Christian Organizer.................................	Lynchburg, Va.
The South Carolina Standard...........................	Columbia, S.C.
Southern Watchman......................................	Mobile, Ala.
The Herald...	Austin, Tex.
People's Recorder...	Columbia, S.C.
The Informer	Urbana, O.
The Messenger..	New Orleans, La.
The American Tribune...................................	New Orleans, La.
Negro World...	Cary, Miss.
Guadaloupe College Recorder...........................	Seguin, Tex.
Advanced Quarterly (National Baptist Convention)...	Nashville, Tenn.
Intermediate Quarterly (National Baptist Convention)	"
Primary Quarterly (National Baptist Convetion)	"
The Teacher...	"
Child's Gems..	"
Easy Lesson Primer......................................	"
Preacher's Safeguard.....................................	"
Zion Church Bulletin.....................................	Denver, Col.
The Journal..	
The Clarion...	Nashville, Tenn.
The Blue Grass Bugle....................................	Frankfort, Ky.
The Moderator..	Louisville, Ky.
The Mission Herald.......................................	Louisville, Ky.
The Trumpet..	Washington, D.C
The Watchman..	Columbia, S.C.
The Pennsylvania Baptist................................	Pittsburg, Pa.
The Florida Baptist.......................................	Fernandina, Fla.

As to the general character of the churches and preachers the following statement, made by the Home Missionary Society about five years ago, seems a fair presentation:

> In the few large cities and towns of the South a minister usually serves one church; in the rural districts and small villages, where three-fourths of the Negro population are found, he has from two to four churches, and preaching "once't a month" is customary. Of the 12,000 churches in 1895, probably not 1,000 have preaching every Sunday. Except in the larger and more progressive churches ministers do very little pastoral work.

About fifteen ministers receive $1,500 or more; one per cent, about $1,000 each; fifteen per cent, from $500 to $700. The great majority get only $200 to $400; while many never see $100 in money yearly. These eke out their scanty salaries by manual labor. The people, generally, are very poor.

Many are noble, high-minded, upright, God-fearing, unselfish, sincere, self-sacrificing, who honor their high calling. Of a great number, however, it must be said in sorrow, that their moral standards are not at all in accord with those of the New Testament for the ministry. They have grown up in an environment unfavorable to the production of a high type of character. The development of a Christian conscience is a fundamental need. In some states and localities it is more difficult than formerly for unworthy men to be ordained.

Forty years ago, the minister who could read was the exception; now, the exception is one who cannot. Many, however, were too old to learn easily and made egregious blunders and understood what they read most imperfectly. Little could they learn in the very inferior country schools, maintained for only three or four months each year. Their knowledge was "picked up." There are sixty per cent, of the ministers whose libraries do not average a dozen volumes. Many, however, take a cheap religious paper. Yet among these are preachers of much native ability.

About 25 per cent have had approximately a fair common school education. Some spent a year or more at an academy or other higher school, where they also had a little instruction in the Bible and in preaching. A few got a start that led to intellectual and spiritual growth and power.

Possibly 20 per cent, have had something like an ordinary academic course. Full college graduates are rare; not 100 Negro Baptist ministers have had a full collegiate and theological course.

There are able preachers, whose sermons compare favorably with the average sermons of white preachers, in substance, diction and delivery. Most of these are the products of our Home Mission schools. They are an uplifting influence to their churches, and to their less favored brethren in the ministry.

But it may be safely said that two-thirds of the preaching is of the crudest character, emotional, hortatory, imaginative, visionary, abounding in misconceptions of scripture, the close of the sermon being delivered with powerful intonations and gesticulations to arouse the audience to a high pitch of excitement, which both preacher and people regard as indispensable to a "good meeting." Two members of a ministers' class recently made these statements to their colored instructor: one had preached that Joshua never had father or mother, because he was "the son of Nun," (none); the other wrought up his congregation mightily by repeatedly shouting: "Mesopotamia." Such instances can be multiplied indefinitely.

The religious phenomenon of this land, if not of this age, is in the fact that while our Negro population increased slightly more than two-fold in forty years, the Baptist increase among them was over fourfold. Negro preachers are remarkable evangelists in their way. Converts with weird and rapturous experiences are quickly baptized. With the survival of old-time notions concerning conversion, probably two-thirds of the churches are made up largely of "wood, hay and stubble." Nevertheless, in these are sincere, devout souls, in whom the Spirit of God seems to have wrought a genuine work and to whom he has given singularly clear views of truth. The process of emancipation from the old order of things is going on, largely under the leadership of men from our schools. Numerous churches maintain most orderly services, have good Sunday-schools, and young people's societies, and are interested in missions. Thousands of church edifices, some well equipped and very costly, bear witness to the zeal and devotion of the people, and to the persuasive power of their religious leaders.

23

The African Methodists

The greatest voluntary organization of Negroes in the world is probably the African Methodist Church. Its beginning had a tinge of romance, and this is the story: *

Between 1790 and 1800 the Negro population of Philadelphia County increased from 2,489 to 6,880, or 176 percent, against an increase of 43 per cent, among the whites. The first result of this contact with city life was to stimulate the talented and aspiring freedmen; and this was the easier because the freedman had in Philadelphia at that time a secure economic foothold; he performed all kinds of domestic service, all common labor and much of the skilled labor. The group being thus secure in its daily bread needed only leadership to make some advance in general culture and social effectiveness. Some sporadic cases of talent occur, as Derham, the Negro physician, whom Dr. Benjamin Rush, in 1788, found "very learned." Especially, however, to be noted are Richard Allen, a former slave of the Chew family, and Absalom Jones, a Delaware Negro. These two were real leaders and actually succeeded to a remarkable degree in organizing the freedmen for group action. Both had bought their own freedom and that of their families by hiring their time—Allen being a blacksmith by trade, and Jones also having a trade. When, in 1792, the terrible epidemic drove Philadelphians away so quickly that many did not remain to bury the dead, Jones and Allen quietly took the work in hand, spending some of their own funds, and doing so well that they were publicly commended by Mayor Clarkson in 1794.

The great work of these men, however, lay among their own race and arose from religious difficulties. As in other colonies, the process by which the Negro slaves learned the English tongue and were converted to Christianity is not clear. The subject of the moral instruction of the slaves

* Taken in part from "The Philadelphia Negro."

had early troubled Penn, and he urged Friends to provide meetings for them. The newly organized Methodists soon attracted a number of the more intelligent, though the masses seem at the end of the last century not to have been church-goers or Christians to any considerable extent. The smaller number that went to church were wont to worship at St. George's, Fourth and Vine. For years both free Negroes and slaves worshiped here, and were made welcome. Soon, however, the church began to be alarmed at the increase in its black communicants which the immigration from the country was bringing, and attempted to force them into the gallery. The crisis came one Sunday morning during prayer, when Jones and Allen, with a crowd of followers, refused to worship except in their accustomed places, and finally left the church in a body.

Allen himself tells of the incident as follows:

"A number of us usually sat on seats placed around the wall, and on Sabbath morning we went to church and the sexton stood at the door and told us to go to the gallery. He told us to go and we would see where to sit. We expected to take the seats over the ones we formerly occupied below not knowing any better. We took these seats; meeting had begun and they were nearly done singing, and just as we got to the seats, the elder said: 'Let us pray.' We had not been long upon our knees before I heard considerable scuffling and loud talking. I raised my head and saw one of the trustees— H. M.—having hold of Absalom Jones, pulling him up off his knees and saying, 'You must get up, you must not kneel here.' Mr. Jones replied, 'Wait until prayer is over and I will get up and trouble you no more.' With that he beckoned to one of the other trustees—Mr. L. S.—to come to his assistance. He came and went to William White to pull him up. By this time the prayer was over and we all went out of the church in a body, and they were no more plagued by us in the church. This raised a great excitement and inquiry among the citizens, insomuch that I believe they were ashamed of their conduct. But my dear Lord was with us, and we were filled with fresh vigor to get a house erected to worship God in."

This band immediately met together and on April 12, 1787, formed a curious sort of ethical and beneficial brotherhood called the Free African Society. How great a step this was, we of today scarcely realize. We must remind ourselves that it was the first wavering step of a people toward organized social life. This society was more than a mere club: Jones and Allen were its leaders and recognized chief officers; a certain parental discipline was exercised over its members and mutual financial aid given. The preamble of the articles of association says:

"Whereas, Absalom Jones and Richard Allen, two men of the African race, who for their religious life and conversation, have obtained a good report among men, these persons, from a love to the people of their own complexion whom they beheld with sorrow, because of their irreligious and uncivilized state, often communed together upon this painful and important subject in order to form some kind of religious body; but there being too few to be found under the like concern, and those who were, differed in their religious sentiments; with these circumstances they labored for some time, till it was proposed after a serious communication of sentiments that a society should be formed without regard to religious tenets, provided the persons lived an orderly and sober life, in order to support one another in sickness, and for the benefit of their widows and fatherless children."

The society met first at private houses, then at the Friends' Negro school-house. For a time they leaned toward Quakerism; each month three monitors were appointed to have oversight over the members; loose marriage customs were attacked by condemning cohabitation, expelling offenders, and providing a simple Quaker-like marriage ceremony. A fifteen-minute pause for silent prayer opened the meetings. As the representative body of the free Negroes of the city, this society opened communication with free Negroes in Boston, Newport, and other places.

The Negro Union of Newport, R.I., proposed, in 1788, a general exodus to Africa, but the Free African Society soberly replied: "With regard to the emigration to Africa you mention, we have at present but little to communicate on that head, apprehending every pious man a good citizen of the whole world." The society co-operated with the Abolition Society in studying the condition of the free blacks in 1790. At all times they seem to have taken good care of their sick and dead, and helped the widows and orphans to some extent. Their methods of relief were simple: they agreed "for the benefit of each other to advance one shilling in silver, Pennsylvania currency, a month; and after one year's subscription, from the dole thereof then to hand forth to the needy of the society, if any should require, the sum of three shillings, and nine pence per week of the said money; provided the necessity is not brought on by their own imprudence." In 1790 the society had £42 9s. 1d. on deposit in the bank of North America, and had applied for a grant of the potter's field, to be set aside as a burial ground for them, in a petition signed by Dr. Rush, Tench Coxe, and others.

It was, however, becoming clearer to the leaders that only a strong religious bond could keep this untrained group together. They would probably have become a sort of institutional church at first if the question of religious denomination had been settled among them; but it had not been, and for about six years the question was still pending. The tentative experiment in Quakerism had failed, being ill-suited to the low condition of the rank and file of the society. Both Jones and Allen believed that Methodism was best suited to the needs of the Negro, but the majority of the society, still nursing the memory of St. George's, inclined toward the Episcopal church. Here came the parting of the ways: Jones was a slow introspective man, with a thirst for knowledge, with high aspirations for his people; Allen was a shrewd, quick, popular leader, positive and dogged, and yet far-seeing in his knowledge of Negro character. Jones, therefore, acquiesced in the judgment of the majority, served and led them conscientiously and worthily, and eventually became the first Negro rector in the Episcopal church in America. About 1790 Allen and a few followers withdrew from the Free African Society, formed an independent Methodist Church, which first worshipped in his blacksmith's shop on Sixth street, near Lombard. Eventually this leader became the founder and first bishop of the African Methodist Episcopal Church of America.

Full figures as to the growth of this institution are not available, but there are enough to show its striking advance in a century from a dozen or more to three-quarters of a million members (see chart on the following page).

In 1818 a publishing department was added to the work of the church, but its efficiency was impaired on account of the great mass of its members being in slave states or the District of Columbia, where the laws prohibited them from attending school, and deprived them of reading books or papers. In 1817 Rev. Richard Allen published a book of discipline; and shortly after this a church hymn-book was published also. Beyond this there was little done in this department until 1841, when the New York Conference passed a resolution providing for the publication of a monthly magazine. But the lack of funds compelled the projectors to issue it as a quarterly. For nearly eight years this magazine exerted an excellent influence upon the ministers with a strong interest. It contained the news in each of the conferences; its editorials breathed a spirit of love and fellowship; and thus the members were brought to a knowledge of the work being accomplished. At length the prosperity of the magazine seemed to justify the publication of a weekly paper. Accordingly a weekly journal, named the "Christian Herald," made its appearance and ran its course for the space of four years. In 1852, by order of the General Conference, the paper was enlarged and issued as the "Christian Recorder", which has continued to be published up to the present time.

The department now publishes the *Recorder*, the *African Methodist Episcopal Review*, and various books.

The financing of so large an organization is a matter of great interest. In the quadrennium, 1896–1900, there was raised for the purposes of the general church organization on the average:

Growth of the African Methodist Episcopal Church

	1816	1826	1836	1846	1866	1876	1880	1900	1901
Bishops	1	2	3	4	4	6	9	13	13
General officers	....	....	....	....	....	3	4	....	12
Presiding elders	....	....	....	....	....	....	....	....	264
Annual conferences	2	2	4	6	10	25	40	....	....
Itinerant preachers	14	17	27	40	185	1,418	1,837	....	6,079
Local preachers	....	....	....	....	....	3,168	9,760	....	9,749
Members	3,000	....	7,270	....	....	172,806	391,044	561,550	688,354
Total members	....	7,927	....	....	....	213,469	402,638	663,746	762,580
Churches	....	....	....	198	285	1,833	2,051	5,630	5,715
Value of property	....	....	86	$90,000.00	$813,000	$3,064,911	....	$8,718,456	$10,360,131
Parsonages	....	....	$13,000.00	....	....	218	402	1,390	2,075
Value of total property	....	....	....	....	....	$3,203,711	$2,448,671	$9,309,973	$11,044,663
Schools	....	....	....	3	....	....	88	....	41
Raised for support of schools	....	....	....	....	$91,593	....	....	....	$125,650
Total money raised	$1,151.75	$1,385.88	....	$7,231.03	(?)	$447,624	....	....	....

Detailed figures showing the operations of seven fairly typical Annual Conferences follows:

Annual Conference Reports

	Virginia	Illinois	Indiana	Iowa	Ontario	Michigan	So. Carolina
Ministers	102	51	74	68	7	22	100
Members	9,116	4,085	4,196	4,237	377	1,345	18,787
Churches	38	74	60	52	9	24	196
Parsonages	35	35	36	26	4	17	52
Value churches and parsonages	$161,215.00	$83,190.00	$159,058.50	$246,265.00	$15,300.00	$280,032.89	$14,147.00
Indebtedness	64,739.61	23,304.44	15,493.77	61,006.42	5,737.90	8,467.29	10,212.14
Pastors' support	18,378.62	17,964.16	17,704.32	22,252.89	1,922.67	11,251.19	31,883.16
Total raised	70,514.67	31,707.00	39,608.95	76,426.85	4,217.52	17,688.40	47,883.38

Each year…………………………………	$ 236,194.79
Each month…………………………………	19,682.89
Each day…………………………………	656.09
Each minute…………………………………	.45

The bishops receive $2,000 a year; the general officers, $1,200. In 1826 the pastors averaged $50 and $60 a year in salary, and often had other work for a livelihood. In 1900 the average salary of presiding elders was $663.72; of preachers $204.18. There is a system of pensions for the widowed and superannuated partially in force. The funds for the church are of two sorts: local monies, raised for the local churches, and "Dollar" money (i.e., one dollar per member), for the general church. The dollar money, which amounts to over $100,000 a year, is divided as follows:

Forty-six percent to general financial department.

Thirty-six percent to the annual conferences.

Ten percent to church extension.

Eight percent to education.

The total amount raised by the church in the four years, 1896–1900, was:

Dollar money…………………………………	$ 403,401.62
Church extension…………………………………	64,474.00
Publishing Department…………………………………	71,313.83
Education…………………………………	270,988.54
Sunday-school Union…………………………………	77,159.46
Preacher's aid…………………………………	2,605.25
Missions…………………………………	64,836.39
Total…………………………………	$ 954,779.09

Salaries of presiding elders…………………………	$ 139,735.37
Salaries of ministers…………………………………	735,796.21
Traveling expenses…………………………………	29,594.00
Salaries of bishops…………………………………	18,000.00
Salaries of general officers…………………………………	12,300.00
Total *…………………………………	$ 935,425.58

Total raised in quadrennium, 1896–1900……………	$ 1,777,948.20
Total raised in quadrennium, 1892–1896………………	1,533,414.01
Total raised in quadrennium, 1888–1892………………	1,064,569.50

* Some of the items in this table are paid wholly or in part from the dollar money above.

Turning to the various departments, we have first the Publishing Department. The *Review* is an octavo publication of about 100 pages, and is now in its twentieth year. It has a circulation of perhaps 1,000 copies. The contents of the New Year's number, 1903, were:

The Mission of the African Methodist Episcopal Church to the Darker Races of the World—By C. J. Powell.

Publications and Literature of the African Methodist Episcopal Church—John E. Hagins.

The Fight of Hagar.—J. A. Adams.

The South Mountain Reservation.—Ralph Elwood Brock.

The Leadership of the Church and the Opportunity of the Ministry.—George W. Henderson.

The Opportunity of the Colored Young Men's Christian Association in the Work of Education.—F. D. Wheelock.

The Preacher at Hill Station.—Katherine D. Tillman.

St. Cecilia.

A New Year—Looking Before and After.—H. T. Kealing.

Joseph Parker's Prophecy.

Women—Life's Mirror; Character in Eyes; Foes to Embonpoint; Tennyson's Egotism.

Sociological—Loves the Game; Alone in Paris; Indian Territory.

Religious.—Some Questions and Answers.

Miscellaneous—Christmas; Christmas in the Orient; Who is Santa Claus? Keep Old Santa Claus; Winter; Music and Old Age; T. Thomas Fortune; The Strength of New England; Things to take to Church.

Editorial—The Review for 1903; President Roosevelt; Thomas B. Reed; Dr. Joseph Parker; You Count for One; The Stars for Us; The Good Old Times Worse than Our Times.

The *Recorder* is a weekly, eight-page paper, and is the oldest Negro periodical in the United States. It is taken up largely with church announcements and reports.

The Philadelphia house received $65,687.98 in the four years, 1896-1900. It is not self-supporting at present, although it has been at various periods in the past.

The outfit, including building and land, is valued at $45,500, on which there is a debt of $15,000. The branch establishment in Atlanta publishes the *Southern Christian Recorder*, a small weekly, at an annual cost of about $1,400.

In Nashville there is located the Sunday-school Union, a publishing house for Sunday-school literature. It has valuable real estate and had an income of $77,159.46 during the quadrennium, or a little less than $20,000 a year.

The mission work at home and abroad has been vigorously pushed in recent years, and in the thirty-six years from 1864 to 1900 this church has spent $2,102,150.75 in mission work. It has today in Africa 180 missions and over 12,000 members, beside missions in Canada and the West Indies. Over $60,000 was raised for missions in the last four years.

There is some indebtedness on the general church property. The total value of churches and parsonages was $9,309,937 in 1900, on which there was a debt of $1,068,995. *A. M. E.*

The African Methodist Episcopal Church began in 1844 to start schools for Negroes. A committee was appointed and founded Union Seminary. Later this institution was united with Wilberforce University, which was bought by the church from the white Methodist Church. Thus Wilberforce, dating from 1856, is the oldest Negro institution in the land. The church has now about twenty-five schools in all. They are supported from three sources: 1. Tuition, etc., paid by students; 2. Donations and bequests; 3. Appropriations from the general fund of the church. From these sources about $275,000 was raised in the four years, 1896-1900; and since 1884, when the general educational department was organized, there has been raised $1,250,000 for education. The figures are:

Schools...............................	25
Teachers...............................	140
Average attendance, four years..	3,693
Acres of land..........................	1,482
Buildings...............................	51
Value of property.....................	$ 535,00.00
Raised and appropriated 1896–1900......	270,988.54
Raised and appropriated 1884–1900......	1,140,013.31

The schools are:

African Methodist Episcopal Schools

SCHOOLS.	Established.	Scholars.	Teachers.	Property.	Receipts, four years.
Payne Theological Seminary, Wilberforce, O...	1891	37	3	$13,000	$15,360.48
Wilberforce University, Wilberforce, Ohio......	1856	311	20	158,000	85,923.23
Morris Brown College, Atlanta, Ga................	1880	350	17	75,000	35,248.69
Kittrel College, Kittrel, N.C.................	1886	136	8	30,000	31,372.46
Paul Quinn College, Waco, Tex....................	1881	203	8	80,000	28,510.56
Allen University, Columbia, S.C..............	1880	285	8	35,000	19,365.05
Western University, Quindan, Kan.................	......	90	10	75,000	15,637.53
Edward Waters College, Jacksonville, Fla.......	1883	172	8	25,000	12,873.85
Shorter University, North Little Rock, Ark.....	1887	110	4	10,250	11,929.44
Payne University, Selma, Ala.................	......	233	9	3,000	5,981.00
Campbell-Stringer College, Jackson, Mo.........	......	100	2	10,300	4,272.85
Wayman Institute, Harrodsburg, Ky............	1891	50	1	2,760	2,618.08
Turner Normal Institute, Shelbyville, Tenn......	1887	79	3	3,500	2,030.36
Flagler High School, Marion, S.C	....	161	3	1,500	700.00
Delhi Institute, Delhi, La....................	......	57	3	3,000	....
Sission's High School, South McAlister, I.T...	....	35	2	....	332.78
Blue Creek and Muscogee High School, I.T.	......	......	......	....	....
Morsell Institute, Hayti......	....	....	....	....	....
Bermuda Institute, Bermuda......................	......	......	......	....	....
Zion Institute, Sierra Leone, Africa.........	......	......	......	....	....
Eliza Turner School, Monrovia, Africa.........	......	......	......	....	....
Cape Town Institute, Cape Town, Africa.......	......	......	......	....	....

In 1901 there were 175 teachers, 6,725 students and 6,696 graduates from forty-one schools, valued at $865,574.

The church extension work received $64,474 during the quadrennium, and there was $1,742.25 paid to preachers' widows. The total ministerial insurance in force amounted to $80,000.

The African Methodist Episcopal Church, however, is chiefly noteworthy on account of its Board of Bishops. A board of thirteen men more or less wield the power directly over 750,000 American Negroes, and indirectly over two or more millions, administer $10,000,000 worth of property and an annual budget of $500,000. These bishops are elected for life by a General Conference meeting every four years. The membership of the General Conference consists of ministerial and lay delegates: the clerical delegates are elected from the Annual Conferences, one for every thirty ministers. Two lay delegates for each Annual Conference are selected by the representatives of the official church boards in the Conference. Thus we have a peculiar case of Negro government, with elaborate machinery and the experience of a hundred years. How has it succeeded? Its financial and numerical success has been remarkable as has been shown. Moreover, the bishops elected form a remarkable series of personalities. Together the assembled bishops are perhaps the most striking body of Negroes in the world in personal appearance: men of massive physique, clear cut faces and undoubted intelligence. Altogether the church has elected about thirty bishops.

These men fall into about five classes. First, there were those who represented the old type of Negro preacher—men of little learning, honest and of fair character, capable of following other leaders. Perhaps five or six of the African Methodist Episcopal bishops have been of this type, but they have nearly all passed away. From them developed, on the one hand, four men of aggressive, almost riotous energy, who by their personality thrust the church forward. While such men did much for the physical growth of the church they were often men of questionable character, and in one or two instances ought never to have been raised to the bishopric. On the other hand, in the case of four other bishops, the goodness of the older class developed toward intense, almost ascetic piety, represented pre-eminently in the late Daniel Payne, a man of almost fanatic enthusiasm, of simple and pure life and unstained reputation, and of great intellectual ability. The African Methodist Episcopal Church owes more to him than to any single man, and the class of bishops he represents is the salt of the organization. Such a business plant naturally has called to the front many men of business ability, and perhaps five bishops may be classed as financiers and overseers. The rest of the men who have sat on the bench rose for various reasons as popular leaders—by powerful preaching, by pleasing manners, by impressive personal appearance. They have usually been men of ordinary attainment, with characters neither better nor worse than the middle classes of their race. Once in office they have usually grown in efficiency and character. On the whole, then, this experiment in Negro government has been distinctly encouraging. It has brought forward men varying in character, some good and some bad, but on the whole decency and ability have been decidedly in the ascendancy, and the church has prospered.

25

The Zion Methodists

The history of the African Methodist Episcopal Zion Church has already been given. * From the 1,500 members of 1821 it has grown until it claimed, in 1904, 551,591 adherents. Some facts about the church, as given at the twenty-first quadrennial session, are:

"In May, 1896, the ordained ministry of the church numbered 2,473; this has increased in four years to 2,902, an addition of 429. The number of church edifices, which were 3,612, has increased to 4,841, an addition of 229. The membership of 409,441 has swollen to 528,461, an increase of 119,020. These, with an approximate transient membership of 12,000, and denominational adherents of 125,000, will give the church a following of nearly 668,000. The increase has been well proportioned in each department of the church. The average increase per year for the ministry is 107; of increase in church buildings, 57, and members, 29,755.

"The valuation of church property, including real estate of every description, church, parsonages, schools, general departments, and other buildings, is estimated at $4,865,372, on which rests a total indebtedness of only $758,400. The rate of reduction of property indebtedness slightly exceeds its increase, the financial wave of 1899 contributing largely to this pleasing result. The African Methodist Episcopal Zion is the least debt-encumbered of any of the large Negro denominations. The growth in material interests has been rapid, while the denominational indebtedness has fallen thirty percent A number of magnificent churches have been erected, completed, or extensively rebuilt or remodeled.

"The African Methodist Episcopal Zion Church ranks fourth in the family of Methodism; second in Negro Methodism, and thirteenth in denominational standing in the United States. Beginning in 1896 without a single denominational Christian Endeavor Society, we have today more

* P.45.

than 600, with a membership of about 30,000. We are happy to say our number of societies and members is constantly increasing.

"Current expenses were per annum, $153,700; for the quadrennium, $614,800; on church debt and building new churches, per annum, $940,999; for the quadrennium, $3,763,996. This, with the general fund, missionary and other revenue to the church, will aggregate for the four years $11,449,800."

The amounts of money for general purposes raised by this connection during four years is as follows, made up of the following items:

Bishops..	$ 64,378.78
Livingstone College.............................	11,421.53
General Secretary.................................	1,516.09
General Steward..................................	1,162.11
Star of Zion..	2,462.65
Book Concern.....................................	1,770.62
Quarterly Review................................	881.10
Sunday-school Department....................	1,077.91
Expenses General Secretary....................	1,230.55
Expenses General Steward.....................	1,148.34
Mrs. J. C. Price...................................	1,669.16
Bishop Jones' estate.............................	417.19
Bishop Moore's estate...........................	1,175.02
Bishop Thompson's estate......................	1,159.03
Funeral expenses.................................	75.00
Superannuated ministers........................	1,746.99
Total...............................	$ 93,292.07

The following sums were raised for education:

School and College Statistics
(Several of the schools had not reported when this report was read.)

NAME OF SCHOOL.	No. of Teachers.	No. of Students.	Amount Collected per Quadrennium.	Value of Plants.
Livingstone College...	14	267	$57,193.05	$117,950
Clinton Institute........ Institute.................	5	202	3,450.00	5,000
Lancaster Institute...	6	277	5,038.00	4,500
Greenville College...	3	125	2,705.66	3,000
Hannon and Lomax	2	80	300.00	1,500

Walters Institute......	2	72	300.00	1,000
Mobile Institute......	.....	......	1,500.00	2,000
Jones University...	.....	......	530.00	....
Money raised by	.....	......	568.50	....
Secretary............				
Totals..........	32	1,023	$71,585.21	$134,950

There were the following additional schools:

Atkinson College, Madisonville, Ky.

Palmetto Institute, Union, S.C.

Edenton Industrial High School, Edenton, N.C.

Lloyd Academy, Elizabethtown, N.C.

Hemphill High School, Crockett, Ga.

Pettey Academy, Newborn, N. C.

Lomax and Rutler Academy, Tampa, Fla

Carr Academy, North Carolina

Lee Institute, Amite City, La.

Pettey Institute, Calvert, Tex.

African Methodist Episcopal Zion High School, Norfolk, Va.

The publishing house had an income of $30,949 in the last four years, and publishes the *Star of Zion*, a weekly paper, the *African Methodist Episcopal Zion Review*, a quarterly, and other literature. The church extension department raised but $1,400, and $2,103 was spent for missions.

26

The Colored Methodists

The Colored Methodist Episcopal Church * started with 80,000 members and two bishops in 1866, and has grown as follows:

	1872.	1896.	1900.
Bishops......................	3	5	6
Itinerant preacher.........	635	1,400	....
Local preachers...........	583	2,500	....
Members....................	67,889	200,000	....

The church collected $145,707 during the four years, 1898–1902. The bishops receive $2,000 a year, and the church supports the following educational institutions:

Name.	Expenditures, Four Years.
Lane College....................................	$ 11,718
Payne Institute [†]..............................	7,466
Haygood Seminary............................	1,794
Homer Seminary...............................	1,927
Texas College...................................	3,157

The Publishing Department expended $12,960 in the quadrennium, and has a plant worth $20,000. This church is often put on the defensive by reason of its origin, but it accepts the challenge boldly:

* Cf. page 46.
† The Methodist Church, South, helps support this school.

"The Colored Methodist Episcopal Church, organized in 1870, is, as you well know, the daughter of the Methodist Episcopal Church, South. We are not ashamed of our origin; nor do we regret the relation which we sustain to that church. We are not forgetful of the fact that the Christianity and Methodism which our fathers enjoyed were largely due to the zeal and labors of Southern Methodist pioneers. The first labors of Bishop John Early were among the slaves of Thomas Jefferson, in Bedford County, Va. Bishop Capers deserves to be called the 'Founder of Missions to the Slaves'; James O. Andrew, ninth bishop of the Methodist Episcopal Church, whose history is pretty well known to these two great bodies of Methodism, frequently rose to superhuman heights of eloquence when pleading for the religious training of the enslaved Negro. Since emancipation no Southerner has done more to ameliorate the condition of the freedman than the author of 'Our Brother in Black.' Bishop Haygood, by his unselfish labors, reflected himself upon the current of the ages as the mountain mirrors itself in the gentle stream which flows at its base. These men, and many others whom I could mention, will ever live upon the tablets of our memory." [*]

Methodists — apparently very against slavery

---

[*] Bishop Phillips, in Fraternal Address to the African Methodist Episcopal Church.

27

The Methodists

All of the above represent branches of Methodism and agree in doctrine and discipline save in a few minor points. There was in earlier times talk of some of them rejoining the parent body; later there have been negotiations looking to the union of the African Methodists and Zionists, and negotiations are pending for a union of the Colored Methodists and Zionists. The chances are that some union will eventually take place, but how soon it is difficult to say. Meantime large numbers of Negroes have remained in the Methodist Episcopal Church, and this colored membership increases. In 1902 we have the following figures:

Methodist Episcopal Church—Negro Membership

CONFERENCES.	Full Membership.	Valuation.	Monies Raised.
Central Missouri..........	6,909	$ 200,606	$ 34,994
Delaware....................	19,288	552,251	104,055
Florida......................	4,490	79,943	14,674
Liberia......................	2,832	75,520	3,346
Little Rock.................	5,018	85,148	15,543
Louisiana...................	14,178	344,820	65,356
Lexington..................	9,558	301,775	49,341
Mississippi.................	18,042	181,070	35,907
Upper Mississippi........	19,721	161,149	38,927
Washington................	26,980	988,193	98,065
Atlanta.....................	13,028	181,138	28,017
Central Alabama..........	5,149	65,700	11,470
East Tennessee..........	4,700	111,380	16,298
Mobile......................	5,546	71,235	11,829
North Carolina............	9,912	116,170	23,481

CONFERENCES.	Full Membership.	Valuation.	Monies Raised.
Savannah..................	7,648	77,442	15,297
South Carolina.............	39,490	408,834	60,548
Tennessee.................	8,598	97,622	22,377
Texas........................	13,045	273,700	35,940
West Texas.................	11,792	193,255	31,935
Total......................	245,954	$4,566,951	$ 717,400

It is of interest to know how much this element contributes to the church. (1) From 1900 to 1903, inclusive, the society appropriated to colored schools $449,119. (2) The colored membership of the church gave of this amount $227,321.53, and beside this they gave as a special contribution towards buildings and debts $55,601.69. Add to this amount their other contribution for Student Help for the same period of $12,599.40 and you have a grand total of $292,522.62 contributed by the colored people in this church towards their education for four years. It must be remembered, however, that the Student Help money passes through the Board of Education. (3) We raised for missions during the same period $83,131.23. The Church Extension Board spent $591,132 in aiding colored churches, 1864–1901, and has collected $81,514 from these churches. The Freedman's Aid Society has spent over $7,000.000 in Negro education. It maintains the following schools:

INSTITUTIONS.	Teachers Past Year.	Students Past Year.	Estimated Value of Property
THEOLOGICAL.			
Gammon Theological Seminary, Atlanta, Ga......	4	48	$ 100,000
COLLEGIATE.			
Bennett College, Greensboro, N.C..................	16	205	60,000
Claflin University, Orangeburg, S.C..............	58	609	110,000
Clark University, Atlanta, Ga.....................	35	603	350,000
George R. Smith College, Sedalia, Mo.........	15	144	50,000
Morgan College, Baltimore, Md..................	24	286	35,000
New Orleans University, New Orleans, La......	25	503	125,000
Philander Smith College, Little Rock, Ark......	17	521	30,000
Rust University, Holly Springs, Miss............	40	334	125,000
Walden University, Nashville, Tenn............	56	1,104	125,000
Wiley University, Marshall, Tex..............	30	501	64,000
Total......................................	320	4,858	$ 1,174,000

INSTITUTIONS.	Teachers Past Year.	Students Past Year.	Estimated Value of Property
ACADEMIC.			
Alexandria Academy, Alexandria, La............	2	122	18,000
Central Alabama Academy, Huntsville, Ala...	5	148	8,000
Cookman Academy, Jacksonville, Fla.........	6	194	21,000
Delaware Academy, Princess Anne, Md......	.....	....	......
Gilbert Academy, Baldwin, La.................	11	219	60,000
Haven Academy, Waynesbor, Ga..............	3	241	5,000
La Grange Academy, La Grange, Ga.........	3	154	8,000
Meridian Academy, Meridian, Miss...........	8	404	8,000
Morristown Academy, Morristown, Tenn...	27	371	75,000
Sam Houston College, Austin, Tex...........	16	252	48,000
Virginia Collegiate and Industrial Inst.,			35,000
Lynchburg, Va...................................			
Total....................................	81	2,105	$ 286,000
MEDICAL.			
Meharry Medical School, Walden University*	.....	339	....
Flint Medical College, New Oleans, La......	.....	....	$ 20,000
Sarah Goodridge Nurse-training	13	72	18,000
School and Hospital, New Orleans, La			
Total....................................	13	411	$ 38,000
Total..	414	7,374	1,498,000

*Faculty included in Walden University.

The history of the Negro in the Methodist Episcopal Church is, however, of far-reaching interest in any study of the relation of the races. This is the one church with a centralized episcopal government which has a large Negro membership, and the efforts to adjust the races in this organization throw light on the problem in the whole country. This history may be graphically illustrated as follows:

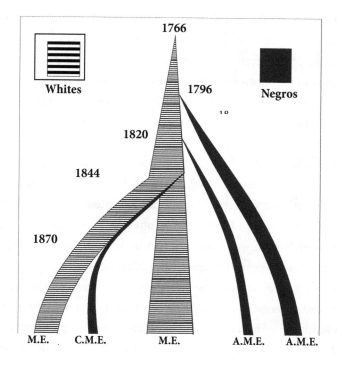

We have clearly discussed the secession of the African Methodist Episcopal, African Methodist Episcopal Zion Church and the setting off of the Colored Methodist Episcopal. These churches, by their individual development, have settled the question of the ability of the Negro in self-organization and self-direction of his religious life. But it was left to the Methodist Church to struggle with the more baffling problem of the relation of the races in one organization. Something has already been said of the Methodists and slavery and the split of 1844. * Even before that serious questions of color had arisen outside the slavery problem. The General Conference of 1800 settled the first of these questions by enacting that bishops could *"ordain deacons of our African brethren* in places where they have built a house or houses for the worship of God," the only limitation being the possibility of finding suitable men. The next question arose after the secession of 1844 had left many Negro congregations in the border states without their usual white pastors; they petitioned the General Conference of 1848 for colored ministers and colored Annual Conferences; the Conference declared "that the organization of such (separate) Conferences" was "at present inexpedient," but it authorized the employment of *itinerant colored ministers* at the discretion of the bishops. No regular appointment was usually made to these congregations, but they were left "to be supplied" by the colored itinerants. In 1852, however, the General Conference directed "that the colored

* P. 21.ff.

local preachers now employed within the bounds of the Philadelphia and New Jersey Annual Conferences be assembled together once each year by the bishop or bishops for the purpose of conferring with the said colored local preachers with respect to the best means of promoting their work and also for the purpose of assigning their work respectively." This was virtually a *Colored Annual Conference* in all but name, and meant the dividing of identical territory with separate Conferences along the color line.

Four years later the color question rose in a different guise. The church had been working in Africa, especially Liberia, and now the members there asked for a *missionary bishop*. The General Conference assented and ordained Francis Burns, a Negro, to the bishopric of Liberia, October 14, 1856; in 1866 the Rev. John W. Roberts, another Negro, was ordained to this same bishopric. These were the first and, so far, the only Negro bishops in the Methodist Episcopal Church. The same Conference of 1856 recognized further the principle of *colored Annual Conferences* all over the land whenever "the holding of said Conference or Conferences shall be recommended by an Annual Conference, and the bishops upon due inquiry, shall deem it practicable and expedient." At the same time it was declared that, "Our colored preachers and official members shall have all the privileges which are usual to others in Quarterly Conferences, where the usages of the comity do not forbid it," otherwise separate Quarterly Conferences could be held. The General Conference also secured Wilberforce University as a seat of Negro education, but afterward sold it to the African Methodist Episcopal Church in 1863 for a nominal sum.

In 1860 the General Conference raised the colored Annual Conferences to full powers and that of 1864 urged the extension of the system to the South, and began to organize the great work of aiding the freedmen. Negroes first sat as *delegates in a General Conference* in 1868 in Chicago. The church spread among the Negroes of the South, many preachers were ordained, and when the General Conference of 1872 met they were faced by a *demand for a Negro bishop*. The question was shelved by declaring the eligibility of Negroes to the office but the absence of any obvious candidate. In 1876 the demand came again, but the General Conference escaped the dilemma by deciding to elect no new bishops. The committee on episcopacy at the Conference of 1880 after considerable deliberation recommended "that this General Conference elect one bishop of African descent, "but the Conference postponed the matter by a vote of 228 to 137. Since this time Negroes have been elected to seven general offices, * involving the superintendence of matters concerning the Negroes,

* These officers are: Rev. M. C. B. Mason, D. D., Corresponding Secretary Freedman's Aid Society; Rev. I. B. Scott, D. D., Editor *Southwestern Christian Advocate*; Professor I. Garland Penn, Assistant General Secretary Epworth League; Rev. G. G. Logan, D. D., Field Secretary Missionary Society; Rev.

and while a Negro candidate for bishop has received a large vote, no Negro has been elected. In all probability the matter will eventually be settled by electing one or more Negroes as suffragan bishops, with special charge of Negro Conferences and churches.

This evolution has been of great interest and will be in the future as showing a peculiar process of adjustment between two groups of people in spite of strong centrifugal forces. May it not in a way prefigure the national struggle?

Robert E. Jones, D. D., and Rev. C. C. Jacobs, D. D., Field Secretaries Sunday-school Union; Mr. W. F. Waters, Assistant Business Manager *Southwestern Christian Advocate*. The last five of these men were elected by the General Boards, the other two by the General Conference: all are official.

28

The Episcopalians

We now come to the churches where the Negro forms but a small percentage of the membership. Archdeacon Pollard gives the following facts concerning Negro Episcopalians in 1903:

> The field of the work among the colored people covers twenty-one Dioceses and three Missionary Districts—all in the Southern States—and ministering specifically to 20,000 persons, of whom 8,000 are communicants, worshipping in 200 churches and chapels, and in charge of more than 100 clergymen. The workers actually number 108 clergymen, 65 laymen and 145 women, or 318 persons in all.
>
> In the entire country today there are eighty-five colored clergymen engaged in the work of the church, about 15,000 communicants, and upwards of $50,000 placed annually as an offering upon the altar. As far as I have been able to trace with certainty, 146 colored men have been admitted to Holy Orders in this church, and two consecrated bishops. The Rt. Rev. James Theodore Holly, D. D., the first bishop of Haiti, was born in Washington, D. C., and consecrated bishop in the year 1874. The Rt. Rev. Samuel David Ferguson, D. D., D. C. L., the fourth missionary bishop of Cape Palmas and parts adjacent, West Africa, was born near Charleston, S. C., and consecrated in the year 1885. Forty-two (42) colored clergymen ordained in this church served their day and generation faithfully and then passed into the paradise of God. Seven (7) felt called to other lands and are now out of the country, but still engaged in ministerial work, while twelve (12), for various causes, were deposed. Some of these last are today among the most active, learned and honorable men in the denominations around us.

Although the Episcopal Church was the first American church to receive Negro members, the growth of that membership has been small. This was the one great church that did not split on the slavery question, and the result is that its Negro membership before and since the war has been a delicate subject, and the church has probably done less for black people than any other aggregation of Christians.

What colored churchmen think of their treatment is best shown in this extract from the *Church Advocate*, one of their organs:

> The Church Commission for Work among the Colored People at a late meeting decided to request the various rectors of parishes throughout the South to institute Sunday-schools and special services for the colored population "such as were frequently found in the South before the war." The Commission hope for "real advance" among the colored people in so doing. We do not agree with the Commission with respect to either the wisdom or the efficiency of the plan suggested. In the first place, this "before the war" plan was a complete failure so far as church extension was concerned, in the past when white churchmen had complete bodily control of their slaves. We are going to quote from the Journals of Conventions of the Diocese of Virginia, since Virginia is a fair type of Southern States.
>
> The Journals of Virginia will verify the contention, that during the "before the war" period, while the bishops and a large number of the clergy were always interested in the religious training of the slaves, yet as matter of fact there was general apathy and indifference upon the part of the laity with respect to this matter.
>
> At various intervals resolutions were presented in the Annual Conventions with the avowed purpose of stimulating an interest in the religious welfare of the slaves. But despite all these efforts the Journals fail to record any great achievements along that line.
>
> In the Convention of 1840, a preamble recited the great and urgent need for such work, and after appealing to the final reckoning as an occasion of condemnation to the master class who have neglected the members of this "degraded race," certain resolutions were presented and adopted: a committee of seven was appointed to consider and report upon the matter. This committee consisted of the two bishops, two clergymen and three laymen. Among other things they were to report to the Convention "the most efficient system of oral religious instruction, both public and private," and further, they were to give such information as would determine the "proper subjects of baptism, both infant and adult."
>
> In the Convention of 1841 the committee was continued.
>
> In the Convention of 1856 the committee reported as follows:
>
> "We commend the establishment of Sunday-schools in our bounds, by the masters and mistresses in our church for colored children, where the instruction would be exclusively oral and governed by the standards of our church:

"In connection with these, and as perhaps more important and auxiliary, the catechetical instruction of young servants by their masters and mistresses of our church, in their families, is strongly recommended. And we further distinctly approve of the plan of making such domestic arrangements as will allow and encourage servants to attend upon the public services of the sanctuary, as well as at family prayers."

Two years later, in 1858, the following action was taken:

"Resolved, That a special committee be appointed to ascertain from the parishes, and to report to the next Convention whether any, and if any, "what provision is made for the instruction of the colored population of their limits."

In the Convention of 1859 resolutions were adopted looking to the maintenance of "missionary services with the slaves," and for building houses of worship for them.

In the Convention of 1860, which met at Charlottesville, a somewhat more elaborate plan of operation was presented and adopted, which in brief may be described as follows: 1. Separate and distinct congregations. 2. Provision of suitable place of worship; trustees chosen by contributors and appointed by the court. 3. A certain number to be taken from the communicants, to assist the minister in the affairs of the congregation, with special reference to the admission, supervision and discipline of church members. In the first place these were to be appointed by the minister. Vacancies to be filled by the communicants, subject to the approval of the minister. 4. The minister always to be a clergyman of the Diocese, either a rector within the bounds, or a missionary appointed by the executive committee of the Diocesan Missionary Society, with the approval of the bishop.

At this same Convention in 1860 a committee was appointed to consider the importance of more generally procuring baptism for children of slaves of members of the church.

So much for ante-bellum relations. So faithful had been the work under such conditions that as late as 1879 there were less than 200 colored communicants reported in the whole state of Virginia. The next ten years in Virginia, 1879-1889, constituted the most glorious period, so far as church extension is concerned, among colored people in the entire history of the Diocese. God richly blessed the efforts put forth so that the list of communicants was increased to nearly 1,000, a native Negro ministry of some ten clergymen raised up. With this auspicious blessing of the Almighty, on the part of some of the white brethren came the "color" question, and the work has never since advanced as before.

At the Convention of 1856, embracing the territory now included in the states of Virginia and West Virginia, there were reported, of colored people, forty-three adult baptisms, 244 infant baptisms, and forty-seven confirmed; the whole number of communicants in this territory being only 235. And four years later, 1860, instead of an increase there was a decided decrease, the figures being as follows: Adult baptisms, 12; infants, 166; confirmed, 22; total number of communicants, 114.

Bishop Johns, in his Convention address of 1860, in his Journal notes in connection with his attendance upon the General Convention which met in Richmond, Va., in 1859, says:

"October 3–23d—During the session of the Convention I was privileged, in common with several of the bishops and other clergy, to address the large and interesting congregations of colored people assembled in the Baptist and Methodist African Churches. We have no such congregations there or elsewhere in the Diocese, and for our delinquency in this I should find it hard to furnish a satisfactory excuse."

What a significant statement! The Episcopal Church, when its white members commanded even the bodies of their slaves, backed by all the prestige and influence of the church in Virginia, failed to any degree to get hold of the colored people.

In South Carolina the complete failure of ante-bellum instruction to result in definite church extension among the Negroes was even more disastrous.

The Journal of the Convention of South Carolina for 1856 shows 424 white baptisms against 975 colored baptisms, and 210 white persons confirmed against 414 colored persons confirmed. There were reported 2,971 white communicants, against 3,022 colored communicants.

In spite of this faithful ante-bellum instruction, when the colored people became free they left the church. They preferred, as they do now, the ministrations of their own, in leadership as well. We might ask the question how well has Archdeacon Joyner of South Carolina succeeded in bringing them back into the church in later days? Let us answer by a few statistics. We take these statistics from official sources, directly the Journals of the Convention of South Carolina.

In 1892 the total of colored communicants in that Diocese was 745. Ten years later, 1902, the total is 859. But of this 859, 356 belong to St. Mark's, Charleston, leaving a balance of 503 pertaining to the Archdeaconry of South Carolina. By this we fail to see any actual gain whatever. But taking the figures of 1903 we have in South Carolina 638 communicants exclusive of St. Mark's congregation. Hence, after deducting 237 communicants of St. Mark's from the total of 745 in 1892, we have as Archdeacon Joyner's portion then 508 communicants. Eleven years later this 508 has become 638.

The auditor who examined the accounts of the Archdeacon for 1892, certified of expenditures amounting to $11,330.25, and for the year 1903 the auditor certifies of expenditures in the neighborhood of $20,000. For the eleven years we have an increase of 130 communicants.

The method of special services for colored people, "colored Sunday-school," not only failed in ante-bellum days, but it has also failed in later years since the war. It is very far from us to contend that these efforts were in vain and without substantial good. Much good was the outcome of such efforts. They helped to mould and build solid characters. But they helped scarcely one iota in church extension or in making churchmen of colored people. The people got the instruction and the material help, and went off to the Baptists or Methodists.

Take an illustration of this same idea in the city of Baltimore. Twelve of fifteen years ago there were large and enthusiastic "colored" Sunday-schools in connection with the following white parishes in Baltimore: St. Peter's Church of the Ascension, St. Michael's and All Angels, and Emanuel Church. At Towson there was both a parish and Sunday-school; also a similar condition obtained at Claggett Chapel, Anne Arundel County, and at West River.

And yet today there is no indication whatever that such Sunday-schools were ever in existence, save here and there a communicant in the two exclusively colored congregations of churchmen in this city. So far as doing good is concerned, a great deal of good was done by these several schools, for many of their former pupils have become reliable and reputable men and women, Christian workers in Baptist and Methodist Churches. But with respect to church extension the idea has been a failure. Twenty years ago the late Rev. Dr. Dashiell, Secretary of the Virginia Council, said:

"In consideration, therefore, of the church's duty to the Negro, we are not deliberating concerning one who will be entirely quiescent. The colored people have the right to speak in the matter and they will assert that right. . . . Again, I say, remember that they are human beings, and it is not in human nature to be content with subordination to those who do not thoroughly understand us, and, therefore, are not capable of complete sympathy with us."

What the church should do. Meeting the issue fairly, honestly and frankly, the church should recognize the fact that whatever may be in the future, at present it is hopelessly impossible to bring together, under one bishop, the white and colored people in Diocesan Conventions in the South. That being a fact, without crimination or recrimination, the church should practically say to the colored clergy and laity, "Organize your own jurisdictional Convention with a bishop of your own race at the head. The bishops and church people in the bounds of your jurisdictional territory are your friends, and they will help and assist you. It may be, in the distant future, when all of us on both sides have advanced more nearly to the true ideal, that this tentative arrangement may lapse, and all of us will be comprehended in one Diocesan system. Until then, although somewhat separated, let us love one another and work for the glory of God. We have confidence in you. We believe that you will accept this as a Providential opportunity and will demonstrate by your successful work in more largely and effectively reaching your race, the wisdom of the arrangement."

The church has lost so many opportunities that we are fearful lest she let slip the present one.

St. Thomas' Church, Philadelphia, was started just before the organic rise of African Methodism. If Bishop White, instead of making Absalom Jones a priest, had consecrated him bishop, to work among his African brethren in this country, the great African Methodist Church today would have been Episcopal and in full communion with the church. The church lost that opportunity. After the late Civil war, if the church had consecrated a colored priest as bishop to work among the African race in this country, following up the "ante-bellum" instruction given the slaves in church families, with the nucleus of former slave communicants, the church of today among the Negroes would be numerically large, vigorous and strong. The church lost that opportunity. For years some of us who have been branded as "up-starts," "heady," "not humble" and "ambitious," for the love that we have in our hearts for our dear Lord and His church, have been content to endure such things while we unfailingly and unflinchingly kept before the church the duty of the hour.

That the church is moving in the direction of this demand is shown by the fact that there are now three annual Diocesan convocations of colored clergy and laity: Southern Virginia, South Carolina and North Carolina. One has already been arranged for Arkansas, which will be effective just so soon as there are sufficient colored clergy and laity.

29

The Presbyterians

The Presbyterian Church, North, began missionary work among the Negroes of the South fully a year before the close of the Civil war. Two committees were at work under the direction of the General Assembly (O.S.) as early as 1864—one with headquarters at Indianapolis, and the other at Philadelphia. The work of these two committees from necessity was confined by military lines, and was chiefly in connection with military and "contraband" camps and hospitals. In May, 1865, the General Assembly meeting in Pittsburg united these committees under one general committee, entitled "The General Assembly's Committee on Freedmen." It met by order of the Assembly in the lecture room of the First Church, Pittsburg, and was organized June 22d, 1865.

Before the re-union there was another work similar in character and purpose with headquarters in New York, carried on as a "Freedmen's Department," in connection with the Presbyterian Committee of Home Missions (N. S.). This "Freedmen's Department" existed only two years, making its second annual report in 1870. When the two Assemblies united in 1870, the work among the Freedmen as carried on from New York and Pittsburg was consolidated and a new committee appointed. This new committee was organized by direction of the Reunited General Assembly, June 10th, 1870, in Pittsburg, Pa.

This committee continued to work without change of plan or reorganization for twelve years; but the question of the ownership of property, necessary to the work, and the handling of bequests made it evident that it would be better to have the committee incorporated. In 1882 the Assembly at Springfield, Ill., sanctioned the change and the committee obtained a charter September 16th, 1882, and became a corporate body under the name of "The Board of Missions for Freedmen of the Presbyterian Church in the United States of America."

This board educates preachers and teachers; maintains ministers in their work and teachers in their schools; builds churches, school-houses, seminaries, academies, colleges and dormitories; prescribes courses of study; looks after the condition of buildings, and orders all repairs and extensions; elects professors and trustees; provides for boarding department all necessary utensils and furnishings; controls the various institutions of learning; receives monthly financial statements from all schools and audits all bills.

Out of confusion, ignorance and poverty there has arisen a system of educational and evangelistic work that commands the attention and demands the support of the entire church.

Schools, academies, seminaries and one large university have gathered within their walls young men and young women to the number of 11,000, who are brought under religious influence, and are being trained in the ways of the Presbyterian Church.

Congregations have been gathered and churches have been organized until now the board has under its watch and care 350 churches and missions containing 21,000 members. Church buildings have been erected and property secured for the use of churches valued at $350,000. School property owned and used by the board in its work is estimated to be worth $500,000. Funds permanently invested for the use of the work amount to $100,000 invested in property and permanent funds. This property, while absolutely necessary to the work of the board, entails a heavy annual expense in the way of repairs and insurance.

As the work has been a matter of growth, and its influence operative from the time it began, the power for good must not be measured alone by this year's work or last year's work, but by all the work that has been done through all these years. Probably 50,000 people have professed their faith in Christ under the preaching of our ministers. The enrollment in our Sabbath schools, adding year to year, must have reached 400,000, and the total enrollment of students in our day schools from the time we began would count up to 250,000.

The indirect influence of our work upon the communities in which our churches and schools have been established is hard to calculate, but the lives of thousands of our quiet, intelligent and order-loving citizens that are the product of our schools and churches must be included in the calculation, if we want to form an estimate of the amount of good that has been accomplished by the Presbyterian Church in its work among these people.

In Virginia there is one colored Presbytery; in North Carolina there are three; in South Carolina three; in Georgia two; in Arkansas one, and in Alabama and

Mississippi one. In these eleven Presbyteries, containing 209 ministers, there are only seven white men and of these all are teachers except two. In Florida we have four colored ministers; in Tennessee fourteen; in Kentucky four; in Missouri one; in Indian Territory five ministers, two of whom are white. The larger part of our work lies in North Carolina, South Carolina and Southern Virginia.

In view of the past history of the work, and of the great good that is being accomplished, the board feels justified in saying that the Presbyterian Church has not yet given annually of its means an amount commensurate with the importance of this cause. The board has received from all sources (including legacies) for the last year about $160,000, whereas $250,000 would hardly begin to meet the reasonable demands of the work.

In 1902 the work of the Presbyterians was reported as follows:

Ministers..................	209	Ministers who preach only.............	149
Churches and missions.........	353	Ministers who preach and teach......	49
Added on examination.......	1,737	Ministers who teach only.............	11
Added on certificate............	206	Laymen who teach......................	24
Whole number..............	21,341	Women who teach......................	188
Sunday-schools..........	350		
Sunday-school scholars	21,299		
Number of schools..............	88		
Number of teachers...........	272		
Number of pupils..............	10,715		421

SCHOOLS.

Boarding Schools.

Biddle University, Charlotte, N. C.
Scotia Seminary, Concord, N. C.
Mary Allen Seminary, Crockett, Tex.
Ingleside Seminary, Burkeville, Va.
Mary Holmes Seminary, West Point, Miss.
Barber Memorial Seminary, Anniston, Ala.

Co-Educational.

Albion Academy, Franklinton, N. C.
Brainerd Institute, Chester, S. C.
Cotton Plant Academy, Cotton Plant, Ark.
Dayton Academy, Carthage, N. C.

Harbison College, Abbeville, S. C.
Haines Industrial School, Augusta, Ga.
Immanuel Training School, Aiken, S. C.
Mary Potter Memorial, Oxford, N. C.
Monticello Academy, Monticello, Ark.
Swift Memorial Institute, Rogersville, Tenn.
Oak Hill Industrial, Clear Creek P. O., I.T.
Richard Allen Institute, Pine Bluff, Ark.
And seventy-one academies and parochials.

To this must be added Lincoln University in Pennsylvania.

"The schools during this year have, almost without exception, done excellent work. Nearly 11,000 pupils have come under, not only Christian, but Presbyterian instruction. Over 1,800 young men and young women have been sheltered in our boarding schools, and have thus been given all the advantages of a Christian home training, as well as daily instruction in the ordinary branches of education."

There are the following Presbyterian churches in the North outside the Mission Board's work:

Fifteenth Street, Washington, D.C.
Madison Street, Baltimore, Md.
Grace, Baltimore, Md.
Knox, Baltimore, Md.
Gilbert, Wilmington, Del.
Pomfret Street, Carlisle, Pa.
Hope, Chambersburg, Pa.
Second, Oxford, Pa.
Fifth, Chester, Pa.
Central, Philadelphia, Pa.
Berean, Philadelphia, Pa.
First African, Philadelphia, Pa.
Washington Street, Reading, Pa.
Grace, Pittsburg, Pa.
Fourth, York, Pa.
Siloam, Elizabeth, N. J.
Mission, Goshen, N. Y.
Mission, Washingtonville, N. Y.
St. James, New York, N.Y.
Mt. Tabor, New York, N.Y.
Liberty Street, Troy, N.Y.
St. James, Rochester, N.Y.
Ninth, Indianapolis, Ind.
Grace, Chicago, Ill.

"There are supposed to be from 10,000 to 12,000 Negro communicants who are members of white churches."

Beside the work of the Northern Presbyterians there is considerable work done by the United Presbyterians through the school at Knoxville, Tenn., and various missions, and the Southern Presbyterians do something. The General Assembly of 1899 of the church declared:

The Assembly is gratified at the evidence of a fresh interest on the part of our people in the religious instruction of the Negroes, as shown in the increased number of Sabbath schools for this race taught by the white people, and commends this work to all pastors and sessions.

In the judgment of this Assembly the time has come for a great forward movement in the work of colored evangelization, and in confirmation of this judgment it calls the attention of our people to the following considerations:

The work has perhaps a wider range than any other to which God has called us. "It includes the entering of a mission field, the erection of churches and manses, establishing and maintaining schools, the support of evangelists and pastors, the selection and training of a ministry—in short, every detail connected with the elevation of a race."

Statistics show the prevalence of immorality and crime among the Negroes. If we are not moved by considerations of pity for them and sympathy with our Lord in his love for the souls of all, we ought at least to remember that the temporal and spiritual welfare of our posterity is at stake. Are our children and children's children to inherit a land crying aloud to heaven because of violence and murder, and lynch law?

The Presbyterian Church believes that it is peculiarly fitted to give the Negro what he needs. His needs are, in our judgment, a soundly educated ministry, sober instruction, simple and quiet rather than ritualistic or emotional modes of worship, a simple and orderly system of church government and discipline, and a "home life in which the children will be carefully trained and instructed in the Word of God and in the faith of the church."

God has opened to us a wide door in Africa. The story of our mission on the Congo may be classed among the wonders of modern missionary annals. How are we to enlarge the work in Africa, so signally blessed with God's favor, except by enlarging the work for the Negroes at home? And how assuredly inconsistent to send missionaries to Africa while we neglect the Africans at our door.

The work of the Southern Presbyterian Church for the Negro has reached the gravest crisis in its history. The few, feeble, and widely-scattered Negro churches, heretofore in organic union with the white churches, have been organized, in accordance with our long-cherished plan, into an Independent African Presbyterian Church. The charge has been brought against us that we have taken this action because of race prejudice, and with the purpose to rid ourselves of the burden of colored evangelization.

Those who bring the charge ignore the fact that it was at the request of the colored ministers and elders in convention assembled that this step was taken. Our critics, too, wherever they are brought into ecclesiastical proximity to the Negroes, manifest the very race prejudice they charge against us. These facts serve as missiles to hurl at those who censure us, but they will not relieve us of the odium in the sight of God and man, if we allow the new-born African Presbyterian Church to perish for want of sympathy and support; we shall be made "a spectacle unto the world, and to angels and to men."

The *Afro-American Presbyterian* thus comments on the development of the church in the South:

The writer and his people were connected with the old Sion Presbyterian Church at Winnsboro, S. C. The very next Sabbath after Sherman's army had swept through that community like a besom of destruction, the pulpit was occupied by the then Rev. W. E. Boggs, now of Jacksonville, Fla., who had unexpectedly appeared on the scene from Virginia. His text was, "God hath spoken once; twice have I heard this; that power belongeth unto God."—Psalms 62:11. He sought to comfort the people by setting forth the superior power of God. From that Sabbath and for months the colored people occupied their accustomed place in the gallery of the church, the minister for the most part being a Rev. G. R. Brackett.

Then the Federal garrison came. The old Methodist Church building was taken possession of Sunday afternoon by a large number of Negroes who had been connected with it. They had been allowed this privilege formerly, some white man being present. Now the meetings became large and noisy. The whites became alarmed. A few Sabbaths later when we approached the entrance to the yard of the Sion Church we were confronted by a Federal soldier, who ordered all Negroes away. It was afterwards learned that the church had applied to the commanding officer for this guard to keep out the Negroes. We all turned away never to feel at home in the old church any more. It was under somewhat similar conditions that the Negroes went out from the white Presbyterian Churches generally. A few hung on, but most of them drifted away.

The Methodist and Baptist Churches among the colored people at the North were already old and strong organizations. The bishops and leaders pushed into the South and gathered in the people by the wholesale, and perhaps 70 percent of the Negroes who had been connected with the Southern Presbyterian Church went into these churches. Many of the intelligent and capable were made preachers and leaders. Exceptions may be pointed out, but the above describes the general condition.

This was the situation when the white Presbyterian missionaries came among the colored people of the Carolinas, Virginia, and Georgia, where nearly all the colored Presbyterians are now found. They came within reach of the scattered fragments which had either gone out or were freezing within Southern churches. They began in a small way by planting a few schools and organizing churches. The schools became centers of influence. Naturally the growth of the churches under the new conditions was rapid to a certain stage.

30

The Congregationalists

The work of the Congregationalists has been done through the American Missionary Association. The fifty-sixth annual report of that Association (1902) gives the following history of the work:

The American Missionary Association was formed in 1846. It is distinctly a Christian missionary society to spread the gospel of Christ wherever it has opportunity. It was organized with pronounced opposition to slavery, which then existed, and against all race and caste prejudice, which still exists. It was preceded by four recently established missionary organizations, which were subsequently merged into it. They were the Amistad Committee, the Union Missionary Society, the Committee for West India Missions among the recently emancipated slaves of Jamaica, and the Western Evangelical Missionary Society for work among the American Indians.

In the foreign field, 1854, its laborers numbered seventy-nine, located in West Africa, Jamaica, the Sandwich Islands, Siam, Egypt among the Copts, Canada among the colored refugees and in North America among the Indians.

The home department embraced two distinct fields, the West and the South. There were 112 home missionaries employed by the Association in 1860, fifteen of them being located in the slave states and in Kansas.

The missions in the slave states give rise to some of the most stirring events in the history of the Association, which has the distinction of beginning the first decided efforts, while slavery existed, to organize churches and schools in the South on an avowedly anti-slavery basis.

The crisis so long impending came at length, and the Union armies, entering the South in 1861, opened the way for the instruction and elevation of the colored people. The Association felt itself providentially prepared to engage in this work, and the first systematic effort for their relief was made by it. Large numbers of "contrabands," or escaping fugitive slaves, were gathered at Fortress Monroe and Hampton, Va., and were homeless and destitute. The Association, on the 17th of September, 1861, established the first day school among the freedmen. That little school laid the foundation for the Hampton Institute which the Association founded later, and was the forerunner of the hundreds that have followed.

The Proclamation of Emancipation, dated January 1, 1863, insured the permanent freedom of Negroes who reached the Union lines. The American Missionary Association rapidly extended its work. At Norfolk the school of the previous year now numbered 1,200 pupils. Teachers were also sent to Newbern and Roanoke Island, N. C., to Beaufort, Hilton Head, St. Helena and Ladies' Island, S. C. and to St. Louis, Mo.; and its force was scattered over the field held by our armies in the District of Columbia, Virginia, North Carolina, South Carolina, Florida, Louisiana, Kentucky, Tennessee, Mississippi, Arkansas, Missouri, and Kansas.

The year 1865 was marked by the close of the Civil war, by the establishment, by act of Congress, of the Freedmen's Bureau, and by the holding of a National Council of Congregational Churches in Boston, which recommended to the churches to raise $250,000 for the work among the freedmen, and designated this Association as the organization providentially fitted to carry it forward. The Association accepted the responsibility, appointed district secretaries at Chicago, Cincinnati and Boston, and collecting agents in other portions of the Northern states. It also solicited funds in Great Britain, and succeeded in securing that year a little more than the $250,000 recommended by the Council. Its receipts from all sources ran up from $47,828 in 1861, to $253,045 in 1866, and $420,769 in 1870.

But in the South there came a reign of terror under the infamous Ku-Klux-Klans—the Thugs of America. The colored people were often assaulted by mobs, dragged from their homes at midnight, and shot down in the streets. But there was no want of courage on the part of our teachers to enter or remain in the field; the number of teachers, which was 320 in 1865, was enlarged to 528 in 1867, 532 in 1868, and 533 in 1870. It was during this very period that the beginnings were made for most of our permanent educational institutions. The Association must train the teachers and preachers for this people.

The Association now sustains as higher institutions Fisk University, Tennessee; Talladega College, Alabama; Tougaloo University, Mississippi; Straight University, Louisiana; Tillotson College, Texas; and J.S. Green College, Georgia, together with forty-three normal and graded schools and thirty common schools scattered over the South and among the mountains, six schools among the Indians, twenty among the Chinese on the Pacific coast, one in Alaska and two in Porto Rico.

Theological departments have also been established in Howard University, Fisk University, Talladega College and Straight University. Industrial instruction first began in Southern mission schools in Talladega, Ala., and was early introduced into many of our schools and has been constantly extended. Talladega College and Tougaloo University have large farms. In all the larger institutions and normal schools mechanical arts are taught to the boys, and household work, cooking, sewing, washing, nursing, etc., to the girls. From these schools go forth annually hundreds of well-qualified teachers and ministers.

Simultaneously with the founding of these permanent institutions the Association began the planting of churches among the freedmen. They were formed mainly in connection with the educational institutions, and were intended to be models of true church life. The work of church-planting has been pressed forward with a steady hand until the churches now number 254, located in nearly all the states of the South, among the Negroes, the mountaineers and the Indians, with most fruitful results. Sunday-schools, temperance efforts and revivals of religion have been marked features in the work. Christian Endeavor Societies were promptly organized and have been rapidly multiplied.

Conferences or Associations have been formed, and of these there are now nine, designated as the Conferences of North Carolina, Georgia, Florida, Alabama, Mississippi, Louisiana, Texas, South Carolina and Tennessee.

As to the churches, one of the corresponding secretaries writes:

"The Congregational Churches, aided by the American Missionary Association, are both few and small in comparison with the great number of Negro churches, but I am happy to say that they are experiencing rapid growth and development. Within the last ten years the number of our churches has increased over 60 percent. Within the last few years the growth has been even more manifest. The peculiarity of this growth is the up-springing of these churches in a great many of the back country regions. Formerly our churches were almost entirely in the immediate neighborhood and under the shelter of our schools. But in different states new movements have arisen spontaneously towards free churches which shall be in fellowship with one another at the same time, while they are not under any centralized ecclesiastical control. Naturally these churches turn to the Congregational fellowship. The indications are that within the next twenty years the number of them will be very largely increased. In many cases they are the natural result of our educational forces. They are not 'Congregational' in any sectarian sense, but they are largely of the nature of 'Union' Churches, except that they do not submit themselves to any centralized church government. Thus they fall within what might be called 'The Congregational Ellipse,' with its two foci of independence on the one side and fellowship on the other."

The Rev. W. N. De Berry of St. John's Church, Springfield, Mass., made an interesting study of these churches in 1901, and has placed the results in our hands. * Reports were received by him from thirty-three representative colored Congregational churches, in seventeen states, both North and South. They were asked the following questions and made these replies:

1. About what percent of the membership of your church is above forty years of age?

ANSWERS:

Less than 10%................................ 3		40%–49%...................................... 7
10%–19%................................ 5		50%.. 3
20%–29%................................ 7		60%.. 1
30%–39%................................ 6		Not known........................…….1

2. What proportion of your members came from churches of other denominations?

ANSWERS:

None.............................. 2		40%...................................... 1
Less than 10%.......................... 7		50%...................................... 1
10%–19%...................... 6		75%...................................... 1
20%–29%...................... 5		95%...................................... 1
30%–39%...................... 5		Not stated..................…... 4

3. Do these persons continue to hold and assert doctrines or beliefs peculiar to the churches from which they came?

ANSWERS:

Yes.................................…......2	To some extent.............................4
No......................................……20	May hold, but do not assert............6
Unanswered..............................1	

* For Mr. De Berry's report see the *Congregationalist*, January 11, 1902.

4. What is the state of feeling on the part of other denominations in your town toward your church?

ANSWERS:

Friendly 19

Hostile.……............................ 6

Growing friendly................2

Jealous and antagonistic..................4

Unity of denominations,
save Baptist... 2

5. Are the Congregationalists regarded as exclusive or "stuck up"? If so, what reasons do you assign for this?

ANSWERS:

Yes.............................22   No..............................…...6

To some extent 5

Some reasons:

(a) Absence of emotionalism.

(b) 1. Lack of information on part of those who regard us as exclusive, and failure to seek that information.

2. Ignorance, which always condemns the intelligent as "stuck up."

3. The lack of Christian grace on our part which would lead us to treat with *special* cordiality these people that we might win them.

4. The large proportion of educated people among us who naturally seek companionship and association among people of like education.

(c) Intelligence and mode of worship.

(d) Intelligence and education.

(e) High religious, moral, and intellectual standard required of our ministers and aimed at in our churches.

(f) Superiority in education and wealth.

(g) Because we condemn ignorance and superstition in pulpit and pew.

(h) Because we sometimes think and act as though we are better than others.

5. What percent of the money required for the current expenses of your church is raised in your own parish?

ANSWERS:

Less than 10%........................ 1	70%–79%................................... 2
10%–19%........................ 1	80%–89%................................... 2
20%–29%................. 2	90%–99%................................... 2
30%–39%................. 6	100%.. 7
40%–49%................. 2	Pay all expenses, save pastors'
50%–59%................. 3	salary, and pay part of that.........2
60%–69%................. 2	Unanswered..........................1

6. Do you regard the amount thus raised as in sufficient proportion to the financial ability of your parish?

ANSWERS:

Yes....................................9	Almost yes 2
No.......................................19	Unanswered.............................3

8. In your opinion, has the progress of Congregationalism among the colored people any peculiar hindrances? If so, name them.

ANSWERS:

Yes.............................. 27	Yes and No.............................1
No............................... 4	Unanswered...............................1

Among the peculiar hindrances the following are mentioned: Lack of denominational knowledge, enthusiasm, loyalty, literature, and effort to increase the membership, the high standards, mental and otherwise, the mode of conducting service, the lack of emotionalism, the lack of denominational emphasis, the low average intelligence of Negro masses, lack of spiritual activity on the part of pastors, and newness of the work.

9. In your opinion, are the prospects for the growth of Congregationalism among the colored people encouraging? If so, upon what do you base your opinion?

ANSWERS:

Yes.............................30	Unanswered.............................1

The prospects are reported encouraging for the following reasons: The increased interest in, and desire for, education, the activity of the ministers, the discontent with the old order of things, the regard for the church and its methods.

Other answers are:

(a) Congregationalism must grow slowly. There is no reason to hope for phenomenal growth in the immediate future.

(b) It depends upon what we mean to do. If the denomination will make the preaching of the gospel and the planting of Congregational Churches on this Southern field its first and main work and put a reasonable portion of missionary money and many more men and women into church work directly, then the prospects are most encouraging and indeed all we can ask. Rapid growth is a foregone conclusion.

10. Suggestions:

The work is new, needs much attention and encouragement; the American Missionary Association schools need to care more about emphasizing the church; the pastors need concentrated organization. It will succeed or fail as interest in education goes.

The statistics of Congregationalism are as follows (1902):

Number of churches..............230	Added on profession............... 1,190
Ministers and missionaries.... 139	Benevolent contributions.........$ 2,813.68
Church members............ 12,155	Raised for church purposes...... 39,397.82
Total additions............... 1,429	Sunday-school scholars......... 17,311

"Last year we enrolled a larger number of new churches than for any year since 1895. The present year has not been marked either by great advances or regressions. There has been steady progress in individual churches, especially in the increased responsibility about management of their own work. The general increase in the number of churches is manifest from the fact that ten years ago our Southern churches numbered 140; they now number 230.

"The improvement of the four-fifths of the Negro population who live in the rural regions is often exaggerated. It is still shadowed with an ignorance which has barely been touched by the light of a scanty school training for a few weeks of the year and with a church life peculiarly infiltrated with superstition. In vast plantation populations the old slave church still stands. Honesty, truth and purity are not taught, because neither people nor preacher have come to realize that these virtues are essential to the religious life. The ethical power of Christianity is scarcely felt, and 'the plantation preacher is the curse of the people.' The time is ripe for a forward gospel campaign in this great, needy black South of the back country."

The figures above include a few white members.

EDUCATIONAL WORK.

SUMMARY.

Chartered institutions................ 6		Instructors......... 480
Normal and graded schools........ 43	TOTALS. {	Pupils.............. 14,048
Common schools.................... 30		Boarding pupils...... 2,055

PUPILS CLASSIFIED.

Theological.......................	95
Collegiate.......................	271
College preparatory...........	365
Normal........................	1,597
Grammar......................	2,916
Intermediate..................	3,245
Primary.......................	5,465
Music..........................	292
Night..........................	66=14,312
Counted twice.......	264
Total..................	14,048

HIGHER INSTITUTIONS.		
	Attendance	
Fisk University, Nashville, Tenn..	498	
Talladega College, Talladega, Ala..	534	
Tougaloo University, Tougaloo, Miss..	502	
Straight University, New Orleans, La..	709	
Tillotson College, Austin, Tex..	148	
J. S. Green College, Demorest, Ga..	498	=6
NORMAL AND GRADED.		
Gloucester School. Cappahosic, Va...	113	
Gregory Institute, Wilmington, N.C...	310	
Washburn Seminary, Beaufort, N.C..	156	
Lincoln Academy, All Healing, N.C..	251	
Skyland Institute, Blowing Rock, N.C.......................................	83	
Saluda Seminary, Saluda, N.C..	123	
Joseph K. Brick Agriculture, Industrial and Normal School, Enfield. N.C.	211	
Bethany School, McLeansville, N.C..	90	
Peabody Academy, Troy, N.C..	135	
Whittier, N.C..	96	
Avery Institute, Charleston, S.C...	352	

Brewer Normal School, Greenwood, S.C.	264	
Beach Institute, Savannah, Ga.	285	
Dorchester Academy, McIntosh, Ga.	357	
Storrs School, Atlanta, Ga.	326	
Ballard Normal Institute, Macon, Ga.	519	
Allen Normal and Industrial School, Thomasville, Ga.	210	
Knox Institute, Athens, Ga.	291	
Normal Institute, Albany, Ga.	349	
Lamson School, Marshallville, Ga.	259	
Cuthbert, Ga.	224	
Normal School, Orange Park, Fla.	139	
Fessenden School, Martin, Fla.	250	
Trinity School, Athens, Ala.	210	
Lincoln Normal School, Marion, Ala.	304	
Emerson Institute, Mobile, Ala.	266	
Green Academy, Nat, Ala.	83	
Normal and Industrial Collegiate Institute, Joppa, Ala.	191	
Cotton Valley, Ala.	234	
Kowaliga, Ala.	195	
Helena, Ark.	165	
Le Moyne Institute, Memphis, Tenn.	612	
Slater Training School, Knoxville, Tenn.	172	
Warner Institute, Jonesboro, Tenn.	120	
Grand View Academy, Grand View, Tenn.	219	
Pleasant Hill Academy, Pleasant Hill, Tenn.	325	
Big Creek Gap, Tenn.	188	
Chandler Normal School, Lexington, Ky.	270	
Williamsburg Academy, Williamsburg, Ky.	277	
Black Mountain Academy, Evarts, Ky.	115	
Lincoln School, Meridian, Miss.	320	
Girls' Industrial School, Moorhead, Miss.	106	
Mound Bayou, Miss.	87	= 43
Common Schools		= 30

The American Missionary Association has stood firmly from the first for unlimited opportunity in education. It was a pioneer in industrial training and at the same time it has refused to abandon higher education.

> "Too much emphasis cannot be laid on the work of our higher institutions, including the normal schools, which contain over 1,500 pupils. We believe in the higher education for those who show ability and aptitude. This is the most important part of the work of this Association. We utterly protest against the position that primary studies and industrial work are all that should be taught the Negro. This Association must not swerve from its object; better facilities and more advanced courses of study should be the aim. An examination of the courses of study in a large number of the educational institutions of the American Missionary Association shows that many of them are abreast of our best Northern schools in modern methods."

31

Summary of Negro Churches 1900–1903.

Dr. H. K. Carroll reports the following membership of Negro church bodies in the United States, not including foreign mission membership, for the year 1903:

DENOMINATIONS.	Ministers.	Churches.	Communicants.
Baptists...	10,729	15,614	1,625,330
Union American Methodists................	180	205	16,500
African Methodists...........................	6,500	5,800	785,000
African Union Methodist Protestants.....	68	68	2,930
African Zion Methodists.....................	3,386	3,042	551,591
Congregational Methodists.................	5	5	319
Colored Methodists..........................	2,159	1,497	207,723
Cumberland Presbyterians..................	450	400	39,000
Total..	23,477	26,631	3,228,393

To these may be added the following figures as already given:

DENOMINATIONS.	Ministers.	Churches.	Membership.
Methodist (Methodist Episcopal)..........	......	......	245,954
Congregationalists............................	139	230	12,155
Episcopalians.................................	85	200	15,000
Presbyterians*	209	353	21,341
Catholics......................................	......	......	......

*Not including twenty-four Northern colored churches.

This would make an approximate total of 3,522,843 communicants in Negro churches not including colored members of white congregations.

The study of the different sects brings out striking facts.

1. *Early tendencies toward race segregation.*

This is shown in the history of the secessions from Methodism. It had the advantage of showing the capabilities of the race, but the disadvantage of separating friends, helpers and co-religionists.

2. *Later tendencies toward race cooperation.*

This has taken several forms. Among the Baptists there has been simple cooperation among independent churches. Some friction has arisen: the white Baptist mission societies have failed to understand the Negro desire for home rule and autonomy, and the Negro recipients have not fully appreciated the help they have received from without; the Episcopalians have insisted on treating the Negroes as wards under age, while the Presbyterians have made them a department in the church.

3. *The failure of mere charity.*

Nothing is more striking or hopeful for the Negroes than the manifest fact that mere charity or patronage, however bountiful, has not satisfied them. The richest church has nearly the smallest Negro membership, not because it does not give to them, but because it does not treat them as equals. The church with the largest Negro membership is confronted by the strange fact that its black members have actually refused its alms, while the Methodist Episcopal Church has a hard time to keep its colored membership from secession despite pecuniary advantages.

4. *Negro ability to organize and control.*

Can Negroes rule? The experience of Hayti is not encouraging, but the experience of the African churches in America is pretty emphatic proof of the affirmative. What causes the difference? The African church is the oldest Negro organization, dating in part from Africa itself, and here Negroes have had the most liberty and experience. Political experience, on the other hand, they almost entirely lacked, and instead of teachers they had hindrances and detraction.

In fact, we have in the history of Negro churches one of the most important examples of the meaning and working of Social Heredity as distinguished from Physical Heredity that the modern world affords.

32

Negro Laymen and the Church.

Some 200 Negro laymen of average intelligence, in all parts of the country, were asked a schedule of questions and answered as follows. The states represented are Georgia, Alabama, Florida, Louisiana, Mississippi, Texas, North Carolina, South Carolina, Virginia, Kentucky, Tennessee, Arkansas, Colorado, Illinois and Pennsylvania. The answers of a few ministers are included:

So far as you have observed what is the present condition of our churches in your community?

Very good..	23
Good...	49
Progressing, improving, prosperous................................	16
Heavy financial burdens hindering spiritual conditions..........	9
Fair financially, low spiritually: more intelligent..............	3
Not so well attended as formerly, but attendants more devoted...........	2
Good, bad and indifferent...	6
Fair, with vast room for improvement..............................	13
Well attended, but mostly in financial straights..................	12
Poor, bad; not what they should be..................................	12
Here and there a sign of improvement..............................	1
Too much involved with financial efforts...........................	5
Lack of piety and true missionary spirit; need of earnest preachers......	2
At a standstill spiritually; not influential enough among the young.......	2
As far as general improvement is concerned, would say, Congregationalists, the Methodists, then Baptists..................	1

Retrograding spiritually... 4

Can't say, don't know; not answered....................................... 5

Is their influence, on the whole, toward pure, honest, upright living on the part of the members?

Yes.. 71

To a very large extent.. 13

To some extent... 17

Room for improvement... 5

Not so on account of preacher... 1

Belief and doctrine advocated too much to have influence for good,
    upright living... 1

Purport simply to bear good influence over the people.................... 1

Not sufficient emphasis laid on Christian living............................ 2

Influence good, but members do not live as they should.............. 2

Cannot say positively yes, though there are exceptions................3

No.. 17

Generally so; much advancement.......................................6

Not answered... 5

Are the ministers usually good men? If not, what are their chief faults? Cite some specific cases, with or without names:

Yes.. 37

Generally good men... 10

Majority good; some exceptions. Faults: Intemperance, dishonesty,
    careless living, selfish ambition, sexual impurity..................... 31

Some good, some bad... 9

Some good, majority bad.. 4

Few good, majority bad.. 3

Not intelligent...6

Fairly good..3

Chief faults: Selfishness and dogmatism.............................. 4

Fault of some: Immorality... 8

Fault of some: Deceptiveness.. 1

Fault of some: Too great love for money……………………….............. 3

Moral status low………………………………………….……….. 1

Faults: Lack of earnestness, sexual impurity, intemperance,
love of worldly things………………………………………….. 6

Proportion of good ones is increasing………………………….… 2

Fault of some: Bigamy… ……………………………….............. 1

Only a few whom I have not heard rumors about………………….. 1

Appear good, but do not know how to influence the young………….. 1

"No better than they ought to be"……………………………….. 2

Some good, but among others the chief faults are sexual impurity,
improper attention to women, and selfishness………………..….... 4

No, not generally so…………………………………………..… 6

Miscellaneous……………………………………………............. 7

Unanswered……………………………………………………… 5

Of the ministers whom you know, how many are notoriously immoral? What direction does their immorality take: sexual impurity, dishonesty in money matters, drunkenness, or what? Cite some particular instances, with or without names:

None immoral; all good men……………………………………. 28

Very few immoral……………………………………….…..… 2

Some few are not what they should be; do not come up to the true
standard………………………………………………............. 4

One or more are lax in financial matters………………………..… 8

Some few are sexually impure and dishonest in money matters;
majority good…………………………………………......…........ 12

Intemperate………………………………………………….… 3

Some intemperate; some cannot be trusted in money matters………… 1

Chief faults of some: Sexual impurity and intemperance……………. 8

Chief fault: Sexual impurity………………………………........... 12

Many guilty of all…………………………………………..…… 6

Not answered……………………………………………...……... 17

Some of the answers are:

Alabama

I can name a few who are said to be immoral, but cannot say from personal knowledge that they are notoriously immoral.—*Girard.*

I believe we have some ministers who are guilty of every fault named in question four, but I think that one of their worst habits is in their tearing down good church buildings; and in their rebuilding they don't seem to have any care for the strain they place upon their members.—*Mobile.*

I think proselyting and exaggerating minor doctrinal differences a real hindrance. Also the loose methods in vogue of conducting church finances—both in collecting and expending—a serious drawback.—*Mobile.*

Two at present in the city. I know others, but they are not preaching here now. Sexual impurity. They are the only ones in the city with the degree of D.D.—one a Methodist, the other Baptist. They both ruined the good names of two young women.—*Mobile.*

Colorado

I know some 500 ministers. Of that number probably about 100 are immoral; 10 percent of the 100 are sexually immoral, 20 percent dishonest, 70 percent drink.—*Colorado Springs.*

Florida

I know of no minister who is notoriously immoral. Yet occasionally there comes a little confusion in the churches here because when money is collected for one purpose, through the minister's influence it is used for another. Such actions always do cause church fusses which last for some time.—*Gainesville.*

I know of five around this city who are grossly immoral. Their immorality takes these directions: intemperance, sexual immorality, and dishonesty in money matters. Two cases of gross immorality came to light recently on two preachers. One preacher has recently been dropped for dishonesty in money matters.—*Jacksonville.*

Georgia

I cannot say how many; perhaps twenty. Women and unfair dealings in money matters. I have known comparatively few who drink, and still fewer who drink to excess.—*Atlanta.*

About one-tenth of all the ministers in that community (Perry, Ga.) are notoriously immoral, especially in the direction of sexual impurity, dishonesty and drunkenness.—*Atlanta.*

One of the most common and general faults against preachers is their failure to pay promptly financial obligations. I know a few who are said to be guilty of sexual impurity, some others who get drunk.—*Atlanta.*

I regret that I know some ministers who are immoral and they are publicly known to be immoral, but they manage to hold congregations and preach (?) to them.—*Augusta.*

The doubtful three might be classified as follows: Two for sexual impurity, one for general looseness, insincerity, questionable methods etc.—*Augusta.*

I know ten and could name more if I would strain my memory who are notoriously immoral. Some of these are sexual impurity, dishonesty in money matters and drunkenness. I have seen this on the streets of Albany. I have not seen any preacher drunk on the streets here in Brunswick.—*Brunswick.*

By common report, yes, Sexual impurity, dishonesty in money matters lead in order given. I know ministers who drink, but they never to my knowledge become intoxicated.—*College.*

I could name as many as ten who drink whiskey and are untruthful. Many are dishonest in money matters. There is a preacher near my home who is a downright drunkard. He first led his members astray by indulging them in this evil habit, so that now it is a corrupt church.—*Jewells.*

About one-third of them are either sexually impure (these being perhaps in the majority), dishonest in money matters and [given to] drunkenness. These are distributed equally.—*Macon.*

I do not know many who are grossly immoral. I have in mind three, two of whom are sexually impure; the other a drunkard, thief, and he was also sexually impure. They say all Baptist preachers in the country drink.—*Newnan.*

Six: (1) three are dishonest in money matters, and are liars; (2) three, whose immorality seems to take almost every direction. I would add that nearly all of the ministers of my acquaintance in the rural districts are distrusted more or less from a moral standpoint.—*Powelton.*

I know several who do not even try to conceal their habits of drink and sexual impurity, as well as being dishonest in money matters.—*Savannah.*

Mississippi

About 10 percent are notoriously immoral; about 2 percent are sexually impure, 2 percent dishonest in money matters, and about 6 percent are liquor drinkers to a very great extent.—*Coffeeville.*

In a radius of five miles of us there are twelve ministers. Five are exceedingly immoral in sexual impurity and drunkenness.—*Westside.*

North Carolina

Confining my answer to this community and to the present time, I know only one man of bad report. He is charged with stealing church funds.—*Charlotte.*

Comparatively few. The Central North Carolina Conference is the largest one that I have—about 100 pastors. During the last ten years we have had an average of not more than one case a year, about equally divided between sexual impurity, drunkenness, and dishonesty in money matters.—*Fayetteville.*

South Carolina

About 10 percent are notoriously immoral. Immorality takes to sexual impurity, drunkenness, and dishonesty in money matters.—*Hartsville.*

Tennessee

Three or four. Their immorality takes all these directions.—*Memphis.*

They drink a great deal, but do not get drunk.—*Memphis.*

Texas

Fifteen notoriously immoral: nine sexually impure, four are drunkards and two are dishonest in money matters.—*Dallas.*

There are but few notoriously immoral. Some are sexually impure, some dishonest in money matters, still fewer drunkards. The great deficiency in the minister's estimated salary causes failure upon their part to meet honest obligations, which places them in an awkward shape.—*Littig.*

About one-fifth. The greatest number belong to the class of sexually impure; a few dishonest in money matters, and there are a few drunkards.—*Paris.*

Virginia

To the first, I say not one. While our ministers do not preach temperance as they should, yet I never heard of one being drunk.—*Frederick's Hall.*

Two of whom I know are immoral. One is not an active minister, but a kind of missionary secretary in North Carolina. The other one was in our community, but is now in Kentucky, in jail, I am informed.—*Lynchburg.*

I know a large number of ministers in this and other states. One out of every four I would regard as being morally bad. In the order named, I would say that sexual impurity holds the first place, drunkenness the next, and money matters third.—*Petersburg.*

None. Some are not careful in the use of other people's money. Some abhor total abstinence and even temperance, while some other are by no means trustworthy.—*Richmond.*

Four: Sexual impurity, 2; dishonesty in regard to money, 1; drunkenness, 1. One was excluded for over-exaction of money in connection with his mother-in-law.—*Rappahannock.*

Is the Sunday-school effective in teaching good manners and sound morals?

Yes, it is effective.. 66

Fairly so. To some extent partially so.. 29

Not as effective as it should be: vast room for improvement.............. 11

The teaching is tending more and more in that direction................... 9

These ends are sought for.. 5

Not generally in manners, but they teach effectively sound morals..........1

The Sunday-schools are doing a good work; greatest hindrance lack of attendance.. 1

To some extent; depends greatly on the home training........................ 2

Where we have teachers and preachers of this stamp they are.............. 1

In part at least too many fail, but on the whole much good is done......... 1

Sunday-school not so effective, but does not much good..........................2

My own exceptionally good in this. Can not speak definitely of others. I think they are good.. 2

Depends on teachers and officials...…... 2

These subjects generally neglected...…. 2

Cannot say definitely..…… 3

No; it is not...17

Some answers were:

I fear that it is not. I think its ineffectiveness, however, is due to the lack of these in the home more than to the teaching. The hour, or hour and a half, out of 168 does not do effectively what the 167 or 166 1/2 hours have failed to do, or undo what they have done.—*Houston, Tex.*

Most Sunday-schools in the West are merely playing at teaching. They lack purpose and thoroughness, interest and soundness.—*Denver, Col.*

It is not generally used for that purpose, but to instill sectarian animosity. There are, however, some blessed exceptions.—*Jackson, Miss.*

With but one exception, the Sunday-schools do not take up questions of morals and manners.—*Troy, N.C.*

Real good manners, an almost obsolete term. Children are catching the spirit of the age. Some schools seem effective towards good manners and good morals.—*Atlanta, Ga.*

Do the churches you are acquainted with do much charitable and reformatory work among the poor in slums and jails or elsewhere? Cite instances.

Yes, some are quite active..11

They aid the sick and the poor...17

To a certain extent. Fairly well...10

Not very much...29

Only one church here can claim any share in the charitable work
of the community.. 17

They help the poor.. 2

They are attentive to the sick, and this is about as far as it goes............ 8

Not generally, but the number engaged in such work is constantly
increasing.. 1

As much as they can according to their intelligence and ability............. 1

No, they do not.. 40

Do not know; cannot say definitely.. 3

Unanswered.. 4

Some answers follow:

Some of them do creditable work along this line. One pastor preaches in a tobacco factory every Saturday.—*Richmond, Va.*

Yes. First Congregational Church, poor-house and jail; Episcopal Church, Orphan's Home. —*Memphis, Tenn.*

Until the meeting of the "Young People's Congress: very little of such work was accomplished, but a goodly number are now actively engaged in such work.—*Memphis, Tenn.*

Yes. When we consider their small means, I think it can fairly be said that they do, in various ways, a large part of the charitable work. Aside from taking contributions, from time to time, for what is usually called missionary work, the churches, as a whole or body, are not doing much, I think, but individual members of churches are doing much individual charitable work in various ways. They feed, clothe, warm and pay house rent for the needy. Twelve persons paid a girl's expenses at Fisk University last year, or half of that expense. The Negro's charity, for the present, consists more in his doing for the needy than it does in his giving.—*Chattanooga, Tenn.*

They have no systematized methods nor regular general organizations for this kind of work. Pastors and individual churches, however, take up such work. We have a Home for Aged Women and an Orphan's Home which we support.—*Allegheny City, Pa.*

There is an Old Folk's Home supported by the Methodist Episcopal Churches, and another supported by the Baptist Churches. I know individuals who do prison work.—*New Orleans, La.*

We have a notable instance in a Baptist colored clergyman, who for twenty years has solicited and distributed some $500 or more in the interests of a Thanksgiving dinner for the white and colored poor in jails and asylums, and has funds left to repeat for both Christmas and New Year's dinners. Funds are given mostly by the whites, if not wholly—a marked instance of general confidence.—*Mobile, Ala.*

In one church a day nursery, a kindergarten, a gymnasium, a kitchen garden, and reading room for boys are carried on with more or less persistence and success. In another church there is a kindergarten.—*Chicago, Ill.*

Do the young people join the church and support it?

Yes; they do..	48
The young join, but do not do much supporting; chief support from the older members..	28
Usually. In the majority of cases they do................................	3
Some do, others do not..	4
Many young people help to support. Many recently joined..............	2
Many join, but few remain in the church. The support is meager......	1
Depends on the church and the minister. Some churches have large numbers of them..	1
About one-fourth...	1
Only a few young members, but they support as best they can.........	1
Very few, a small proportion. Majority of them do not..................	2
They do not support the church...	1
Not as much as they did a few years ago................................	1
To some degree. To a limited extent.....................................	4
The accessions from among the young people are increasing rapidly...	1
The young are too much bent on pleasure................................	3
No; they do not...	2
Unanswered..	4

Some answers are:

The great masses who come into the church are young people. They make the best members, all things considered.—*Richmond, Va.*

I think the young people need to be disciplined a great deal along that line.—*Richmond, Va.*

They do to a degree commensurate with their home training.—*Lynchburg, Va.*

They are being trained toward supporting churches and schools.—*Bowling Green, Va.*

Not as I would wish, but more than is generally thought. About two-thirds of the girls and boys who come to our school are members of churches and support the church in a fairly good manner.—*Austin, Tex.*

Many of them join the churches and make big promises but, as a rule, do but little. Some will pray, but won't pay; others will pay, but won't pray; a large number won't pay nor pray, and a blessed few who both pray and pay.—*Chattanooga, Tenn.*

They join during revivals and leave at the close. They contribute often because they like to go up to the table. If this were stopped our churches would suffer financially.—*Darlington, S. C.*

The young people when they have attained the ages of fifteen or twenty join the church, but as to supporting the church, I think those of the less aristocratic churches do more in the line of support for the church. In the aristocratic churches the older folks support the church.—*Charleston, S.C.*

They delight in Sunday-school, Christian Endeavor, Young People's Union and church work. Are enthusiastic over it. The churches are largely made up of young people.—*Allegheny City, Pa.*

Fairly well, but they are hindered by the old members and often caused to become discouraged and indifferent by the actions of the leaders and influential members.—*High Point, N.C.*

Not generally among the men; more among the women. Church-going has degenerated into a fashion.—*Jackson, Miss.*

In those churches where the organization and training have been carefully done they do. In others I fear they do not systematically nor to the proper extent.—*Augusta, Ga.*

Not to the desired end, but there is being more and more thought and said concerning this very important duty.—*Atlanta, Ga.*

What is the greatest need of our churches?

An earnest, consecrated, educated, wide-awake, intelligent ministry...24

An educated, well-trained Christian ministry............................ 25

A good, pure ministry.. 6

True conversion, practical religion, true Christianity.................... 4

Honest, upright leaders, both preachers and officers..................... 9

Earnest, educated, consecrated Christian workers......................... 5

Consecrated ministers and faithful members.............................. 5

More money and better preachers... 5

The spirit of Christ and the Holy Ghost................................. 2

Some answers are:

I think there is need of improvement in intellect and in a financial way.—*Vincent, Ark.*

A practical knowledge of right and wrong.—*Mobile, Ala.*

Regard for spiritual ideals.—*Mobile, Ala.*

A more perfect knowledge of the requirement of Jesus upon his followers.—*Colorado Springs, Col.*

Downright seriousness and actual missionary spirit and efforts.—*Denver, Col.*

High-toned Christian ministers in the pulpits and teachers of the same kind in Sunday-schools.—*Atlanta, Ga.*

Able and pure men as pastors and a warm oratory to reach and hold the masses.—*Atlanta, Ga.*

I should say more spiritual life. This lack is very general in our churches of today.—*Atlanta, Ga.*

First of all, better men in the ministry. It would follow that the members would be better.—*Augusta, Ga.*

They need so many things it is hard to say dogmatically what is the greatest need.—*Augusta, Ga.*

The greatest need is to live up to what we preach. Do away with so much emotion and do practical work. "If ye love me keep my commandments."—*Brunswick, Ga.*

1. Properly trained minister. 2. Upright, cultured and Christian officers who possess business knowledge. 3. Bibles for congregational reading. 4. Song books for congregational singing.—*Macon, Ga.*

Decidedly, an educated ministry and a higher standard of morality.—*Rome, Ga.*

1. Pure ministry. 2. Less costly edifices. 3. More charitable work. 4. Practical sermons, i.e., how to live, etc.—*Savannah, Ga.*
Thoughtful workers.—*Thomasville, Ga.*

Moral ministers who are able to chastise immorality.—*Princeton, Ky.*

1. The Holy Spirit's power. 2. Clean, heroic, unselfish pastors who love God, righteousness and souls. 3. Deacons who fill the scripture standard. 4. Members who fear God because they are really new creatures in Christ.—*Jackson, Miss.*

The continued emphasizing of intelligent worship, spirituality instead of formality, and efforts to keep them from substituting respectability and high social forms for Christian piety.—*Allegheny City, Pa.*

Good preachers, who read, study, and can apply what they read. Thinkers who will make the churches attractive. Church boards composed of those who are not afraid to hold their preacher to a certain standard or get rid of him.—*Darlington, S.C.*

Less emphasis on financial matters and more practical preaching as to economy in living and home-getting.—*Florence, S.C.*

A broad, able and educated ministry, capable of entertaining the congregation, from the most illiterate to the most scholarly, with practical, common-sense doctrine.—*Houston, Tex.*

Punctuality, business sense, stability, devotion, ideals and tact, a faithful, a well-enlightened, and a religious pew.—*Littig, Tex.*

Men of high intellectual, moral and religious standings.—*Paris, Tex.*

A pure ministry rather than an educated one. Spirituality. The abolition of questionable methods of raising money, such as festivals, entertainments, excursions, etc.—*Paris, Tex.*

A large membership of solid, sensible, exemplary men, who will take a lively interest in the religious life of the church as well as its business matters.—*Prairie View, Tex.*

More liberal support on the part of the church members.—*Achilles, Va.*

Money to support pastors, and the Holy Spirit to enlighten the inner man.—*Bowling Green, Va.*

Better learned ministers and punctuality.—*Chula Depot, Va.*

Possibly education.—*Frederick's Hall, Va.*

I am of the opinion that the greatest need is morally and intellectually trained leaders, especially pastors: and when I say "morally and intellectually," I mean all that those terms can imply in the highest institutions of learning and under the best influence. Nothing that is really good for a white person is too good for a Negro. I am of the opinion that when this is recognized and the Negroes have leaders accordingly, we shall be a long distance on the way to the solution of the so-called "problem."—*Richmond, Va.*

Cooperation and sympathy with each other. This would make the work more effective and extend it more widely among the people.—*New Orleans, La.*

Are the standards of morality in your community being raised or lowered in respect to sexual morals, home-life, honesty, etc.?

They are being raised.. 81

They are being raised gradually.. 8

Raised to some extent, yet room for improvement.......................... 14

Some answers follow:

I think the standard is being raised, which is due mainly to increase in good schools.—*Augusta, Ga.*

There is less intemperance in the new-made homes than formerly existed in the old homes. This is largely the work of the school teacher.—*Augusta, Ga.*

To this question I must sadly admit it is not what it was twenty-five years ago.—*Brunswick, Ga.*

It is being raised. Young men and women coming from our colleges are marrying and are setting the standard in their communities for higher moral living. Their home life and honest dealing in the community are helpful, and are being diffused in all the homes to some degree.—*Brunswick, Ga.*

We have several homes that are models of purity and good morals.—*LaGrange, Ga.*

There is some effort being made toward a higher standard which, if supported and encouraged, will result in much good in that direction.—*Rome, Ga.*

The church has influence on its members and they all live uprightly.—*Princeton, Ky.*

A good condition generally obtains in the churches, and where suspicion rests the parties are made to feel uncomfortable owing to the popular sentiment.—*Allegheny, Pa.*

As to the lower classes I do not know, but the educated few are being raised. Charleston is not as great an educational center as it ought to be and for this reason, I think, for the masses it is not doing as much in respect to sexual morals and home life as it might.—*Charleston, S.C.*

It is being raised. The church and the schools are the levers. —*Hartsville, S. C.*

The very best sign we have of the Negro's substantial progress is his rapidly increasing respect for the marriage vow, and the many living, beautiful, happy illustrations of his determination to keep that vow. There are hundreds and thousands of pure homes and beautiful, well-ordered families among us now, whereas, thirty-five years ago there were but few.- *Chattanooga, Tenn.*

Yes, positively. An able, eloquent minister was forced to leave one of our churches here recently because there were "rumors" and a "belief" that he was immoral.—*Austin, Tex.*

Yes, I think so—perhaps more through the influence of the schools than otherwise. —*Prairie View, Tex.*

Under conditions our people compare favorably with any other people. —*Petersburg, Va.*

33

Southern Whites and the Negro Church

The difficulty of getting valuable expressions on the Negro churches from Southern white people is that so few of them know anything about these churches. No human beings live further apart than separate social classes, especially when lines of race and color and historic antipathies intervene. Few white people visit Negro churches and those who do go usually for curiosity or "fun," and consequently seek only certain types. The endeavor was made in this case, however, to get the opinion of white people whose business relations or sympathies have brought them into actual contact with these churches. A few of the names in this list are of Northern people, but the great majority are white Southerners. The circular sent out was as follows:

> Your name has been handed to us as that of a person interested in the Negroes of your community and having some knowledge of their churches. We are making a study of Negro churches and would particularly like to have your opinion on the following matters:
>
> 1. What is the present condition of the Negro churches in your community?
>
> 2. Is their influence, on the whole, toward pure, honest life?
>
> 3. Are the Negro ministers in your community good men?
>
> 4. Are the standards of Negro morality being raised?
>
> We would esteem it a great favor if you would give us your opinion on these points.

Some of the answers follow:

J. M. Wilkinson, President Valdosta Southern Railway Company, Valdosta, Ga:

1. In fair condition.

2. Good.

3. Most are.

4. Yes, I think so.

Alfred D. Mason, Memphis, Tenn.:

1. Good. I believe they are doing good, faithful work.

2. Yes.

3. Yes, all that I know are.

4. Yes, I am quite sure they are.

W. W. Dexter, Houston, Tex., publisher:

1. Very good.

2. Yes, among better class; but the greater influence is "fear of the law."

3. Many good ones; but as a class are of questionable repute.

4. Yes, possibly, on the whole.

W. T. Jordan, Colorado:

1. Fair. They average with the white churches.

2. Yes.

3. So far as I know.

4. Yes.

Rev. J. E. Ford, pastor of Zion Baptist Church, is president of the Denver Baptist Ministers' Conference, and is a first-class pastor, preacher and manager. Rev. Mr. Peck of the Methodist Episcopal Church is another minister of the same type. The Negro churches in the whole state are doing fully as well as the white churches and many of them a great deal better.

Rev. J. M. Filcher, Corresponding Secretary Baptist General Association of Virginia, Petersburg, Va.:

1. Excellent.

2. Yes.

3. Yes.

4. No.

R. A. Morris, Austin, Tex.:

1. Fair.

2. In part.

3. Some are.

4. Not much.

The most of them voted the anti-(Prohibitionist?) ticket which, I think, is bad.

P. W. Meldrim, Savannah, Ga.:

I answer all of the foregoing questions in the affirmative, so far as a general answer may be given. To the first question I beg to say that it is too vague to enable me to reply.

James B. Gregg, minister First Congregational Church, Colorado Springs, Col.:

1. Very fair.

2. Yes.

3. Yes.

4. I can't say very definitely. There has been of late years an influx of Negroes into our town and there are more signs of immorality among them than when that population was small. But the ministers are decidedly above the earlier ministers of that race here and that, I should say, indicates a higher tone in the Negro churches, if not in the Negro population, as a whole.

R. B. Smith, County School Commissioner of Greene County, Woodville, Ga.:

1. Not good.

2. No.

3. No.

4. No.

I have given you my candid opinion of such churches and ministers that I know. There are some exceptions to the above. 1. There is a Presbyterian Church in Greensboro that has an intelligent pastor who is a good, true man. 2. I also think that the Methodist Church of same place is also doing pretty good work. A large portion of the ministers are ignorant and in some instances are bad men. I am truly sorry to have to write the above, but it is too true.

W. J. Groom, Princeton, Ky.:

1.   Very slow, if any advancement.

2.   No.

3.   Very few.

4.   No.

I regret to say, in my opinion, the Negro race has not advanced religiously, morally or financially. They have some few commendable ministers, but the majority are immoral and dishonest.

J. H. Icosh, Nashville, Tenn.:

1.   They are making advancement, slowly but surely.

2.   I think so.

3.   So far as I know.

4.   Yes.

It is not easy to give satisfactory answers to such questions without going into detail. I have answered, as seems to me, in accordance with the facts in the case. But information given in the way is not sufficient to furnish a basis for an intelligent view. Am glad to work in any way to help the Negro brothers.

James C. Stanley, Houston, Tex.:

1.   Upward tendency for education, morality, and mutual advancement on American protective lines.

2.   _____.

3.   All I know, yes.

4.   Considerably.

I have lived and been in newspaper business here for thirteen years. I have attached my answers to your questions above as to impressions made by experience. The memberships of churches are larger, the number of churches more; the schools are having greater attendance and teachers are of higher education and practical plane than when I first came here. There are 100 to one in business also. The careless pull all to a common level in race prejudice. I know of none seeking social equality, but many educational and legal and property rights equality.

J. H. Kilpatrick, White Plains, Ga.:

1. Lack of discipline and not harmonious.

2. I think so.

3. Some are and some are not.

4. I think not. I see no decisive evidence of it.

Geo. Wm. Walker, President Paine College, Augusta, Ga.:

1. A healthy spiritual condition.

2. Yes.

3. Yes.

4. Yes.

Prof. Burnell, Emerson Institute, Mobile, Ala.:

1. Improving, as I believe.

2. Yes.

3. The majority are; many notably so.

4. Yes.

Geo. Standing, South Atlanta, Ga.:

1. Their influence is, on the whole, good.

2. The ministers are good men.

3. The morality of the people generally is very good.

Wm. N. Sheats, State Superintendent Public Instruction, Tallahassee, Fla.:

1. Buildings fair, some good, some neglected and some poor. The proportion of really pious members is about on average of white churches.

2. Certainly, but like other churches, the black sheep are too numerous.

3. Some are, and some are the greatest drawback to real piety and the spread of the gospel.

4. Yes, I think so, but entirely too slow for their good and the good of all.

John D. Jordan, Pastor First Baptist Church, Savannah, Ga.:

1. Medium to good.

2. Yes.

3. Most of them; I really know no exceptions.

4. I think so.

I take pleasure in sending favorable answers to all your questions. I wish well for our Brother in Black.

J. Reese Blair, Troy, N.C.:

1. They are on the upgrade, but in need of better leaders.

2. Good.

3. Some not what they should be.

4. I think so.

In this county I consider the Negroes very much improved in the work of their teachers and churches.

J. W. Newman, Pastor Methodist Episcopal Church, South, Talladega, Ala.:

1. Fairly good.

2. Yes.

3. Generally.

4. Yes.

T. C. Moody, Marion, S.C.:

1. Good.

2. Yes.

3. Yes.

4. Very much.

I hope the above answers will satisfy you, as they are the true condition of the churches here. The Negro race is improving in every way.

J. W. Kein, Richmond, Va.:

1. Good and membership increasing.

2. Yes.

3. They are.

4. Yes.

W. L. Tillman, Columbus, Ga.:

1. They bring about idleness among the Negroes.

2. No.

3. Some may be.

4. No, getting worse.

In many churches are too many so-called preachers. They demoralize the Negroes and keep them from regular work by their constant preaching night and day, and require them to give up the last coin they have. Some of the preachers are very good, but a large portion of them are bad men. The Negroes morally are growing worse.

W. G. Bradshaw, High Point, N. C.:

1. Fairly good.

2. Yes.

3. Yes.

4. Doubtful.

E. H. Leidy, Memphis, Tenn.:

1. Good.

2. Yes.

3. Yes.

4. Yes.

On the whole, I think our Negroes will compare with those of any section in this country.

J. M. Collman, County School Commissioner, Putnam, Ga. :

1. There are too many—about three churches to one school. Buildings generally poor; creeds bitter against each other. Some churches established seemingly by local authority for "revenue only," the wandering priest dropping in and preaching and then a collection.

2. Not as a whole, but in part.

3. Some are, numbers are not.

4. Yes, but much too slow.

In my opinion, here, where the teachers are selected by the County Board of Education, they are doing more for the race than the preachers. They are far better educated and, as a whole, better men and women.

Sam Smitherman, Troy, N. C.:

1. They are, as a whole, bad.

2. No.

3. No.

4. No.

We have one good, honest and reliable Negro preacher in our community, and he is trying to raise the standard of living among his race. But he has an up-hill business to do so. The old Negroes, as a whole, are a long ways better than the young ones. The Negro preacher that I refer to is O. Faduma. Everyone that is acquainted with the Negro race knows that a Negro is better off without an education than he is with one, for when he has an education he begins then to want to do some mischief. He will either go to preaching or stealing or both. Of course there are some better than others.

John N. Rogers, Professor of Agriculture, Dahlonega, Ga.:

A large majority of the church buildings have been much improved in the past five or six years.

The good sufficiently dominates to warrant their encouragement. The majority are good men and exert an elevating influence on the people among whom they labor. A few are a disgrace to the church and to their race.

In answer to question No. 4, I would say that there is quite a noticeable improvement among the females, but among the males, young and old, there is quite a lack of regard for a high standard of virtue, either among themselves or for the opposite sex with whom they associate. The average colored man does not regard it as anything against him to be seen in company with the lowest woman of his acquaintance. In my seven years experience as school superintendent of the county, I had only two complaints of immorality of female teachers. I had four or five of male teachers.

The lowest state of morals is found on the large plantations where the houses throw the families in as close contact as is usually the case in cities. The greatest improvement is noted in families living on small farms (either rented or owned by them) where only one or two families live in close contact.

J. G. Collinsworth, Eatonton, Ga.:

I do not believe any race with the same environments could have made more progress since their emancipation. They deserve great credit for what they have accomplished, intellectually and educationally. They have two churches in Eatonton that are good buildings and in fair repair. These churches have marvelous influence for good. It is characteristic of the

Negro to be scrupulous concerning his church vows. Their ministers, from external appearances, are capable, God-fearing, consecrated men.

J. J. Lawless, Richmond, Va.:

We have in our town two colored churches and they are fairly well supported by their members. They are gaining in numbers and getting stronger financially from year to year. They have in them some members whose lives are such as to impress outsiders with the sincerity of their Christian professions, but unfortunately they allow members to remain in their churches who ought to be turned out, and thus cause reproach to fall upon the whole body.

My opinion is that both of the Negro ministers in our town are good men.

The President of the City National Bank, Austin, Tex.:

I have deliberately delayed answering until now that I might more fully prepare myself to answer intelligently the several questions you ask me in your said favor of March 19th. What I write is principally the result of my own observation and reflection, but partly after conference with several intelligent colored and white men, in whose judgment and candor I have confidence. I will answer your questions in the order in which they are asked.

"1. What is the present condition of the Negro churches in your community?"

To this I answer, in the main the church buildings of this community are in every way reputable. They are principally rock or brick buildings, of good architecture, and neatly, comfortably and tastily finished and furnished. As to the membership in the main it is clean and self-respecting. Most of the colored churches here are either out of debt or are paying their debts with reasonable promptness. Some of the colored churches are in debt and poorly administered, but as a rule the membership and physical condition and supervision of the Negro churches are good.

"2. Is their influence, on the whole, towards pure, honest life?" In answer to this question I will say that, on the whole, their influence is decidedly towards pure and honest life.

"3. Are the Negro ministers in your community good men?" To this I will say that, in the main, they are, but some of them are very sorry men. They are deadbeats, and have no regard for their word nor for their obligations, and they are low in their moral instincts and acts. They have neither regard for truth nor honesty. They are particularly unscrupulous in politics. But speaking of this community, I sincerely believe that this character of colored preachers is decreasing. They are greatly better men, and more intelligent men than they were ten or twenty years ago. Speaking of this community, again, I would say that the unworthy colored ministers are rather the exception than the rule, and I think I know what I am talking about.

"4. Are the standards of Negro morality being raised?" To this I will say that, in my opinion, they certainly are. I think there is a higher standard of morality amongst colored men as well as colored women.

A Real Estate Agent, Florence, S. C.:

The Methodist Episcopal Church, North, and the Baptist Church: these churches were well attended, and one reason was that the ministers were their political leaders. Of late years a good many men who have learned to read and write have been going about preaching, some I know of no character. The consequence has been that many new congregations have been started, and although not large, the tendency has been to do more harm than good. These Negro ministers (so-called) are too lazy to work, and make their money in an easy way, principally from the most ignorant Negro women. At present, I think the Negro ministers at the established Methodist Episcopal Church, North, the African Methodist Episcopal Church and Baptist Church are very good men; have not heard anything against their characters. But my opinion is that for real religious training of the Negro the Episcopal Church and Roman Catholic Church would be the best for the Negro, the first named from the example and training, and the latter the confession they would have to make to the priest—the latter more from fear. My opinion, again, is that the Negroes are more immoral, as they read and know what has been done and is being done by the immoral, unreligious white men of the country, and I believe that the example set by the white men of low character has been the greatest cause for the immorality of the Negro. Take for example that crime of rape. I don't know of a section where the whites are refined, nice people and treat the Negroes nicely, but let them know their places, where such an attempt has occurred. How can you expect the Negro women to be virtuous when the white men will continue to have intercourse with them? How can you blame the Negroes for committing murder when the example is set them by the white man?

assuming a very one-way influence here

We must face the truth. If any dirty work is to be done a white man hires a Negro to do it for him. If a member of a church does not wish to be seen going to buy whisky he sends a Negro. If these are facts, what an example to set to an inferior race! And they are facts and a shame on our white race. It seems to me that the Negroes are more immoral here than they used to be and the fault is due mostly to the example set them by the white men.

A. C. Kaufman, Charleston, S. C.:

1. There are a number of Negro churches in Charleston that are prospering. The great trouble, I apprehend, is in the multiplicity of churches with the colored as the whites. In my judgment, a church should not be established until there is actual need for it.

2. This is a difficult question for me to answer, but as far as I know their influence is for the betterment of the race.

3. I believe that the Negro ministers here are generally good men. I have no reason to state to the contrary.

4. The standard of Negro morality I am sure is being raised. The young men and women, under proper environments, are beings raised along these lines. In the lower strata of society things may be different.

H. M. Willcox, Willcox Hardware Co., Marion, S. C.:

Your letter received. In answer to your questions will state:

1. That the Negro churches are in good condition here.

2. That the moral and religious trend is upward.

3. That the present colored ministers are above the average in every way, both in relation to intelligence and as to morals. I have had business with them all, and the present incumbents seem to be a very reputable set of men. I will state that several who preceded them in the last ten years cast a moral blight by their lives while here upon their church community.

4. I think we have a very good class of colored people and that from a moral standpoint they are improving.

J. E. Woodcox, High Point, N. C.:

Replying to your favor of 22d, beg to say that the condition of the Negro churches in this community, in my opinion, is improving.

The influence of their churches is much better than formerly, with less sectarianism.

We have some Negro ministers in our town who are splendid, good men.

The standard of morality among the Negroes here is much better than formerly. The fact is, I have often remarked, that High Point is blessed with the best Negro population of any place I have seen in my life. Many of them own their own homes and have some credit and standing in the community.

A. E. Owen, Portsmouth, Va.:

1. The present condition of the Negro churches in this community is fairly good.

2. I do not hesitate to say that the influence of nearly all the Negro churches is toward a purer, honest life. Of course in many instances their teaching is above their practice.

3. The Negro preachers are fairly good men. Sometimes some suspicions rest upon them.

4. I am sure that the standards of morality, especially among the church members, are being raised.

The Negroes are doing well. I think if people who speak and write about Negroes would keep in mind the fact that Negroes *are* Negroes, it would keep them from being led astray. Negroes are religious, and many of them are faithful church members. Negroes should not be compared with the best conditions of the white race. But still the Negroes are improving. They are getting clearer ideas of purity and honesty, and I believe the Negro race, as Negroes, will rise to a higher plane of religion and integrity.

Such a weird mix of racism and... level-headedness?

J. R. Peppers, Memphis. Tenn.:

1. The Negro churches in Memphis, so far as the buildings are concerned, are considerably better than five or ten years ago, which shows that more attention is being given to the houses of worship used by them, and their gifts are liberal.

2. My observation is that their influence is toward pure and honest lives and I think the pastors of the churches, as a rule, strive towards this end.

3. So far as I know the ministers in our community are good men. I know of no irregularities at present among them.

4. I think the standards of morality among the Negroes are being raised, though, of course, in no such degree as their friends would be glad to see.

W. H. Banks, Merchant, Hartsboro, Ala.:

In answer to your first question, will say that their houses of worship are not in very good condition. They are manifesting some spirit of improvement in the respect however, and have done what they could to improve their church buildings. The religious life of their churches is not of a higher order. They are emotional and demonstrative and, I feel sure, are generally sincere. Many of them are really religious people, but they have standards of their own, and they are low standards. For instance, the average Negro Christian would consider it a grievous sin to play the "fiddle" or dance, but would regard it as a small offense to drink too much whiskey or to cover up a theft committed by some one of his race, or to do many other things that you would regard as grave violations of the moral law.

Question 2. I hope so. Progress in this direction is slow, and the Negro is not wholly to blame. Public sentiment among his own race and among his white neighbors, and the non-enforcement of law against inchastity, are great hindrances to his progress toward pure living. The laws against bigamy, seduction and adultery, are a dead letter so far as the Negro is concerned. The Negroes' religion does act more as a restraint upon them in their business dealings. Many of them pay their debts and meet their financial obligations well. In these respects the Negro has the support and stimulus of law and public sentiment.

Question 3. A few of them are, I think, but many of them I am afraid are not.

Question 4. In some respects I am sure that they are, and in all respects I hope there is some improvement.

Wm. Hayne Leavell, Minister, Houston, Tex.:

I am sorry to have to answer you that since coming to Texas I have not been able to know anything of the Negroes or their churches. Out here they seem to be a very different sort from those among whom I was brought up, and in whom I have always been interested and by whom always been well received. Here they are altogether to themselves, and I do not think I know personally a solitary Negro minister. It is true I have for ten years been a man busily driven, but the one or two attempts I have made to help the Negroes have not encouraged me to try again. I know only that there are very many church organizations of the various denominations, but of their quality I know nothing.

W. J. Neel, Attorney at Law, Rome, Ga.:

I doubt if I am sufficiently informed on this subject to give you any definite or satisfactory information. It is a matter in which I am interested and I occasionally attend service at Negro churches, but I cannot say that I have information sufficient to meet your inquiry. However, I will undertake to answer the four questions submitted by you in their order.

1. As to the present condition of the Negro churches in Rome: It does not seem to me to be quite satisfactory. It has not been long since there was a serious split in the leading colored Baptist Church of Rome, resulting from differences between the pastor and a majority of his congregation: and within the recent past one of the leading colored Methodist Churches in this city was greatly disturbed on account of the conduct of its pastor, who was charged with misappropriating church funds. It resulted in an indictment and prosecution in the courts. So I cannot think the condition of the Negro churches here is what it should be.

2. To this question I would answer: Yes, but with a mental reservation as to individual instances.

3. For the most part, I believe the Negro ministers in our community are fairly good men but there are exceptions, and the exceptions are rather too numerous to be reassuring. Some of our Negro preachers, especially those of the cheaper sort, are too much inclined to drift into local politics, which seems to be always more or less corrupting and to leave a stain on their good name. A Negro-preacher-politic-boss is not a very wholesome or helpful citizen in any community. But, happily, I believe his shadow is growing less.

4. To your fourth question, as to the standards of Negro morality, I would answer: Yes and no. In individual instances, I believe Negro men and women are rising in the moral scale and setting their faces firmly and hopefully to better things: but, if I am to be entirely candid, I will be compelled to say that the standards of morality among the Negroes in this section, and especially among the younger generation, do not seem to be rising. I regret to have to admit that the tendency appears to be in the other direction. I wish it were not so. The Negro is in the South, as I believe, to stay, and we of the South are mightily interested in his elevation and betterment as a citizen. He is here either to hinder or to help in the general progress and prosperity of our country, and his progress, up or down, necessarily affects us all.

A White Layman, Cuckoo, Va.:

In most of the churches the membership is very large, but, on a whole, I think they have very little conception of what true religion is. I think a number are trying to lead honest lives, but the majority do not know the meaning of true religion.

I think some of the ministers are by no means what preachers ought to be. I think a few are trying to do the best they can. I have attended the church nearest me occasionally and I regard the pastor as a man of ability and fine character and calculated to much good. I wish I could say this for them all.

Answer 4. I am afraid not.

Clarence Cusley, Houston, Tex.:

1. The present condition of Negro churches in this state is altogether encouraging, though there is a vast room for improvement in the character and education of many of the preachers.

2. Their influence, on the whole, is toward a better life, but the preaching is still too much emotional and too little addressed to the practical problems of living.

3. Of the Negro ministers of my acquaintance many are earnest and godly men, some are ignorant, and a few I fear are insincere.

4. The standards of Negro morality are being raised in many respects and being lowered in others. Among the more intelligent class, there is decidedly a tendency toward purer domestic life. Many Negroes whom I know I believe to be thoroughly virtuous and honest. On the other hand, among the less intelligent class there is a very dangerous, not to say fatal, drift towards the worst forms of domestic vice.

On the whole, I believe that on this account the race is not multiplying at a normal rate.

A. J. McKelway, Editor, Charlotte, N.C.:

I am interested in the welfare of the Negro race, and know somewhat of their churches. The Presbyterian Churches in Charlotte and Mecklenburg County, I commend most highly, not because I am a Presbyterian, but Charlotte is located in a Presbyterian section, and the old families were largely Presbyterian, and the best Negro stock is the same. Biddle University, near by, is a helpful influence, too, in training educated ministers. I can also commend the Congregational Church here, but the Methodist Episcopal and Baptist Churches are the average emotional congregations, with but little connection between morality and religion. Some ministers among them are good men, some are not. I think the standard of Negro morality is being raised: that is, the standard to which the best are trying to attain: at the same time there is a great tendency in the other direction among the worst element.

Rev. G. Lyle Smith, Paris, Tex.:

1. A considerable majority of adult Negroes are church members, a fair condition of peace prevails in the congregations, but denominational prejudices and wranglings are too frequent and violent, and a petty contentiousness is too common in individual organizations.

2. Yet, all in all, it may be said truly that their influence, on the whole, is toward a good, pure, honest Christian life.

3. Yes, with comparatively rare exceptions, the Negro preachers are good men so far as known to me. They certainly get into serious trouble far more frequently than white ministers, yet the general statement would stand that Negro preachers are good men.

4. Yes, it is manifest that the standards of morality are being steadily raised, especially if we take into view any considerable period of time. Advancement is as rapid as could reasonably be expected, all things considered.

E. C. Moncure, Judge County Court, Bowling Green, Va.:

First, I have great sympathy with the Negro race and my opinion if anything, I fear, will be a little biased in their favor.

The Negro seems to be naturally a very religious person, full of emotion and human sympathy, mixed up with some superstition and suspicion.

The Negroes are devoted to their churches and will undergo many privations to contribute to church building. They have great pride in their churches, and to be turned out of church is the most humiliating condition in their minds. A Negro convicted of larceny will suffer under the burden of his humiliation from being "turned out of the church" much more than from his disgrace of criminal conviction. Of course that remark does not apply to those who are the leaders of the church. Twenty-five years ago the Negro churches were controlled by much inferior men than today. The Negro churches in any community of today are quite well organized, with well-attended Sunday-schools, and are progressing. They have an over-zeal in building church houses, and are striving to emulate the white people in having good and neat houses. Their church discipline is rather loose. This, in a measure, comes from the great number of unconverted persons in their churches, for all Negroes must belong to the church; and a great many of their preachers are not educated and not of the highest character, so that they are not particular enough in receiving candidates into their communion. But, in my opinion, the Negroes are gradually improving along many lines. The trouble is with us white people, who, setting a judgment on their progress, expect and demand too much in a small space of time. But the influence toward pure, honest lives, upon the whole, is good; that is, the preponderating influence.

Of the colored registered vote lately voting on a local option in my county, the abridged electorate, consisting principally of the educated and owners of property, nearly as a unit voted against whiskey.

Not all of the Negro ministers of my community are good men. In the main, they are, but some are ignorant and superstitious. But with all this, I am clearly of the opinion that the standards of Negro morality are being slowly and gradually raised.

To sum up, I do not think that Negro education and evangelization are failures by any means. In my acquaintance there are some noble examples of progress, faithfulness and devotion to principle.

C. C. Brown, Pastor, Sumter, S. C.:

1. One of the four Negro churches in Sumter is doing a good work. I seriously question whether the other three are accomplishing much. They suffer from poor leadership and from having too many preachers, who are always hanging around, seeking a pulpit in which they can preach.

2. I think the tendency is towards a better and more honest life. Too many supposed converts go into their churches upon the basis of emotion, and hence vital religion is to a large extent wanting.

3. Two Negro preachers here are unfit for their high place: four others are good and honest men, as far as I have had an opportunity to judge them.

4. Yes, among a certain class of Negroes. Good Negroes are getting better, and evil Negroes are getting worse. The great vice is adultery, which is winked at in many cases, and the social atmosphere can never be clarified until the harlot is no longer given recognition by those whose lives are clean. The Negro needs lessons about home life far more than he does lessons about church life. The fact that Negroes have little or no confidence in each other lies at the bottom of many evils. This lack of confidence is general, and even the preacher has to contend against it. It weakens his power as a preacher and takes all authority away from his preaching and teaching.

But, on the whole, I am inclined to believe the Negroes are making strides towards a better condition. I am willing to be patient and live in hope. I am also willing to condone some existing evils, and to charge these things to the long years of history which lie in the past.

Edward S. Elliott, Savannah, Ga.:

1. The present condition of the Negro churches in this community is, on the whole, improving.

2. The influence, on the whole, is towards pure and honest life.

3. In my judgment, some of the Negro ministers in this community are good men and some are not.

4. The standards of Negro morality are being raised very slowly and among some. I regret that I have not been able to give this matter a careful investigation, and the above opinion is expressed merely from casual observation.

Rev. J. T. Plunket, D.D., Augusta, Ga.:

1. I am not fully advised, but from all that I can hear or see I think, in the main, the present condition of the Negro churches here is very good.

2. I think the influence of the Negro churches is, on the whole, good and helpful toward purity and honesty of life.

3. So far as I have heard with few exceptions.

4. The moral improvement of any race must necessarily be gradual and slow. A fair judgment upon such an issue can only be made from broad and dispassionate observation rather than from a too narrow and prejudiced view. My judgment is that the racial standard of morality is being raised.

34

The Moral Status of Negroes

As to the mass of Negroes in the United States there is much confusion of evidence as to their moral condition. This is perfectly natural. Many of them are suffering from the effects of well-known tendencies to decadence of the second generation; at the same time their economic and educational advance is undoubted. What has been the resultant? Two answers are usually given to this question. One declares that the advance has been great and uniform in all moral relationships; the other answer is typified by the assertions of men like Thomas* that the Negro race is thoroughly corrupt and that "soberly speaking, Negro nature is so craven and sensuous in every fiber of its being that a Negro manhood, with decent respect for chaste womanhood, does not exist." For the purpose of getting some valuable opinions on these points and especially on Thomas's assertions, a committee of the Hampton Conference, in 1901, under the chairmanship of the Rev. Francis J. Grimke of the Fifteenth Street Presbyterian Church, Washington, D. C., made an investigation, a part of the results of which are here printed:

> With a view of reaching those who were best qualified to give the desired information, the committee sent out to the American Missionary Association, the Presbyterian Board of Missions for Freedmen, the American Baptist Home Mission Society, the Home Mission Board of the National Baptist Convention, the Freedman's Aid and Southern Education Society of the Methodist Episcopal Church, and to many individuals of prominence in all the denominations, the following request:
>
> "Will you be kind enough to send us a list of the teachers and preachers of your denomination laboring among the colored people in the South whose opinion touching their moral condition would carry most weight?"

* W. H. Thomas: The American Negro.

The list of names thus secured was also supplemented by consultation with others who were in a condition to know, and also by consulting the History of the Medical Department of Howard University, recently published, which contains a list of all of its graduates.

We sent out in all nearly a thousand circulars. These were sent to teachers, preachers, lawyers, physicians and business men, both white and colored, located in Maryland, Virginia, West Virginia, North Carolina, South Carolina, Georgia, Florida, Alabama, Mississippi, Louisiana, Kentucky, Tennessee, Texas, Arkansas, Kansas, Missouri, the District of Columbia, and also in some of the Middle and Eastern states. Of the replies received only two agree wholly with Mr. Thomas.

One Southern white man writes from Atlanta:

> Your circular letter received and in reply to your request as to whether, as far as my knowledge extends, the statements copied from the *American Negro* are true or not, I beg leave to say they are true.

The other is from a Northern white woman, who has lived for some time in the South, and who has been working among the colored people for a number of years, some dozen or more years in her present locality. She writes:

> Your circular received as I am leaving for Denver. I have labored among the colored people for nearly twenty-two years in South Carolina and Tennessee. It is with sincere sorrow that I have to admit that those statements are true and correctly represent the present condition of the race.

Miss Sarah A. Collins, 110 East Center street, Baltimore, Md., writes:

> Replying to you out of an experience of eighteen years among the humbler classes of the race I have not, by observation, found those statements true. Human weakness, under the unfavorable conditions of poverty and ignorance, has furnished examples of moral downfall, I must admit, but I have never considered them peculiarly racial nor have I noted any such downfall that has not had an offset under conditions equally unfavorable of noble chaste womanhood.
>
> Among the cultivated class my observation has had a more limited area, but those with whom it has been my good fortune to come in close contact have furnished some of the most beautiful examples of dignified, unspotted womanhood, whose lives might be read, page by page, without revealing one spot or blur. I have known, and do know, of homes among both the cultivated and ignorant whose sanctity is unbroken and whose atmosphere is as pure as true manhood, faithful womanhood, and innocent, happy childhood can make it.

Miss Nannie E. Grooms, 523 West Lanvale street, Baltimore, Md., writes:

My work in a large city has covered a period of nearly fourteen years. Thousands of girls have passed under my observation, many of them have already begun their careers, several are teachers in the Baltimore city school system, and are doing their part in life. The home life of all these individuals was not of the best kind, but with this much to be deplored in their condition I believe the percent of immorality to be low.

At this writing, my work is in a veritable slum. Degradation of every kind is rampant. In the next block above us houses of ill fame line both sides of the street. The occupants of these places are white. In a street parallel to this are houses occupied by both white and colored. Many of our children come from these places. The greatest percent of degradation I have ever witnessed exists here. What the harvest shall be only Providence knows; but taken all in all, I believe that 8 percent would cover the mathematical reckoning as far as figures may be taken indicative of conditions of society.

I believe the statements made in the *American Negro* are false. William Hannibal Thomas must have spent his time entirely among the degraded, depraved and vicious.

Dr. Lucy E. Moten, Principal of the Normal School, Washington, D.C., writes:

I have had eighteen years' experience, with the closest observation, with girls of the race, average age eighteen, graduating not less than 400, and I am proud to say that not one, so far as I know, has in any wise cast a shadow upon her Alma Mater.

The Rev. Owen Waller, Washington, D.C., writes:

I was bred in England, during my most impressionable years, among the sturdy, moral, upper middle class, and now after ten years' work among the colored people, I can truly say that, class for class, circumstances compared, expect for differences of complexion, one would not realize the change, certainly not in conduct and morals. One is especially impressed with the real modesty of the colored woman, and how she can be ingenuously assailed in this respect is both absolutely and relatively inexplicable.

Dr. H. B. Frissell, the Principal of the Hampton Normal and Industrial Institute, Hampton, Va., writes:

I have had an experience of twenty-one years with colored people, during which time I have been intimately acquainted with a large number of them at Hampton Institute. I have gone into their homes and have had perhaps as much opportunity as most any white man for knowing intimately their life.

I am glad to bear witness to my knowledge of the clean, pure lives of a large number of whom I have known. I have often said, what I believe to be true, that it would be hard to find in any white institution in the North the freedom from low talk and impure life as is to be found at Hampton, where 1,000 young people of two races are brought together. The colored race is not degraded. Many of the young people who came to me years ago and had no conception of the wrong of certain lines of conduct and who, since they have gained that knowledge, have lived up to what they know. I have seen young people coming from one-room cabins, where morality seems well nigh impossible, who sloughed that old life, and have made good use of the cleared knowledge which they have gained at Hampton.

I have often said that my own boy would be less likely to hear low talk here than in most Northern institutions for the whites. My own judgment in the matter is confirmed in the experience of others. For a number of weeks an English gentlemen, who is making a most careful study of the race, has been staying at the school. He has mingled with the boys in their play, in their workshops and in their dormitories, and he confirms my impression and that of my disciplinarian, who himself is a colored man, living in close contact with the young people of the school.

I have seen in my years of work in the South a steady improvement in the whole community in which I live. The standards are being raised, and there is a marked improvement in the matter of purity of life.

The President of the State Normal School, Petersburg, Va., writes:

We have graduated 106 girls from our Seminary and following the lives of these graduates with careful and constant interest, we have known of only one who has gone astray.

Mr. W. McKirahan, Principal of Norfolk Mission College, Norfolk, Va., writes:

I have been laboring among the colored people for five years. The roll of our school carries about 700 names yearly, about 450 of these being girls. To my knowledge about five or six go astray yearly, or about one in each hundred.

Mrs. Orra Langhorne, a Southern white woman, 710 Church street, Lynchburg, Va., writes:

I was born among colored people, have always been surrounded by them and believe this man Thomas grossly exaggerates the actual conditions. It was the most sorrowful part of slavery that there could be no legal marriage for the slaves, no protection for the virtue of women. Even now there are no laws to protect the colored girl, such as have always existed for her white sisters. In discussing any question that relates to the Negroes, regard should be given to the rapid formation of classes among them. There is a respectable class, and this class is increasing, where married parents live virtuous lives, guard the sanctity of their homes, and strive to bring up their children in the path of virtue. I go among the colored people of all classes and see many signs of encouragement. We must all work and hope for the elevation of the race, and prove to the world the falsity of Thomas's cruel and odious book.

Rev. D. Webster Davis, colored, of Richmond, Va., writes:

I recall ten cases coming under my personal observation where mothers, living in vice, have put their children in boarding schools, Catholic homes, and in good families, when they could succeed in doing so, and these girls in most cases have been reared without having visited their mothers' homes since babyhood. In fact, it is the rule rather than the exception that mothers, leading lives of shame, do all in their power to prevent their children leading the same lives.

Dr. Charles F. Meserve, white, President of Shaw University, Raleigh, N. C., writes:

I believe that there are in every community large numbers of colored women that are as chaste and pure as can be found in communities made up of other races.

I believe that a large percentage of colored boys and girls over fifteen years of age, who have been properly trained, are clean and pure.

I have found, as a rule, that Negro fathers and mothers are more than anxious that their offspring should lead pure lives. Whatever truth there is in this statement can apply only to the degraded tenth.

I have spent over seven years in educational work among the colored people of the South, have seen them in school and at home, and in practically all of the Southern states. When I consider that they have come from over 250 years of enforced slavery, with all the degradation and darkness that this means, the wonder to me is that there is such a large number of pure, refined, industrious, intelligent men and women as there is. There is, as every one knows, a dark picture, but it is only what is to be expected. It is a picture that is growing brighter year by year, and although there are discouragements and obstacles, from time to time, that come up, on the whole, the race is making substantial and remarkable progress, and the outlook ought to be considered by all careful observers and lovers of the human race as hopeful and encouraging.

Dr. D. J. Satterfield, white, President of Scotia Seminary, Concord, N. C., writes:

> When a Southern white man told my predecessor that all Negro women were impure his reply was, "I suppose you know, I don't." I have seen Negro women who I have good reason to believe are living virtuous lives under conditions of trial such as our virtuous white women as a class know nothing about. Through my sainted wife I know of examples of colored women whose firmness in resisting temptation makes them worthy to represent any race.
>
> Of those same women I can speak without reserve on all these points. Their modesty and genuine worth are conceded by white, as well as colored; their marital fidelity is above question. Many of them have passed through the stage of courtship and entered married life under my own personal observation, and even the most fastidious could find nothing but what was proper and pure. We have Negro women around us here who are for duty's sake remaining single, though sought by the very best of our young men.
>
> One of the most touching things to come under my notice has been the many mothers who come to beg us to take their girls, saying, I know I am not what I ought to be, but I don't want her to be like me. We could fill Scotia over and over again every year with girls whose parents want them in safe place, so that they may grow into good women. In these nearly fifteen years we have not had the basis of a scandal involving a member of this school inside of our grounds, and we believe that our record as a school both for honesty and purity, will bear comparison with the female schools generally.
>
> It would not be wise however in our zeal to refute the false assertions in Mr. Thomas's book to overlook the fact that many of them are in a measure true. We cannot do our duty to the Negro while we keep ourselves ignorant of his true condition, and no Thomas or any other man can overdraw the picture of the morals of the uncared for masses of the Negro in the South, not because they are Negroes, but because they are uncared for.

Prof. George A. Woodard, Principal of Gregory Normal Institute, Wilmington N.C., writes:

> I have been laboring among the colored race for sixteen years, and we have had three hundred colored youth in our Institution yearly. I cannot be made to think that the majority of them are devoid of morality. We would not keep a pupil in school known to be unchaste. The expulsions for this cause have not averaged one case per year.

Rev. A. B. Hunter of St. Augustine's School, Raleigh, N. C., writes:

I have no doubt that W. H. Thomas's picture is an overstatement and exaggeration of the facts, but the facts are such as to stimulate us all to secure a betterment.

Thirteen years' work here has convinced me of the truth of Prof. DuBois's statement (College-bred negroes, page 57) that "without doubt the greatest social problem of the American Negro at present is sexual purity, and the solving of this problem lies peculiarly upon the homes established among them."

Dr. L. M. Dunton, white, President of Claflin University, Orangeburg, S. C., writes:

In reply to your circular letter permit me to say that I have read W. H. Thomas's book on "The American Negro". I have labored for nearly thirty years among the colored people of South Carolina, and I believe that Mr. Thomas is either wholly unacquainted with the Negro or else he has deliberately undertaken to get up a sensation and possibly a market for his book, by the wholesale denunciation of the race. His statements cannot possibly be true.

Rev. A. C. Osborn, President of Benedict College, Columbia, S. C., writes:

I have been president of this college for six years, with hundreds of girls under my care, and I have not the remotest reason to believe or even to suspect that a single girl connected with this school has committed an act of immorality or has led either before coming here or while here, or afterwards, other than a virtuous life.

Rev. Thomas H. Amos, D.D., Principal of Ferguson Academy, Abbeville, S.C., writes:

The statement with respect to Negro virtue cannot be true. We have 113 boys and girls in our boarding department. They range in age from fourteen to thirty years, and never have we known of any indecent conduct on the part of either sex toward the other. I frequently inspect the walls and fences that are marked in crayon or pencil and not more than twice have I seen in eight years any writing or drawing of an indecent nature. Our young men once thrashed a boy at their building for introducing some reference to a girl's character, and when I asked them about their conduct, said that they had only one rule in the whole building. It was that no one should speak of the school-girls slightingly, and whoever did so should be first, thrashed, second, reported to the faculty, and thirdly, expelled from the building. The facts I have in hand release 75 percent of Negro women from most of what Mr. Thomas says. At least 50 percent live above the slightest suspicion, and I think it fair to say 50 percent of those who are suspicioned are not guilty.

Miss Ellen Murray, of St. Helena Island, near Beaufort, S. C., one of the noblest of white Christian women from the North who have consecrated their lives to the upbuilding of this race, writes:

I have been for nearly forty years the Principal of the Penn School, Superintendent of a Sunday-school, President of a Temperance Society, Leader of a Woman's Meeting among the Negroes of St. Helena Island, on the southern coast of South Carolina. There are 6,000 Negroes on the island, who were called the lowest of all the Negroes, and incapable of improvement.

In our school of 270 there are at least 100 young people from fifteen to twenty-two and they are living lives as pure as any white people, however high or refined. The age at which they marry has, since freedom, changed from fifteen to eighteen, on an average. After marriage, the rule is fidelity. I scarcely know a case in which the wife is unfaithful, and the more educated and intelligent the men grow, the more moral they become. I have talked with numbers of teachers from many of the colored schools of the freed people, and I do not believe that any such state of things as Thomas asserts can be found in them. It would be impossible. There are on this island 6,000 Negroes, thirty whites, one constable, one justice, and such a thing as an attack on a white woman has not been known in all these forty years.

The mothers have steadily grown more and more careful of their daughters, providing for them a separate room, seeing that they are not out late in the evening; the churches are stricter on the matter; fathers are sterner with their sons. I do not claim that they are perfect. They were treated as brutes by their owners, who counted on their increase, as a Negro woman said to me bitterly, "just like we count for our chickens." Girls and women were alike forced into sin by the whip. In the two-roomed huts where three or four families crowded, there was no chance for modesty or decency. Hampered by heredity, burdened with poverty and contempt, and vexatious laws to oppose them, with many a stumble and many a fall, they are, nevertheless, pressing up, longing for learning, desirous of re-spectability, taking with eager gratitude all the help they can get. I wish those who talk of the Negro deteriorating could see, in contrast with the floorless huts of slavery, the homes of these people here. Five rooms, floors with rugs, papered walls, chairs, lounge, lamp, sewing machine, dresser with its china, table set with a white cloth and dishes, beds with white spreads and mosquito nets, plain indeed, cheap indeed, but comfortable and paid for.

Miss Mary L. Deas, 83 Morris Street, Charleston, S. C., a teacher in the Avery Institute of that city, writes:

> I think I may safely say that I am well acquainted with the school system of South Carolina. My work for the past fourteen years has been in one of the best known of the schools. I know nearly all of the educators of the colored people of the state, but I do not know one who would knowingly allow a girl sustaining immoral relations with any man to remain in the school, much less to have him pay her expenses. White men pay the tuition of many students, but these students are their children, not their mistresses, and many of these girls grow up honorable and pure women, in spite of their home surroundings. The lessons of chastity taught them in the schools bear fruit in their lives. Avery Institute, where I teach, has over 300 graduates, but not one of whom is living a dissolute life. During the past fourteen years there has been but one case of immorality known to the school authorities. The girl was expelled. All the schools of which I know anything make for purer lives.
>
> Conditions are bad enough, but 90 percent is far too large an estimate for the immoral class. Fearing that my position would cause me to have too optimistic views, my associates being women pure in word and deed, I consulted two men whose business brings them in contact with all classes. They both said that even 50 percent was too large for the vicious of this city. The large class of people who move in good society here regard chastity in women as one of the essentials. The women who have been proven guilty of a fall from sexual virtue are dropped by their former friends. The men of this class show their respect for pure women by seeking them for wives, and by guarding their sisters whenever possible. It is true that fallen women sometimes marry, but they nearly always marry below their rank.

Miss Harriet E. Giles, white, President of Spelman Seminary, of Atlanta, Ga., writes:

> I have been laboring among the colored people for more than twenty years. I am sure there is a steadily growing sentiment against immorality. I think of the girls who have been trained in Christian schools at least 95 percent live moral lives. By this, I mean those who have remained in the schools for several years.

Mr. Fred W. Foster, white, Principal of Dorchester Academy, McInstosh, Ga., writes:

> There are thousands of Negroes who would fight to the death to preserve the purity of their own women or that of white women deserving their respect.

No doubt there are educated Negroes who "presume to be refined" who are licentious, but to say that education and refinement are no barriers against this evil, that there is no refined class of colored people who maintain their marriage vows unspotted, is too far-reaching and glaring a misstatement to go unchallenged.

I have lived and worked among the colored people twelve years, during which time I have tried to get as fair and just an idea of the average Negro character as possible, as well as to learn that which is best, and I have had opportunities of seeing and knowing somewhat of the worst side.

The Negro is the product of generations of entire freedom from restraint, to which has been added the effects of the unrestrained lust of a stronger race; but despite these things there are multitudes of the colored race in America whose lives are as pure, whose regard for the marriage vow as great, and "whose respect for chaste womanhood" as strong as of any other race in our land.

Miss Lucy C. Laney, Principal of Haines Institute, August, Ga., writes:

I have been interested a number of years in noting, as I have passed through the country, to find what a large number of Negroes are true, and have been true, to their marriage vows. It is not an unusual thing to find those who have lived faithfully together for fifty, sixty and sixty-five years. Those of us who have worked for twenty years among the colored people note marked improvement. Nothing cheers our hearts more than to see the large number of fathers who come and enter their children in school, make constant inquiry as to their progress, and who, accompanied by their wives and children, attend the public exercises of the school. This interest is real; they want to know the moral status of their children, they labor for and desire the best for their children, children of one wife. In our kindergarten of forty-five children there were only three illegitimate children.

T. DeS. Tucker, President of Florida State Normal and Industrial College, Tallahassee, Fla., writes:

I have been engaged for nearly thirty-five years, more or less, in duties which have brought me in close contact with our people in every walk of life. When the depths of depravity from which they emerged are taken into consideration the marvel of their advance in morals is simply phenomenal. Specimens of pure womanhood and exalted manhood are to be found among the race today in every village and hamlet in the land. While we have much to struggle for in generations to come, the assertion may be safely ventured that in the light of our past attainments in virtue, our future is safely assured.

Rev. R. C. Bedford, white, who is connected with Tuskegee Institute, writes:

> I have been working for colored people now nineteen years. For eight
> years, 1882 to 1890, I was pastor of a colored church in Montgomery, Ala.
> I have traveled in every Southern State among the graduates of Tuskegee
> and have taken careful note of conditions everywhere I have gone, and
> instead of things being as represented by this book, I have found myself
> wondering all the time how they could be so good. Virtue, not vice, has
> been the characteristic most pronounced everywhere. In the eight years
> I was in Montgomery I made a thorough study of things in the city, and
> while there was much vice in certain localities, the marvel was that there
> were so many absolutely pure homes. During all the time I was there, we
> had not a single case of immorality connected with our church. I have
> been intimately associated with the work here for nineteen years. I know
> every graduate that has gone out of the school, and many of the 5,000
> others who have been students here, and I have been constantly delighted
> with the freedom from anything like gross immorality on the part of a
> very large majority of these people. Things mentioned in the circular are
> the least of our troubles here. I have in mind one of our branch schools, lo-
> cated in a very dark county of Alabama, with eighteen teachers and about
> 400 students. I have just come from the Commencement exercises there
> and during the whole year, though fifteen of the teachers are unmarried,
> there has not been even a breath of scandal.

Miss Charlette R. Thorn, white, Principal of the Calhoun Colored School,
Calhoun, Ala., writes:

> I have been for thirteen years working among, for and with, Negroes. The
> first four years' work and life were at Hampton, and I will say nothing
> much about that, for the Hampton teachers have a better and larger knowl-
> edge of students and graduates than I have. I would say, however, that it
> was because I saw such positive proof of high-mindedness and beauty of
> a character among the Negroes and because we saw, year after year, the
> coming in of earnest, self-respecting boys and girls, that Miss Dillingham
> and I felt we must go out and show the way of light to some who lived in
> dark places and had never had a chance to know what really was the right
> in any part of life.
>
> It was because we had firm belief in the Negro that we came, and each
> year but carries deeper conviction that we were then right. We came here
> (Calhoun) in 1892. During the nine years since I have been constantly
> filled with admiration of the people who, with but little to work for and
> with constant and deep temptations, are able to withstand the temptation
> and struggle on to get a precarious living, in the strength of high convic-
> tions and deep and ever-increasing self-respect. When we came we felt

that the free living represented sin, but in a very few months we believed it represented the natural life of a group of people who had never been shown or taught life on a higher plane. After a few months of life among them they took hold of what little we could do and began to reconstruct their lives. Of course we found many whom we then believed, and still feel, were leading pure, good lives, merely from inborn instincts.

In regard to the morality of our girls at school, I do not want to omit a statement which, knowing the community, seems to be almost miraculous. In the last twelve months only two girls who have ever been in our school have been known to go wrong. One was of mixed Indian, Negro and white blood. She has been brought up in a house of vice and brutality, has heard bad language and low talk and seen low life and brutal living ever since babyhood; has been brutally beaten and knocked about, and it was small wonder that she died last week in sin of every sort. The other, a girl of sixteen, is feeble-minded, so that after trying to teach her for four years we found she knew but little more than when she started in school. These two cases had not been in school for several years, and are the only ones out of many hundred who have attended who have gone astray.

Our boys and young men from sixteen to twenty-five years of age are upright and self-respecting in the majority of cases. Of course, in this community, one of the worst in the whole South, when we came here we found all kinds, good and bad, but there is a daily evidence of desire and strivings for high standards of living, and victories over self that are marvelous.

The statement of William H. Thomas regarding the morals of the race, according to my knowledge, are false when applied to the Negro race as a whole. Of course, no one claims that the race has not its low and bad—all races have these—but the Negro's natural instincts are refined and sensitive.

Rev. H. N. Payne, D. D., white, President of Mary Holmes Seminary, West Point, Miss., writes:

For the past sixteen years I have been continuously engaged in Christian work for and among the colored people.

From that knowledge I say without hesitation that it is not true that "a Negro manhood with decent respect for chaste womanhood does not exist." It is untrue that "marriage is no barrier to illicit sexual indulgence."

That there is a great and saddening amount of immorality among the Negroes is frequently admitted, but that it is universal is unhesitatingly and absolutely denied. I glory in the purity of my own race, though there are some sad, yes, monstrous cases of moral degradation among white women. It has been my good fortune to be personally acquainted with many colored women who were morally as pure as any white women I have ever known. This I say with tender respect and reverence for some who have been very near and dear to me.

Rev. F. G. Woodworth, D. D., white, President of Tougaloo University, Tougaloo, Miss., writes:

The trend and tendency are very decidedly towards better things in the moral life, and it has been in existence long enough to have molded a very considerable portion of the Negro people to a nobler life than Thomas seems to know about. The more I study the matter the more I am convinced that with all the evils resultant from slavery and from the sudden freedom, the indictments brought against the race now have never been fully true, and it is less true now than formerly.

I have had fourteen years of experience and observation in teaching in the heart of the black belt of Mississippi.

There is an increasing number of men who have a high regard for chaste womanhood, who are earnest in the desire to protect women from impurity of every kind. They welcome and forward such agencies; for the promotion of purity is the White Cross with its pledge of reverence for women.

The number of girls who would resent solicitations to evil is not a small one and among those who have been carefully reared, who have had something of moral training, the percentage of those who go astray is a small one. The number of homes where the pure ideal of family life exists has increased constantly since I have been in the South. There are some pure homes among the poor and illiterate. Among those who are educated the dishonored homes are few.

Mrs. Sylvanie F. Williams, white, 1438 Euterpe Street, New Orleans, La., writes:

I have been laboring among the colored people since 1870, and as far as my experience goes, I am prepared to say that there is a decided improvement in the moral status all along the line. I have consulted with other teachers of experience who have taught in public, private and prominent boarding schools, and none of them have ever discovered conditions such as Mr. Thomas names in his exploration of "Negro training schools of prominence." As to illegitimate motherhood of Negro women, I will state that when I first began teaching among the freedman, I was much surprised to find that in a family of several children each had a different name. I have watched that phase of the situation, having an annual register to make each year, and have been pleased to see how they have improved, until today I find, in my school, families of six or more children having the same father, and the celebration of crystal and even silver weddings is quite common. I speak of the lowly people who are laborers, whose children attend the public school up to the fifth grade, because they are not financially able to remain at school beyond that period. The school of which I speak numbers 900 pupils, ranging from six to eighteen years of age. I do not pretend to say that the entire roll is virtuous, although I have no reason to think otherwise, but I do say that the great majority of them are a living refutation of every assertion made by Thomas.

Rev. M. R. Gaines, white, President of Tillotson College, Austin, Tex., writes:

I have been nearly five years in my present position. We have had an average of 200 students a year. There are about fourteen of us white teachers in pretty close touch with this body of young people. Of course, they do not lay their secret thoughts open to us. I do not believe they are so honeycombed with moral depravity and sensuality as these extracts would lead us to suppose.

When I think over cases of known violation of laws of immorality and chastity, I am free to say that the record here will not suffer in comparison with what I could name of experience along similar lines elsewhere. My intimate acquaintance with young people as teacher covers several decades.

Rev. P. B. Guernsey, white, President of Roger Williams University, Nashville, Tenn., writes:

I personally know from letters received and conversations with parents of girls entrusted to this school, that the mothers of our girls are as deeply concerned for the morals and general reputation of their girls as any mothers could be. They have never failed to sanction unreservedly any restrictions and precautions felt to be desirable to protect the girls from even the appearance of evil. I am glad to say that this institution, which has for more than thirty years educated young men and young women side by side in the same classes and upon the same campus, has been, I can safely say, as free from scandal along that line as any co-educational institution that I know anywhere. I have worked in at least one co-educational institution in the North attended entirely by white students, where I saw more to criticise in the relation of the sexes than I have ever seen here. While the moral standards of many colored people are sadly defective, the surprise to me is that, considering all the circumstances and the institution of slavery, the standards should be as high as they are.

Rev. C. A. Isbell, United States Jail Physician and Surgeon, 723 South Sixth Street, Paducah, Ky., writes:

I have been for the past ten or twelve years in contact with the Negro, and have had direct dealings with him. The statements made by W. H. Thomas to my knowledge are not true. The race is misrepresented. We have among us men and women of the highest character. We are not as a race at the top of the ladder in morals, but we are on the way to it.

Mr. W. H. Hunton, Secretary of the International Committee of Young Men's Christian Associations, Colored Men's Department, writes:

After fourteen years of constant laboring among my people throughout the South, especially among young men in the cities and students in boarding schools of all grades, I am firmly convinced that a heroic and successful fight is being waged against immoral tendencies inherited from centuries of debasing slavery. Of course there is much dross yet to be burned away before we can have only pure gold remaining.

I confess with great sorrow of heart that there are some members of my race, and possibly a large proportion, who could be put down as fitting one or more of the foul characteristics of Mr. Thomas, nor do I seek to cover this acknowledgement with the fact that in every other race on the earth, individuals can be found equally low in life and character. But there are various classes among the freedmen as among other people.

Born and reared in Canada, and having spent three years just prior to my coming South in 1888 as a civil servant at Ottawa, where I mingled freely in church and social life with some of the best of white Canadians, I find myself greatly encouraged as I compare my experience of the past fourteen years with those of my earlier life, and especially the three years referred to above. I have met in all sections of the country hundreds of colored women whose bearing has been as suggestive of good as that of the women of the fairer race in the North. I have also come into close contact with thousands of young men whom I know to be struggling against unfortunate inherited tendencies and unfavorable environment.

It is true that only a few of the Negro race have yet attained to the degree of perfection possible among men, but between those few and the submerged masses is a promising and inspiring host of men and women in various stages of moral, intellectual and industrial evolution.

35

Children and the Church

We turn now to the two questions of the training of pulpit and pew for the Negro church. Much might be said of human training, but perhaps the testimony of children themselves would be of some interest. In the colored public schools of Atlanta last May, 1,339 children were asked questions as follows and wrote at the following answers:

Are you a Christian?

AGE.	Yes.	No.
Seven years........................	7	10
Eight years........................	15	31
Nine years........................	27	50
Ten years.........................	42	124
Eleven years.....................	40	140
Twelve years....................	78	156
Thirteen years..................	87	142
Fourteen years.................	89	105
Fifteen years....................	62	57
Sixteen years....................	36	28
Seventeen years...............	10	2
Eighteen years.................	1	....
Total........................	494	845

One-third of the children were church members; of the more mature, 11–18 years of age, 60 percent belong to the church. Nearly all go to church, however.

Do you go to church?

AGE.	Yes.	No.	Some-times	?
Seven years.....................	14	2	....	1
Eight years.....................	45	1	....	....
Nine years.....................	78	1	1	....
Ten years.....................	156	10	3	1
Eleven years..................	172	5	3	....
Twelve years..................	135	7	6	....
Thirteen years..............	224	2	3	....
Fourteen years............	192	1	5	....
Fifteen years............	138	2	....	....
Sixteen years............	59	1	3	....
Seventeen years.........	12	....	....	....
Eighteen years............	1	....	....	....
Not given..................	10	....	....	....

Do you like to go to church?

AGE.	YES.	NO.	SOME-TIMES	?
Seven years..................	16	1	.....	.....
Eight years.....................	45	.....	.....	1
Nine years.....................	75	1	.....	3
Ten years.....................	159	8	.....	3
Eleven years..................	174	5	.....	1
Twelve years..................	247	1	.....	.....
Thirteen years..................	227	.....	.....	2
Fourteen years..................	197	1	.....	.....
Fifteen years..................	137	2	.....	1
Sixteen years.....................	62	.....	1	.....
Seventeen years..............	12	.....	.....	.....
Eighteen years..................	1	.....	....	.....
Not given......................	10	.....	.....	.....

Nearly all like to go to church.

Nearly all go to Sunday-school and like it.

Their denominational affiliations were determined by all sorts of considerations:

Why do you like a certain church the best?

AGE.	On account of parents or relatives.	Because I am a member.	Because I have never attended any other.	Because they treat me nicely there.	Because I go there.	?.	Because it helps me.	Because I think Christ was of that denomination.	Because I believe in that denomination.	Because it is a good, nice church, or very large.	Because they have good services.	Because it has the best method.	Because my girl goes there.	Because the people are good	Because I was converted there.	Because I can do more good there.	Miscellaneous.
Seven years	13	...	...	...	2	2	...	...	...	...	...	...	...	...	...	...	...
Eight years	35	...	...	1	5	2	3	...	...	...	...	...	...	...	...	...	...
Nine years	54	1	...	4	6	7	7	...	...	...	...	...	...	...	...	...	...
Ten years	91	3	3	5	15	26	10	1	10	...	2	1	1	...	...	...	...
Eleven years	113	11	5	4	7	22	4	2	5	3	1	...	1	2	...	...	...
Twelve years	131	13	4	3	28	26	8	2	19	6	2	2	...	2	...	1	...
Thirteen years	121	17	3	1	32	17	3	8	14	8	5	...	...	...	...	...	...
Fourteen years	99	19	2	...	17	19	3	8	16	5	2	...	...	...	3	2	6
Fifteen years	67	8	2	...	11	14	1	6	23	2	...	...	...	1	3	1	1
Sixteen years	23	6	1	...	5	4	...	3	19	...	...	...	...	...	...	1	1
Seventeen years	8	1	...	...	2	...	...	...	...	...	...	...	...	...	...	...	1
Eighteen years	1	...	...	...	...	...	...	...	...	...	...	...	...	...	...	...	...
Not given	4	2	...	...	...	2	...	...	1	...	...	...	...	...	1	...	...

The chief interest, however, lies in their conception of Christianity, as there the answers showed plainly their training. The answers to the question, "What does it mean to be a Christian?" fall into five chief groups. First, then, are the answers which make Christianity simple, moral goodness, such as a child easily comprehends. Such answers were thirty-three in number:

ANSWERS.	AGE, IN YEARS.												
	7	8	9	10	11	12	13	14	15	16	17	18	?
To be good...............	4	10	9	49	32	53	37	18	14	5	...	...	1
To be kind, honest, etc	...	...	2	1	7	4	3	1	...	...	...	...	...
To live a better life...	...	...	...	4	7	10	12	3	5	1	...	...	1
Total.................	4	10	11	54	46	67	52	22	19	6	...	...	2

Some others had the idea of goodness, but added the phrase, "and live for Jesus," although it is not clear just what this addition meant to them. The ages of these were:

Seven years................................... 9

Eight years.................................. 19

Nine years................................... 10

Ten years..................................... 8

Eleven years................................. 7

Twelve years................................. 5

Fourteen years.............................. 1

Total.. 59

Others considered Christianity as the obeying of the ten commandments:

Eight years.................................. 1

Nine years.................................... 2

Ten years..................................... 1

Eleven years................................. 1

Twelve years................................. 10

Thirteen years.............................. 4

Fourteen years.............................. 7

Fifteen years................................ 3

Sixteen years................................ 3

Total.................................... 32

The idea of love for persons as an expression of Christianity was mentioned. Several said it meant "To love everybody"; two said, "To save others."

Seven years................................ 1

Eight years................................. 1

Nine years.................................. 1

Ten years................................... 3

Eleven years		10
Twelve years		15
Thirteen years		8
Fourteen years		9
Fifteen years		11
Sixteen years		2
?		1
Total		61

Others answered, "To serve God," but it is doubtful if they understood by this, ordinary work for anyone, although two said, "Work for God." Most of them probably meant church service:

Eight years		4
Nine years		14
Ten years		30
Eleven years		43
Twelve years		36
Thirteen years		29
Fourteen years		26
Fifteen years		20
Sixteen years		6
Seventeen years		2
Total		210

From this point the answers became more mystical and figurative. Doubtless they had more or less meaning to the writers, but they were repetitions of common phrases and had certain vagueness:

ANSWERS.	AGE, IN YEARS.												
	7	8	9	10	11	12	13	14	15	16	17	18	?
Child of God...	...	1	...	5	4	6	10	6	2	3	....	..	...
Christ-like.....	....	...	...	...	...	6	5	10	6	6	1	..	1
Follow Christ...	...	...	4	7	7	4	11	12	3	3	1	..	...
Soldiers of Christ..........	...	...	...	1	1	1	...	...	...	...	....	..	...
Love God......	...	6	10	9	14	26	26	18	4	4	1	..	11
Believe in Christ	1	1	7	9	18	44	44	43	18	18	7	1	1
Sins forgiven	...	...	...	...	...	5	1	3	1	...	....	..	...
Total......	1	8	21	31	44	80	97	92	66	34	10	1	13

These were followed by phrases which were without doubt theological and understood by few who used them. Some of these phrases were:

"To have true religion and honor God's word."

"To be a member in Christ."

"To be born again."

"To have the Love of God in your soul."

"To honor the Lord Jesus Christ."

"To keep the faith."

"To trust in the Lord."

"To honor God."

Those giving these answers were:

Nine years......................	2
Ten years......................	5
Eleven years....................	6
Twelve years....................	5
Thirteen years..................	13
Fourteen years..................	8
Fifteen years...................	5
Sixteen years...................	3
Total....................	47

A few looked for certain signs of Christianity, as baptism, joining the church, "getting religion," or "being changed":

Seven years.	1
Ten years.	5
Eleven years.	2
Twelve years.	9
Thirteen years.	5
Fourteen years.	5
Fifteen years.	7
Total.	34

Few naturally spoke of the desire for happiness or reward: five mentioned heaven, and one child of eleven, with unconscious socialism, defined a Christian as "a poor man!"

Ten years. 2

Eleven years. 2

Fourteen years. 2

Total.   6

Thirty-seven children answered frankly that they did not know what Christianity was, and seventy-six left the quarry unanswered for lack of knowledge or time:

	AGE, IN YEARS									
ANSWERS.	8	9	10	11	12	13	14	15	16	?
Don't know.............	0	0	9	10	7	4	5	0	1	1
Unanswered...............	4	4	12	9	16	7	9	7	6	0
Total...................	4	4	21	19	23	11	14	7	7	1

Analyzing these answers further they reveal some interesting facts.

ANSWERS.	7–12 years	13 years and older
Moral and altruistic…	296	148
Higher will and phrases..	387	505
Miscellaneous……..	21	19
Unanswered, etc.…	123	97

The children of twelve and under had the clearer and simpler idea of the direct connection of goodness and Christianity. The older children tended more toward phrases which sought to express the fact that religion had reference to some higher will. Indeed this was the more popular idea, and 70 percent of the children spoke of Christianity as "Love for God," "Belief in Christ," or some such phrase. Clear as such phrases may be to some minds, they undoubtedly point to a lack in the moral training of Negro children. They evidently are not impressed to a sufficiently large extent with the fact that moral goodness is the first requirement of a Christian life.

A few typical answers, given *verbatim*, follow:

What does it mean to be a Christian?

AGE 13.

(a) It means that you love God, the church, and the people, and all good things, but hate evil things.

(b) To be kind, honest, and trustworthy.

(c) To be a Christian means to live and die the same.

(d) It means to serve God in a true way and live above suspicion.

(e) To live as God would have you live.

(f) To give your heart to God.

(g) To praise the Lord.

(h) Holy and happy.

AGE 14.

(a) To believe in God and not only be called a Christian, but to live the life of one.

(b) To tell the truth, to have a clean heart, and to keep the church laws.

(c) To change your mind to do right.

(d) To live for Christ and try to help others to come to Him.

(e) To live for Christ and obey the word of the Lord Jesus Christ, who died to save us.

(f) To have your sins pardoned by God and to be washed in the blood of the Lamb.

(g) When the Lord has forgiven you of your sins and you know it and you mean to follow Him the balance of your days and do all you can to make others come to Him.

(h) To keep in the right path.

(i) To obey the laws of the church.

(j) To hold love in your heart toward God and all mankind and work on earth for the upbuilding of God's cause.

(k) To believe that Jesus is the Son of God, and that all power is in His hand.

(l) A Christian means something more than praying.

AGE 15.

(a) To be a holy person.

(b) To be truthful and never swear.

AGE 16.

(a) To be true and honest.

(b) If I am not a Christian in the day of judgment my soul will be lost, because Christ has said that if a man is not born again he cannot enter the kingdom of God. Therefore, I serve and love the Lord.

36

Training of Ministers

There are in the United States the following theological schools designed especially for Negroes:

Atlanta Baptist College, Atlanta, Ga., Baptist........................	1867
Union University, Richmond, Va., Baptist..............................	1867
Biddle University, Charlotte, N.C., Presbyterian......................	1867
Howard, Washington, D.C., non-sectarian	1870
Lincoln University, Pennsylvania, Presbyterian.....................	1871
Talladega, Talladega, Ala., Congregational...........................	1872
Stillman, Tuscaloosa, Ala., Presbyterian.............................	1876
Gammon, Atlanta, Ga., Methodist Episcopal........................	1883
Braden, Nashville, Tenn., Methodist Episcopal.......................	1889
King Hall, Washington, D.C., Protestant Episcopal..................	1890
Fisk University, Nashville, Tenn., Congregational.....................	1892
Wilberforce, Wilberforce, Ohio, African Methodist Episcopal......	1891
Straight University, New Orleans, La., Congregational................	?

The detailed figures as to these schools are as follows:

	Howard.	Braden.	Lincoln	Atlanta Baptist.	Stillman	Talladega.
Length of course	3, 4	3	3	4	3	3
Length of session	34	32	28	26	35	35
Teachers	*4	1	+3	2	2	2

* Three others assist partially.
+ Five others teach partially.

	Howard.	Braden.	Lincoln	Atlanta Baptist.	Stillman	Talladega.
Students	61	20	61	28	18	17
Students with A.B. and B.S. degrees	1	0	38	0	0	0
Total number graduates	199	..	330	48	60	55
Prospective graduates of 1903	7	10	16	0	4	4
Value of grounds and buildings	...	..	$36,000	$75,000	$10,000	$4,500
Endowment fund	$45,100	..	144,000	1,000	0	13,000
Total income	4,261	..	...	...	2,500	2,815
Volumes in library	1,400	500	...	2,500	3,000	2,000

	King Hall.	Fisk.	Union University.	Wilberforce.	Biddle.	Straight.	Gammon.
Length of course	3	3	3	3	3	....	3
Length of session	35	37	33	36	35	....	30
Teachers	2	2	5	2	±2	1	5
Students	16	2	62	4	17	....	62
Students with A.B. and B.S. degrees	0	0	0	....	13	2	6
Total number graduates	17	9	150	40	102	9	177
Prospective graduates of 1903	1	0	5	....	2	2	12
Value of grounds and buildings	$30,000	$30,00	$300,000	$12,000.00	$200,000	0	$100,00
Endowment fund	....	4,033	70,000	....	85,000	0	562,096
Total income	....	....	6,000	3,731.89	....	....	20,000
Volumes in library	3,000	1,000	7,000	2,800	12,800	500	12,500

This shows thirty-three teachers and 368 theological students. Of these students sixty are college graduates. The total number of theological graduates is 1,196, and sixty-three more graduated in 1903. The reported value of grounds and buildings was $797,500 and the endowment amounted to $944,229, of which $562,096

± Two others assist partially.

belonged to one institution. The income was reported only partially and amounted to $39,307.89. The libraries held 49,000 books. In many cases of omitted figures the items are not differentiated from the general figures relating to the institution, of which the theological school is a part. The reports from certain of the schools speak of their present condition and work.

ATLANTA BAPTIST COLLEGE. – The great difficulty in theological training is, that aspirants for the ministry, who have such literary training as would fit them to pursue a theological course with profit, find themselves able to meet the demands of most congregations without such training, and those who have not that literary training can take only the most elementary course in theology. The result is, speaking generally, that few of our students are able to complete a course in theology, and the average ability of the students of that department is not high. This means, of course, that the demand is for general culture and rhetorical ability in the pulpit rather than theological training. I think there is an increasing demand for more culture in the pulpit but not for specially theological training. In view of the fact that so large a number of the Negro ministry are uneducated, I am convinced of the fact that a most important class of theological training is that given in local ministers' institutions, of short duration, and dealing with exclusively Biblical topics.

FISK UNIVERSITY. – We have no regular Theological Department this year. Mr. Morrow taught some college students who took a theological elective in the fall term.

We have had no applications that we considered at all worth the considering. Insufficient preparation and other circumstances have turned down all that we have had.

GAMMON – Some of the students who come to us from other institutions of theological training show that in some of them the instruction is of a very low grade. From other evidences, I believe, however, that, considering all the circumstances, a fair standard is maintained, but there should evidently be an effort made to secure more college-prepared students, and a more advanced course for them.

Wide observation and reports from our students from nearly every part of the nation convince me that the Negro's religious condition is steadily improving and that there is still room for large advance.

BRADEN SCHOOL OF THEOLOGY. – I have been engaged in the work of the Christian ministry for more than a quarter of a century, and will say without hesitation that I have never seen a more hopeful outlook for the moral uplift of our people than now. Better homes, higher appreciation of public instruction, the schools and colleges established and fostered by various religious denominations, with the constantly elevating standards of the Christian ministry are among the potential factors in the marvelous change in the religious sentiment of the Negro.

To meet the increasing demand of this transitional church and to direct the religious energies of this most emotional race, means an increasing output of our theological seminaries or schools which devote their time to this special work. But this preparation must be based upon the most enlarged views of the vast spiritual needs of the race. It must be broader than a mere denominational predilection. It involves a world-wide preparation for a world-wide salvation. While our theological schools are doing a magnificent work it must be admitted that the supply is not equal to the demands. The facilities for the kind of work required ought to be increased a hundredfold. Even then it would tax the energies of those directing affairs to meet the imperative demands for the thoroughly trained ministry.

VIRGINIA UNION UNIVERSITY. – A very small proportion of those who are entering the Negro ministry are receiving a broad, thorough training similar to that given in any Northern theological seminary. The weak points in this training are the same as in the training of Northern schools. I believe there is not enough attention given to relating the truth which is learned to life and the conditions with which the pastor will be surrounded. The theological student is not trained sufficiently in the problems of the community, the possibilities of increasing the welfare of the people, in practical ethics, in the practical hand to hand use of the Bible in effective public speaking. But notwithstanding these failures, the record of our school shows, at least, that men with ordinary ability and such training as has been given have proved very useful in winning converts, in building up the character of the church and in improving the conditions of the communities. I think their record as useful ministers of the gospel would bear comparison with the record of the graduates of any Northern theological seminary.

As for the demand for this kind of education, our students, if they have ability, find no difficulty in securing wide fields of usefulness. We therefore feel that there is a large demand for men trained in this way. I do not believe that the character of the training should be changed, but I do believe that added emphasis should be placed on some things. I cannot see how a preacher can be a specialist in matters of religion without being able to get the foundations of questions, without knowing how to use his Greek and Hebrew Bible, without knowing church history, theology and homiletics. I believe he needs these things, but with them he needs more knowledge of modern conditions and methods and the possibilities and ideals of individual and community life.

WALDEN. – This school was formerly known as Central Tennessee College. Rev. John Braden, who was for nearly a quarter of a century its president, organized, in 1889, a theological department which was continued under his supervision for nearly ten years. His death occurred in 1899, which closed the department. It is not possible to furnish you with correct data as to the school during the last three or four years of the life of the late Dr. Braden.

The change in the name of the school from Central Tennessee College to Walden University was followed by the election of Rev. Jay Benson Hamilton, D.D., as president to succeed the lamented Dr. John Braden. The theological department has been reorganized and is now known as the Braden School of Theology of Walden University, thus perpetuating the name of its founder.

STRAIGHT UNIVERSITY. – Most of our students take only a partial course, and for this reason do not appear among our graduates. The total attendance this year is eleven. Seven of these are pursuing studies in other departments.

I am without assistance at present. Our work is not well developed, but much good has been done and the future looks more hopeful.

My judgment is that hardly sufficient attention has been given to the education of our ministry. Still good foundations have been laid, and the importance of the subject is better understood. The demand is increasing. Churches which a few years ago were satisfied with uneducated men now search the country for men of high character and intelligence.

As to the success of the educated ministers that has been fully settled. The old assertion oft repeated that educated ministers could not preach successfully to churches of ignorant people has been thoroughly discredited in the city and the country. As to the education itself, the conception of religion as including all life within its scope and the duty of the minister to interest himself in sociology and the material and educational progress of the people should be insisted on.

KING HALL. (a) The success of theological training in the past has been, considering the conditions, unparalleled. I doubt if history records another instance of a slave and subject population producing in so brief a space so many intelligent, progressive and high-minded men as are to be found in the pulpits of the Negro churches. It cannot be denied that there is still much ignorance and that a very lofty standard of morality is not always upheld, yet in view of historical and social convictions, the dominant emotions may be pride and thanksgiving for past achievement.

(b) The present condition of theological training gives ground for hope that conditions in the future will be superior to those in the past. The rule in former years has been that any man who evinced a slight degree of rhetorical or oratorical aptitude, or gave any promise of becoming useful to his denomination, was admitted to the ministry with little or no regard to his academic or theological preparation, but that method is the exception rather than the rule today. All of the religious denominations now demand some sort of intellectual preparation as a preliminary to ordination or licensure, and the rapid multiplication in these latter years of theological seminaries prophesies increase in the numbers of a well-trained ministry. Moreover, the diffusion of popular intelligence and the educational advance of the race will more and more demand an educated ministry, just as the steady quickening and strengthening of the ethical sense in the race will more and more demand moral purity and piety in those who minister at the altars.

(c) The direction it should take:

It should be dominantly and emphatically ethical and spiritual. The race must have clean, pure, high-minded men in her ministry, or it is doomed. Like priest, like people, and morality is the basis of the race's life. It must be soundly intellectual. There should be broad culture and a thorough scholarship. The bombastic and pretentious must be barred, at any rate sternly discouraged. If the alternative is broad and thorough academic, or merely theological training, I would say, choose the former, for with that any deficiency in the latter can be easily remedied.

The tendency has been, and it is, to reverse this order. There is no training like that of the college and there is no people who stand in so much need of it as Negroes, and hence they must resist every effort to rob them of its advantages.

The training of the minister should also be practical. The race needs good, educated men, but it needs, and needs sorely, leadership in all that pertains to race development, and mere goodness and intelligence are not always guarantees of practical power. The Negro minister needs to know and do more than merely preach and pray. He must be possessed of public spirit and have the capacity to cooperate in educational and other social movements which promise present as well as prospective salvation. He must fit himself to preach and also practice the scripture that hath the promise of the life that now is as well as that which is to come.

The course of study at one school is subjoined as fairly typical of the courses offered in all the schools:

Virginia Union University

Bachelor of Divinity Course

FIRST YEAR

First Term.	*Second Term.*
Biblical Introduction	Biblical Introduction
Hebrew Language	Hebrew Language
Greek Interpretation	Greek Interpretation
Sacred Rhetoric and Elocution	Sacred Rhetoric and Elocution
Vocal Music	Vocal Music

SECOND YEAR

Church History	Church History
Hebrew Interpretation	Homiletics
Greek Interpretation	Christian Theology
Sacred Rhetoric and Elocution	Sacred Rhetoric and Elocution
Vocal Music	Vocal Music

THIRD YEAR

Biblical Introduction	Pastoral Duties
Homiletics and Church Polity	Theology and Ethics
Christian Theology	Electives
Sacred Rhetoric and Elocution	Sacred Rhetoric and Elocution

Candidates for the degree of Bachelor of Divinity, before entering upon the theological course, must have completed in a satisfactory manner the common school studies, namely: Reading, Spelling, Writing, Grammar, Geography, United States History, and Arithmetic. They must also have done faithful work for at least, one year of eight months, with five recitations a week in each of the following subjects and groups of subjects and must pass a satisfactory examination in at least eleven of these subjects before entering upon the theological course, two of which must be English Literature and Rhetoric and Composition. The subjects and groups of subjects are as follows: English Literature, Rhetoric and Composition, English History and General History, Physical Geography and Botany, Physics and Physiology, Algebra, Geometry, Civil Government and Ethics, and Industrial Training.

In addition to the required English studies, candidates for the degree of Bachelor of Divinity, before entering the classes in Hebrew and Greek, must pursue a course in Greek, which shall include Greek Grammar, Composition, and three books of the Anabasis.

Candidates for the degree of Bachelor of Theology, before entering upon the studies of the theological course, must possess the same English qualifications and pass the same tests upon English subjects as are required of candidates for the degree of Bachelor of Divinity.

Negroes have also attended theological schools in the North. It has been impossible to get a full account of these, but some figures are available:

INSTITUTION.	NEGRO GRADUATES.
Christian Biblical Institute, Stanfordville, N.Y........	Two.
Presbyterian Theological Seminary, Omaha, Neb......	Some.
Rochester Theological Seminary, Rochester, N.Y......	One.
Tufts College, Divinity School, Tufts College, Mass...	One.
Episcopal Theological School, Cambridge, Mass......	Two.
Chicago Theological Seminary, Chicago, Ill...........	Four.
Seabury Divinity School, Faribault, Minn..............	Two.
New Church Theological School, Cambridge, Mass...	One.
Allegheny Theological Seminary, Allegheny, Pa......	Four.
Ryder Divinity School, Lombard University, Galesburg, IL...................................	One.
Reade Theological Seminary, Taylor University, Upland, Ind....................................	Some.
Lane Theological Seminary, Cincinnati, Oh...........	Few.
Princeton Theological Seminary, Princeton, N.J......	Some.
St. Joseph's Seminary, Baltimore, Md..................	Four.
Union Biblical Seminary, Dayton, O....................	Some.
General Theological Seminary of Protestant Episcopal Church New York, N.Y..........	Six.
Eureka College, Bible Department, Eureka, Ill........	One.
Union Theological Seminary, New York, N.Y.........	About twelve.
University of Chicago, Divinity School, Chicago Ill....................................	Eight.
Meadville Theological School, Meadville, Pa.........	One.
Oberlin Theological Seminary, Oberlin, O.............	Twelve (?).
St. Mary's Seminary, Baltimore, Md.....................	Three.
Shurtleff College, Theological Department, Upper Alton, Ill..........	One.
Yale Divinity School, New Haven, Conn................	Ten (?).
Hamilton Theological Seminary, Colgate University, Hamilton, N.Y.	Two.
Xenia Theological Seminary, Xenia, O..................	Three.
Reformed Presbyterian Theological Seminary, Allegheny, Pa.........	Two.
Moravian Theological Seminary, Bethlehem, Pa.......................	One.
Hillsdale College, Theological School, Hillsdale, Mich.................	Five.
Evangelical Theological Seminary, Gettysburg, Pa.....................	One.

Concordia College, Springfield, Ill..	Two.
McCormick Theological Seminary, Chicago, Ill..........................	Three.
Union Christian College, Theological Department, Merom, Ind........	Seventeen.
Hartford Theological Seminary, Hartford, Conn.........................	Eight or ten.
Newton Theological Institution, Newton Center, Mass..................	Twenty-five.
Divinity School of the Protestant Episcopal Church, Philadelphia, Pa..	Ten or twelve.
Drew Theological Seminary, Madison, N.J..............................	Some.
Auburn Theological Seminary, Auburn, N.Y...........................	"
Drake University, Bible Department, Des Moines, Ia...................	"
Western Theological Seminary, Allegheny, Pa..........................	"
Pacific Theological Seminary, Oakland, Cal............................	"
Nashotah House, Nashotah, Wis...	"
Andover Theological Seminary, Andover, Mass........................	Three (?).
Boston University, School of Theology, Boston, Mass.................	Ten.

The following schools in addition have had Negro students, but so far as known no graduates:

Theological Seminary of the Reformed Church............	New Brunswick, N.J.
St. Vincent's Seminary...	Beatty, Pa
Kenyon College Divinity School.............................	Gambier, O.
Susquehanna University Theological Department.........	Selinsgrove, Pa
Greenville College School of Theology.....................	Greenville, Ill.
Augustana Theological Seminary............................	Rock Island, Ill.
German Evangelical Lutheran Seminary, Capital University...	Columbus, O.
Crozier Theological Seminary.................................	Chester, Pa.
Theological Seminary of Reformed Church.................	Lancaster, Pa.
Temple College of Philadelphia, Theological School.......	Philadelphia, Pa.

The color line is, of course, evident in such institutions in spite of religion. The schools above admit Negroes. The following schools would admit them if they applied, but they never had applicants:

St. Paul Seminary............	St. Paul, Minn.
St. Lawrence University........	Canton, N.Y.
St. Joseph's Seminary.........	Yonkers, N.Y.
St. Charles's Seminary	Overbrook, Pa.
United Church Seminary	Minneapolis, Minn.
Augsburg Seminary.........	Minneapolis, Minn.
Western Theological Seminary........	Holland, Mich.
Cobb Divinity School.........	Lewiston, Me.
Bangor Theological Seminary..................	Bangor, Me.

Wartburg Seminary..........	Dubuque, Ia.
Charles City College.........	Charles City, Ia.
Union Biblical Institute........	Naperville, Ill.
Chicago Lutheran Theological Seminary......... ..	Chicago, Ill.
Berkeley Divinity School.........	Middletown, Conn.
San Francisco Theological Seminary...........	San Anselmo, Cal.
Concordia Theological Seminary.........	St. Louis, Mo.
Redemptorist College of Ilchester...............	Ilchester, Mo.

In the following schools there have been no Negro applicants, and it is not certain whether Negroes would be admitted.

Church Divinity School of the Pacific..........	San Mateo, Cal.
Western Theological Seminary................	Atchison, Kan.
Mt. St. Mary's Theological School............	Mt. St. Mary's, Md.
St. John's University.........	Collegeville, Minn.
Theological Seminary of the Evangelical Lutheran Church...	Philadelphia, Pa.
Erskine Theological Seminary.........	Duewest, S.C.
Union Theological Seminary.........	Richmond, Va.
German Lutheran Seminary.........	St. Paul, Minn.
Heidelberg Theological Seminary.........	Tiffin, O.
St. Bernard's Seminary.........	Rochester, N.Y.
Louisville Presbyterian Theological Seminary.........	Louisville, Ky.
Red Wing Seminary.........	Red Wing, Minn.
Ursinus College School of Theology.........	Philadelphia, Pa.
St. Paul's College.........	St. Paul, Minn.

The following schools are non-committal on the question:

Hartwick Seminary.........	Hartwick Seminary, N.Y.
Eugene Divinity School........	Eugene, Ore.
Kenrick Theological Seminary.............	St. Louis, Mo.

The following schools do not receive Negroes for obvious reasons of languages, etc.:

German Martin Luther Seminary.........	Buffalo N.Y.
Norwegian Danish Theological Seminary.......... .	Evanston, Ind.
Jewish Theological Seminary........	New York, N.Y.
German Theological School of Newark.......... ...	Madison, N.J.

The following schools do not admit Negroes:

Denver Theological Seminary...............	Denver, Col.
St. Viateur's College....................	Kankakee, Ill.
St. Meinrad's Ecclesiastical Seminary........	St. Meinrad, Ind.
Grand View College.................	Des Moines, Ia.
Presbyterian Theological Seminary...........	Danville, Ky.
Southern Baptist Theological Seminary........	Louisville, Ky.
Westminster Theological Seminary...........	Westminster, Md.
Redemptorist Seminary of St. Louis Province...	Kansas City, Mo.
Central Wesleyan College................	Warrenton, Mo.
Seminary of the Immaculate Conception.......	South Orange, N.J.
St. Mary's College	Belmont, N.C.
St. Charle's Seminary...................	Carthagena, O.
Presbyterian Theological Seminary...........	Columbia, S.C.
Evangelical Lutheran Seminary	Mount Pleasant, S.C.
Grant University....................	Chattanooga, Tenn.
Southwestern Presbyterian University	Clarksville, Tenn.
Vanderbilt University	Nashville, Tenn.
University of the South	Sewanee, Tenn.
Episcopal Theological Seminary	Theological Seminary, Va.
Provincial Seminary of St. Francis of Sales	St. Francis, Wis.
Evangelical Lutheran Theological Seminary	Wauwatosa, Wis.
Theological Seminary of Eden College........	St. Louis, Mo.
Mission House of the Reformed Church	Franklin, Wis.
Evangelical Lutheran Theological Seminary	Saginaw, Mich.
Christian University Theological Department...	Canton, Mo.
St. Stanislaus Seminary	Florisant, Mo.
St. Mary's Theological Seminary	Cleveland, O.
St. Vincent's Seminary	Philadelphia, Pa.
Rio Grande Congregational Training School...	El Paso, Tex.
Kansas City University, College of Theology....	Kansas City, Kan.

We have, therefore, a record of at least 185 Negro graduates of Northern theological schools. They have not gone to these schools in large enough number to allow any very valuable conclusions to be drawn, but the authorities of the schools have returned answers to several questions:

How have your colored students compared with others in ability?

> They have been quite average in ability. Mr. _____ was *quite* scholarly. Mr. ____ did not take readily to accurate scholarship, but good in gaining

general information. He used what he gained quite effectively. – Christian Biblical Institute.

The one student was of fair ability and compared with others in his class. – Presbyterian Theological Seminary.

Those we have had are so few in number that no conclusions with regard to the ability of the race can be drawn from them. If I were to judge only from those who have come to the Seminary I should be obliged to say that they were far below the average of our white students. – Rochester Theological Seminary.

We gave _____, a young Baptist minister, the B.D. since graduation. We felt that we owed something to his race. – Tufts College, Divinity School.

They have compared well. One was an excellent scholar, but no more than some whites. – Episcopal Theological School.

About up to average. One was an African chief, was a man of force; a second was weak as a scholar, but had unusual dramatic power; the third is a successful pastor. One, a B.A., we dismissed because he could not keep up with the work. Others left for similar reasons. – Chicago Theological Seminary.

Favorably. – Seabury Divinity School.

Favorably. – New Church Theological School.

Very well. – Allegheney Theological Seminary.

Mr. _____ was an excellent student, both in scholarship and character. He has been for some years an influential member of the faculty of Guadalupe College, Seguin, Texas. – Ryder Divinity School, Lombard University.

Nearly equal. – Reade Theological Seminary of Taylor University.

Equal in diligence and regularity, superior with average in memory; below average in logical precision, and below average in orderly arrangement of knowledge. – Lane Theological Seminary.

Not unfavorably, although some of them have proven unable to pursue our course owing to lack of preliminary education. – Princeton Theological Seminary.

Two of our colored boys were among the best. The others were average students. Remember that the students of this house attend the lectures at St. Mary's Seminary, the National Seminary of the United States, in which are about 240 students, all whites. – St. Joseph's Seminary.

Their previous advantages were poor, and they themselves not of the best in natural adaptation. – Union Biblical Seminary.

They have been quite equal to the average white student in ability. – General Theological Seminary.

About average. – Eureka College, Bible Department.

This is a difficult question to answer and all the reply that is possible must be based on the individual opinion of the one entertaining it. There is no one person living who knows all of the colored students who have attended this Seminary. Personally I have known about six. Three of these were men of good ability, two of them above rather than below the medium line. Three others were below the average, two of them being distinctly inferior to the white low grade. But, on the other hand, it should be added that one of the six graduated with the diploma of the Seminary. He was above the ordinary average. – Union Theological Seminary.

Fairly well. Some of them have been able, some rather bright, but shallow, and two or three weak. A greater diversity than among whites. – University of Chicago, Divinity School.

Most of our colored students have been "specials," i.e., not members of our regular classes (Junior, Middle and Senior), but taking a partial course in connection with their service of the African Methodist Episcopal Church in this place. Their pastoral duties, of course, absorbed most of their time. Perhaps their average ability, as manifested to us, was hardly equal to that of our other students as scholars. – Meadville Theological School.

During the ten years of my teaching here the grade of men has been very good indeed. We get some of the best and very rarely any of the poorest. I mean that they grade with our other students, though no colored man has ever led the Seminary in scholarship. They have taken second and third grade scholarships, but not a first. – Oberlin Theological Seminary.

The three graduates have stood well up among the first third of their classes. –St. Mary's Seminary.

Most not up to average. One very much excelled in ability. – Shurtleff College.

They have varied greatly. It has seemed to depend largely upon the school at which they prepared. – Yale Divinity School.

They were not college men, as our students universally are, hence were at a disadvantage. Notwithstanding, they worked honestly and did well. – Xenia Theological Seminary.

These men were educated in the North; one, _____, was born in Allegheny, Pa. – Reformed Presbyterian Theological Seminary.

He compared well; was their equal in many respects, only somewhat less logical in thought and expression, and perhaps less logical and independent in ideas. – Moravian Theological Seminary.

Not above the average. – Hillsdale College

Four of these compared favorably with the other students in some respects; the others were total failures. – Concordia College.

No difference appreciable. – McCormick Theological Seminary.

Somewhat below the average of white students. – Union Christian College, Theological Seminary.

They have not equaled the average of our other students, except perhaps in two cases, but they have not usually fallen far below. – Hartford Theological Seminary.

Their ability has been from fair to good. That of a few of the men may be called very good. – Newton Theological Seminary.

Only a few have compared favorably. One alone, if I am rightly informed, can be ranked among the *very* able men which this school has graduated. – Divinity School of the Protestant Episcopal Church.

They have maintained a good average. – Drew Theological Seminary.

In ability the average of the colored students has certainly not been below that of others. – Auburn Theological Seminary.

As far as I can learn they have. – Drake University, Bible Department.

Very favorably in most cases. During the past six years while I have been connected with the institution, we have had two colored students. One took a very high stand in the class and was elected president of the class. The other was so deficient in intellectual powers that he was dropped after six weeks' trial.—Western Theological Seminary.

This man, an ordained minister, with a church in San Francisco, took only special studies for one year. Of average ability with others of his class. But was irregular because of pastoral duties.—Pacific Theological Seminary.

He was above the average in scholarship, and took the degree of B.D.—Nashotah House.

How have they compared in character and morals?

Very well. Quite on an average with the white students. They were respected by the white students without the regard to their color.—Christian Biblical Institute.

We never knew any criticisms on earlier.—Presbyterian Theological Seminary.

We cannot complain of any positive infractions of immorality on their part. There has been weakness of purpose, over-sensitiveness to others' opinions, considerable vanity and love of display.—Rochester Theological Seminary.

Compared well in this respect.—Tufts College, Divinity School.

They have been without exception men of good morals and of manly character.—Episcopal Theological School.

Fairly well with others. Though in two or three cases of men who did not graduate there was a lack of determination and persistent effort. One had trouble in his family which led us to advise him to leave the Seminary.—Chicago Theological Seminary.

Favorably.—Seabury Divinity School.

Favorably.—New Church Theological School.

They were not inferior.—Allegheny Theological Seminary.

Very favorably.—Ryder Divinity School, Lombard University.

Not as strong in character.—Reade Theological Seminary of Taylor University.

Well.—Lane Theological Seminary.

Favorably.—Princeton Theological Seminary.

The blacks are just as good as the whites.—St. Joseph's Seminary.

Not so favorably with the white students.—Union Biblical Seminary.

They have been, so far as I know, uniformly excellent in character and morals.—General Theological Seminary of Protestant Episcopal Church.

Much above the average.—Eureka College, Bible Department.

As all of these men were candidates for the ministry it is to be supposed that a reply to this question is superfluous. I have no reason to make any unfavorable comparisons.—Union Theological Seminary.

Generally the equals of the whites. Two or three have been careless about financial honor, and one was dismissed for presenting for his own sermons taken from others.—University of Chicago, Divinity School.

They have compared favorably with our other students in morals and character.—Meadville Theological Seminary.

Our Seminary men have been on the very best—earnest Christians, sane, modest. Nothing in these respects has been left to be desired.—Oberlin Theological Seminary.

Very well.—Shurtleff College, Theological Department.

I have noticed no difference when each had the same chances.—Yale Divinity School.

Quite favorably. All three were earnest and devout.—Xenia Theological Seminary.

He was irreproachable in conduct and bore a good moral character. – Moravian Theological Seminary.

Well. – Hillsdale College, Theological School.

Those educated in our colored Lutheran mission schools in the South compared well. The rest proved to be unsatisfactory. – Concordia College.

No difference. – McCormick Theological Seminary.

Average, good. – Union Christian College, Theological Department.

Very well, as a rule. – Hartford Theological Seminary.

Favorably for the most part. I think it is a strain upon character for them to take their course here, since some of them are inclined to estimate themselves highly and to be ambitious for place. – Newton Theological Institution.

Equal to the white students. All of them better than some of the white students. – Divinity School of the Protestant Episcopal Church.

They have been men of good character so far as I know. – Drew Theological Seminary.

In character and morals they compare evenly in the case of the best men. In other cases they are not very uneven, except that an abnormally large number of colored men borrow money and fail to pay. – Auburn Theological Seminary.

They compare well. – Drake University, Theological Department.

Very favorably. I believe there has been only one case where discipline was necessary. – Western Theological Seminary.

During the vacation of his last year he was charged with immoral conduct by a young woman of his congregation. The matter came into the public press, but the charge was denied by student. – Pacific Theological Seminary.

What has been their success in after life?

Good. – Christian Biblical Institute.

One of these left us at the end of his first year and we have never been able to learn anything from him since. A second was so feeble in scholarship that we had to dismiss him to another institution. The third succeeded in graduating, and has been doing useful service from that time until now. – Rochester Theological Seminary.

Mr. _____ is now in his senior year in Medical School of Tufts College, Boston, Mass. He wants to be doubly prepared for missionary work. – Tufts College, Divinity School.

One is the successful minister of a colored church in Washington, where he has been for nine years, ever since graduation. Another had difficulty in getting a suitable place, but now is well settled. The third is just going out. – Episcopal Theological School.

The four graduates did well. One died in Africa, a second is a professor in a Southern college, the third is a pastor in Washington, D.C., the fourth is a pastor in the South. – Chicago Theological Seminary.

If anything, above the average man of their class. – Seabury Divinity School.

Good. – New Church Theological School.

Not especially noticeable, but very fair. – Allegheny Theological Seminary.

Quite useful. – Reade Theological Seminary of Taylor University.

Two are priests. A third teaches school under his father in New Orleans, La. The fourth is a school teacher in Oklahoma. – St. Joseph's Seminary.

Good, those who remained in the ministry. – Union Biblical Seminary.

As a rule, quite as good as the white fellow students. – General Theological Seminary.

So far as known, satisfactory. – Eureka College, Bible Department.

The one mentioned above as a graduate took a church in New York and made a success of it despite heavy odds. He worked so hard, however, that he undermined his health and died at an early age, respected and beloved by the members of the Presbytery with which he was connected. Most of the others I have not been able to trace. They have belonged to various denominations and I have not had the time to look them up specifically. – Union Theological Seminary.

Some have had marked success; some have done fairly well and a few have proved failures, but I judge as large a proportion have succeeded as among our white students. – University of Chicago, Divinity School.

So far as I have been able to judge from rather scanty information, they have had a fair degree of success in their work. – Meadville Theological School.

All, without exception so far as my own knowledge extends, have been exceptionally faithful and successful. But my personal knowledge does not cover all the cases. – Oberlin Theological Seminary.

They are all doing quite well. – St. Mary's Seminary.

Only two have had a marked success. – Shurtleff College.

Our regular graduates have been successful men. – Yale Divinity School.

So far as I know, it has been good. They are useful and influential men. – Xenia Theological Seminary.

He served as a missionary in Dutch Guiana, South America, disagreed with his superiors, became discontented and was dismissed from the church service because of unsuitable marriage connection, after it had been decided to give him a call in the West Indies. – Moravian Theological Seminary.

Fair. – Hillsdale College, Theological School.

Know not, except in case of Bishop D.A. Payne, whose history belongs to the public. – Evangelical Lutheran Theological Seminary.

Two are missionaries among their own people and, as the reports say, are doing well. – Concordia College.

Fair. – McCormick Theological Seminary.

Not striking. A limited number have made a splendid record – some as teachers, some as soldiers in the United States Army. – Union Christian College, Theological Department.

So far as we know their careers have varied greatly, but we judge that they have generally carried themselves at least with credit. – Hartford Theological Seminary.

Very creditable. – Divinity School of the Protestant Episcopal Church.

So far as I have known they have done well and have proved useful ministers of the people. – Drew Theological Seminary.

Tested numerically, too large a proportion of the colored men have either died young or have thus far failed of being distinctly successful. Of the fifteen two-thirds are successful, and some of the others may become so. The list is too short, however, and the instances too peculiar to make the numerical showing very decisive.—Auburn Theological Seminary.

The one whose name I give is reported as doing good work. – Drake University, Bible Department.

It compares favorably with that of our other graduates. Most of them are laboring under the Board of Freedmen in the South. – Western Theological Seminary.

Other schools say in general:

Of the colored men who have graduated from Boston University, School of Theology, J.W.E. Bowen, Prof. Wm. B. Fenderson, Prof. M.M. Ponton, are perhaps the most prominent. J.A.D. Bloise is a strong preacher (graduate Livingstone College) and A.W. Thomas who graduates tomorrow is a brilliant student. – Boston University, School of Theology.

Harvard has had three students. One excelled in philosophical studies. Two stood low. One of these was "of high character and morals", the other was probably an "imposter" – Harvard University.

In the last twelve years I can remember of about three, no one of whom graduated. They have not been well prepared for our work nor have they been of average ability. – Garrett Biblical Institute.

We are expecting great things of our one colored student who is now with us, and I should like to see our school become a larger factor in the solution of the race problem in the South. – Meadville Theological School.

We have never had a colored student graduate from the Theological Course, though we have had many take the course in part. The difficulty has always been that they come to the course unprepared and have fallen by the wayside. We had one colored student who very successfully completed our Law Course, but he was better prepared to begin the work.

It is very difficult to make the colored students realize that they must have a good foundation before beginning the study of theology. They desire to study theology before they know how to spell or before they have any knowledge of English grammar. So far as our observations have gone, we have never had any complaint to make of them morally, and they are generally very earnest. – The Temple College.

37

Some Notable Preachers

Certain early preachers among the Negroes have been noted in the eleventh and twelfth sections of this treatise. A word ought to be said as to some of their successors. Of the more notable preachers, the African Methodists have furnished Bishop Daniel Payne, a pure Christian and able executive officer, and perhaps the greatest of the bishops of that church; the Baptists have given us D.W. Anderson and Leonard A. Grimes, men of vigor and daring; the Episcopalians are proud of the clean character and learning of Alexander Crummell. Henry Highland Garnett was an eloquent Presbyterian, and the greatest of the Zion Methodists was the late J. C. Price. These men are all noteworthy as upright, able men, eloquent speakers and notable leaders and organizers.

Of living Negro preachers some are worthy of mention: there are the bishops of the three Methodist bodies, of which the foremost character is undoubtedly Bishop Benjamin F. Lee, a worthy successor of Daniel Payne, and a type of man too seldom put to the front; with him may be mentioned Bishop B. T. Tanner. Among the Baptists are two notable organizers, E.C. Morris, President of the National Baptist Convention, and R. F. Boyd, the head of the publishing house. The Presbyterians have in the Rev. Francis J. Grimke a man of power and upright character, and the Negro priest of longest service in the Episcopal Church is one of the most valuable social reformers of the day, the Rev. H. L. Phillips of Philadelphia. The Methodist Episcopal Church has Dr. J. W. E. Bowen, a man of ability and dignity, while the Congregationalists have the Rev. H. H. Proctor.

The men mentioned are not the better known to the public, but they are the ones who are doing the work and leading the best elements of the Negroes. [*]

[*] For the lives of these men, Cf. Simmon's Men of Mark.

38

The Eighth Atlanta Conference

The Eighth Atlanta Conference, to study the Negro Problems, met Tuesday morning, May 26, 1903, in Ware Memorial Chapel, Atlanta University. The subject for study was the NEGRO CHURCH, and the following programme was carried out:

First Session, 10 A.M.

President Horace Bumstead, presiding.

Subject: "Young People and the Church."

Address – Rev. W. H. Holloway, of Thomas County, Ga.

Address – Rev. Dr. Washington Gladden, President of the American Missionary Association.

Second Session, 3 P.M.

Mrs. Anna Wade Richardson, of the Lamson School, Marshallville, Ga., presiding.

Subject: "Women and the Church."

Music – By the pupils of the Mitchell Street School

Address – Mrs. Mary Church Terrell, First President of the National Federation of Colored Women's Clubs.

"Children and the Church." – Report of the Secretary.

Third Session, 8 P.M.

President Horace Bumstead, presiding.

Remarks of President Bumstead.

"How the Religion of Negroes may become more Practical." Rev. C. B. Wilmer, Rector of St. Luke's Protestant Episcopal Church, Atlanta, GA.

"Religion as a Solvent of the Race program." Professor Kelley Miller, of Howard University, Washington, DC.

Symposium: "The Negro Church." Ten-minute speeches: Rev. J. W. E. Bowen, Rev. G. W. Moore, and others.

Resolutions.

Mr. Holloway's address is printed in this treatise as section fifteen, and that of Dr. Gladden as section thirty-nine. Professor Miller's paper has been accepted for publication in the *North American Review*.

The Rev. C. B. Wilmer, representing the Southern white people, said in part that the country owed a debt to these Conferences and that it was a pleasure for him to take part:

"Religion is the chief means of uplifting mankind, but the Negro church is not the power for good that it ought to be. God never made a race incapable of responding to the motives of the gospel. Your past proves this of you, and today there is no higher hero than the Negro who lives a clean, upright life.

"Let the Negro preacher get God's truth into his mind and heart, and then let him get it into the minds and hearts of his hearers. This involves his understanding his people and understanding the truth as it is and as it ought to be applied to their needs.

"In general, the Negro possesses the primal virtue of loving what is above him. That virtue implies the capacity for all virtue. If I speak now of your weaknesses it is only that I may help you. They seem to be, mainly, emotionalism, sensuality, in the wide sense, and lack of perseverance. But, in particular, your having come out of the experience of slavery, exposes you to peculiar temptations. You have passed from childhood into youth, and are passing into manhood. The youth is apt to mistake 'sassiness' for courage, mannishness for manliness, and false pride for self-respect.

"What next, then, are some of the things your preachers should say to you and omit to say? Let the Negro preacher

"(1) Keep politics out of the pulpit.

"(2) Quit trying to reform white folks. Let the white minister raise a crusade against lynching and the Negro against crime.

"(3) Leave off talking about rights for a while and direct attention to duties.

"On the positive side let the Negro preacher

"(1) Inculcate good will toward all men, especially white folks. No cause is rendered easier of solution by hate.

"(2) Insist that only the truth can make you free. Sin is a worse task-master than any man could be.

"(3) Insist that nothing worth the having can be had by a jump, but must be climbed for. This is where perseverance comes in.

"(4) Above all, and finally, let the Negro preacher impress on his congregation that salvation does not mean acquittal from punishment, 'getting off,' nor is it the luxury of emotionalism. It is, negatively, deliverance from sin, and positively, the power of righteousness and service of our fellow men."

39

Remarks of Dr. Washington Gladden

You are citizens, by the definition of the constitution, and you are bound to be good citizens—intelligent citizens, law-abiding citizens, loyal citizens. From these obligations I am sure you do not wish to escape. You mean to do your part in contributing to the peace, the order, the security, the welfare of this great commonwealth in which you live.

In my counsels to the young people of Columbus, O., I went on to say that those to whom the duties as well as the rights of citizenship are entrusted ought not only to fit themselves for their discharge, but to discharge them solemnly and conscientiously, when the time comes for their performance. What shall I say to you who find yourselves obstructed in the performance of these duties? I do not wish to make any inflammatory suggestions; I doubt whether the question of your political rights can be settled by violence. But this much I am safe in saying: people who are thoroughly fitted for good citizenship, and who show by their conduct that they have the disposition and the purpose to be good citizens, are not going to be permanently excluded, in any part of this country, from the responsibilities and duties of citizenship. That is as sure as tomorrow's sun-rising. It cannot be that in the United States of America, young men who are thoroughly intelligent, who know what citizenship means, who love their country, who are working to build up its prosperity and to secure its peace and who are ready to shed their blood in its defence, are going to be forbidden to take any part in its government.

What I have said, therefore, applies to you, I think, even more closely than to the young people of my own state. To you, in an exceptional and impressive way, this truth ought to come home. The more strenuously men oppose your participation in political affairs, the more zealous and diligent ought you to be in qualifying yourselves to take part in them. You are not wholly shut out from such duties and whenever you have a chance to exercise them, let every man see that they are performed with exceptional intelligence and exceptional conscientiousness; that the black man holds the suffrage as a high and sacred trust; that he cannot be bribed or led astray by the arts of the demagogue; that he puts aside his own personal interests when he votes; that he will not even use the suffrage as a means of extorting benefits for his own race at the expense of the rest of the community, but will always keep in view the general welfare; that he is always and everywhere a patriot in his political action; that when he holds an office he discharges its duties more faithfully and honestly than the white man does. I have heard of some instances of this nature since I came to Atlanta—of men in public station whose white neighbors testify concerning them that their conduct is blameless and their service of the highest order. Let such instances be multiplied. Hold up the standard everywhere; rally round it all your people. Let it be your constant endeavor, your highest ambition to infuse this spirit, this purpose, into the thought and the life of all colored men. Before such a purpose as that the barriers of political exclusiveness are sure to go down.

Do not understand me as justifying or excusing those exclusions. I think they are utterly many. But I am pointing out to you the kind of weapons with which you can surely batter them down.

And now, very briefly, what can we say of the relations of the young people to the church? Here are these 1,210,481 young people under twenty-one. They are all citizens of Georgia; they all belong to the state. Do they all belong to the church? No; I fear not. They all belong to God; they are all His children; they owe Him love and reverence; if they are filial children, prodigal children, they are all God's children; they cannot, if they renounce and forswear it, rid themselves of the obligation of allegiance to Him. We may say of them, that they all belong in one sense to the kingdom of God....

Here again I find myself in some doubt as to the fitness of these words to your peculiar circumstances. To those of you who live in Atlanta I can speak with confidence for I know that you can find a church here of which all that I say is true, in which you can find the kind of instruction and inspiration you need, to which you can attach yourselves with intelligent enthusiasm, with which you can join in the work of uplifting humanity. I suppose that there are churches of the same sort in many of the Southern cities in which you could be welcome. Doubtless there are a great many churches in all the Southern states which are far below this ideal, in which the religious instruction you would receive would be imperfect, in which the prevailing idea of religion would be one that no intelligent and conscientious person could accept. Many of you will find yourselves in communities in which the only churches are of this kind. I am not familiar enough with the situation in such communities to give you any very positive counsel respecting your conduct. I had hoped that I might be able to attend the whole of this conference, and that then I might be able to gain some information which would enable me to form a clearer judgment upon these questions. What I say about it now must be very provisional and tentative.

1. In the first place, it seems to me that you are bound to do all you can for the purification of the ideal of the Christian church. What the Christian church is, what it ought to stand for, you have some clear idea. You know that it stands, above all things, for pure conduct and high character; that its members ought to be men and women of blameless lives; that its ministers ought to be examples of virtue and honor and nobility. You know that conversion is no mere ebullition of religious emotion; that it is a change of mind and heart and life; a change from untruth to veracity, from impurity to chastity, from selfishness to unselfishness, from the spirit which is always asking, "How much am I going to get out of this?" to the spirit which is always saying, "Where can I give the most to those who are neediest?" You know that a Christian church ought not to be a company of men and women whose main business is having a good time—by getting happy and convincing themselves that they are sure of going to heaven—but whose main business is bringing heaven down to earth by showing men how to live such clean, beautiful, unselfish lives that the wilderness and the solitary place are glad for them, and that flowers of Paradise spring up in their path wherever they go. And I think it is your first duty to enforce this high and true ideal of what a church ought to be upon all the people with whom you come in contact. You will have to be wise about it. It will not do to be harsh and censorious in your judgments of the ideas and practices of those whom you are trying to lead into the light; you must persuade them by lifting up higher ideals before them, rather than by condemning and denouncing their ways. But I am sure that the young men and women who go out from such schools as this can do much, if they are wise and kind, to purify and elevate the ideals of the church in the communities where they live.

2. In some cases, doubtless, it will be found impracticable to improve the conditions of the existing churches, and it will, therefore, be necessary to organize new churches in which the essentials of Christianity can be maintained and exemplified. This will call for hard and self-condemning work. It will demand faith and courage and patience and gentleness; but it may be work of the highest value and productiveness, and you must be ready for it.

3. Finally, let me express my belief that no other kind of work can be more vital or more fruitful in the elevation of the Negro race than the work of the ministry when it is exercised with intelligence and fidelity and devotion to the highest standards of Christian conduct and character.

There are few positions in which a young man can do more harm than in the leadership of a church which is the exponent of nothing better than a mere emotional religionism; in which pietism is divorced from character and made the cover of all kinds of immoralities. But, on the other hand, there are few positions in which a young man can do more good than as the pastor of a church in which clean living and unselfish service are exemplified; a church which stands for all the great verities of manhood and womanhood and lifts up a standard around which the elements that make for social and civic righteousness may gather and do heroic battle for God and home and native land. I do not believe that such churches as these are likely, in the present order of things, to be very popular all at once. It is probable that young men who undertake to organize and lead them will have to be content with the hard work and small compensation. They can find softer places and betters salaries in churches where the standards are different. But no man can afford to lower his ideals for the sake of pelf or popularity. The elevation of the Negro race will wait a long time under such leadership. But men who are not looking for such berths, men to whom life means service, can find, in the Christian ministry, a great opportunity to serve their race and their country.

Such are the ideals which will, I trust, commend themselves to your choice as you go out to the work of life. For men and women with such purposes and aims the church has need and the state has need, and great rewards are waiting for them. I want you to win success, the true success—that which is won not by outstripping our neighbors but by helping them to get on their feet and keep in the way of life. That is not what the world means by success, but it is the only true success, believe me. Now is the time for you to get this truth firmly fixed in your own minds, not only as a pleasing sentiment, but as a working theory of life.

40

Resolutions

The Eighth Atlanta Conference is impressed by the great crying need of a strengthening of religious effort and moral inspiration among the masses of the Negro people.

We are passing through that critical period of religious evolution when the low moral and intellectual standard of the past and the curious custom of emotional fervor are not longer attracting the young and ought in justice to repel the intelligent and the good.

At the same time religion of mere reason and morality will not alone supply the dynamic of spiritual inspiration and sacrifice.

We need, then, first the strengthening of ideals of life and living; of reverent faith in the ultimate triumph of the good and of hope in human justice and growth.

We need this for the sake of the family, the moral standards of which need lifting and purifying. Upon the *women* of no race have the truths of the gospel taken a firmer and deeper hold than upon the colored women of the United States. For her protection and by her help a religious rebirth is needed.

We need it for the sake of our race, which, in the midst of repression and discouragement, is so easily apt to drift into crime and listlessness.

And finally, we need it for the sake of the state. Despite the present unrighteous denial of political rights to black men it is true, as Dr. Washington Gladden has said to this Conference, that—

"People who are thoroughly fitted for good citizenship and who show by their conduct that they have the disposition and the purpose to be good citizens are not going to be permanently excluded in any part of this country from the responsibilities and duties of citizenship. This is as true as tomorrow's sun-rising. It cannot be that in the United States of America young men who are thoroughly intelligent, who know what citizenship means, who love their country, who are working to build up its prosperity and to secure its peace and who are ready to shed their blood in its defense, are going to be forbidden to take any part in its government."

The great engine of moral uplift is the Christian church. The Negro church is a mighty social power today; but it needs cleansing; reviving and inspiring, and once purged of its dross it will become as it ought to be, and as it is *now*, to some extent, the most powerful agency in the moral development and social reform of 9,000,000 Americans of Negro blood.

The Negro of America needs an Age of Faith. All great ages are ages of faith. It is absolutely necessary for a new people to begin their career with the religious verities. Religious and moral qualities are independent of the eventualities of the race problem; no matter what destiny awaits the race, Religion is necessary either as a solvent or as a slave.

Religious precepts would rob the white man of his prejudices and cause him to recognize the Fatherhood of God and the brotherhood of man. Christianity is contrary to the spirit of caste—spiritual kinship transcends all other relations. The race problem will be solved when Christianity gains control of the innate wickedness of the human heart, and men learn to apply in dealing with their fellows the simple principles of the Golden Rule and the Sermon on the Mount.

(Signed)   MARY CHURCH TERRELL,
KELLY MILLER,
W. E. B. DU BOIS.

Index